Thirteen Questions

PETER LANG
New York • Washington, D.C./Baltimore • San Francisco
Bern • Frankfurt am Main • Berlin • Vienna • Paris

Thirteen Questions

Reframing Education's Conversation

Second Edition

Edited by
Joe L. Kincheloe &
Shirley R. Steinberg

PETER LANG
New York • Washington, D.C./Baltimore • San Francisco
Bern • Frankfurt am Main • Berlin • Vienna • Paris

Library of Congress Cataloging-in-Publication Data

Thirteen questions: reframing education's conversation / edited by
Joe L. Kincheloe, Shirley R. Steinberg. — 2nd ed.
   p.   cm.
   Includes bibliographical references.
   1. Education—United States—Aims and objectives.
2. Educational change — United States. I. Kincheloe, Joe L.
II. Steinberg, Shirley R.
LA217.2.T48   370'.973—dc20   94-44299
ISBN 0-8204-2769-1 (PBK)   CIP

Die Deutsche Bibliothek-CIP-Einheitsaufnahme

Thirteen questions: reframing education's conversation / ed. by
Joe L. Kincheloe; Shirley R. Steinberg. - 2nd. ed. - New York; Washington,
D.C./Baltimore; San Francisco; Bern; Frankfurt am Main; Berlin; Vienna;
Paris: Lang.
   ISBN 0-8204-2769-1
NE: Kincheloe, Joe L. [Hrsg.]

Cover design by Nona Reuter.

The paper in this book meets the guidelines for permanence and durability
of the Committee on Production Guidelines for Book Longevity of the
Council on Library Resources.

© 1995 Peter Lang Publishing, Inc., New York

Printed in the United States of America.

To our mothers, Libby and Marianne

Contents

Preface to 2nd Edition

If a purpose of education is to provoke response and elicit action, we feel like we "musta done something right." Our editor, Michael Flamini, phoned us several months ago and said he had sent some returned volumes of *Thirteen Questions* to us for examination. Evidently one batch of books had some pages missing and, after the semester, a professor returned the books to Lang for credit. This situation as it stood was obviously forgettable; however, what Michael felt worth recording was the margin notes that the students had written in a dozen or so of the volumes.

When we received the books, we spent time leafing through the familiar chapters marked with yellow, green and pink high-lighter with emotional expletives and inflamed statements that the authors were full of "bullshit," comments like "yeh, yeh—no way, this is all philosophy shit," questions of "what? are they kidding? how?" and challenges to "prove it, asshole." The phe-nomenologists in us demanded that we thematically arrange where we found the comments: in articles by women that talked about male dominant culture; in an article that criticized the white curriculum for marginalizing Blacks as the "other;" in articles whose focus was power and the recognition of power within culture; and articles with strenuous objections to any criticism of the New Right or the Reagan-Bush agendas. Our discovery led us to believe that the students who responded with ire a la the margins were furious with our challenges to their own grand narratives of white, male curriculums and with our audacity in naming and demanding revelation of power structures within our educational society. Wow. *Thirteen Questions* (at least at the university that returned the books) was rocking the boat.

Michael also has informed us that *Thirteen Questions* was one of Lang's top-selling books and that it had been nominated for various and sundry awards (none of which we received).

The fact that we are in our second edition and went through three printings of the first edition is a testimony to the idea that someone out there wants to discuss educational reform without the warm, fuzzy language of liberal educators, without the dogma of conservative educators, and without governmental agencies warning us where we are at risk and listing models: critical solutions to present problems and reminding us that we must be number one and competitive with other nations. This volume is a collection of thoughts from some of the United States and Canada's best thinkers/writers/teachers—we have added new chapters, and replaced several in keeping with the times. These authors gave readers the license to write in the margins, they pull no punches, still name names—and the conversation continues. . .

Shirley R. Steinberg
Joe L. Kincheloe
Penn State University

October, 1994

Acknowledgements

We would like to thank those that surround us and make our daily lives rich: our children, Ian, Meghann, Chaim and Bronwyn; our mothers, our friends, Jeanne Brady, Lee Woods, Cindy Fetters, Laurence Axtell, Elaina Chinea, Dan Marshall, Patrick Slattery; our students; the production staff at Peter Lang; and special thanks to our contributors, for their insight, assistance and expertise in putting together this volume. A separate and heartfelt thanks to Michael Flamini, our friend, confidante, springboard, devilish advocate and editor.

Thank you to the many students and educators who have given us excellent feedback to the first volume. We appreciate every response we received about the book and invite both individuals and classes to enter into our conversation by contacting us at Penn State College of Education.

Introduction: The More Questions We Ask, The More Questions We Ask

Joe L. Kincheloe
Shirley R. Steinberg

The study of education is a confusing and complex undertaking —we understand how unsettling it can be. How do we begin to decipher and make sense of the purposes of schooling, especially when we hear diametrically opposing opinions expressed by different "experts?" Just as this book was going to press the waters of American education were further muddied by the publication of *The Bell Curve: Intelligence and Class Structure in American Life*. Claiming to cover new ground, the authors, Richard J. Herrnstein and Charles Murray present "evidence" to support claims that African Americans are not as intelligent as white Americans, or at least score lower on I.Q. and other standardized tests. These low-scorers, they argue, receive too much attention in the nation's schools, in the process taking attention away from the cognitive elite (the gifted). It is this group, the upper two or three percent, that most needs a good education. After all, the authors conclude, these are the kids who will run the country: "the students with the most capacity to absorb education should get the most of it" (Herrnstein and Murray, 1994, p. 418).

Such thinking provides an eerie backdrop to the issues raised by the authors of this volume. In almost every chapter authors respond to the *scientific* irrationality of Herrnstein and Murray's sugar-coated eugenics. Written before the publication of *The Bell Curve*, this book, nevertheless, addresses many of the questions it raises. How is this possible? Though they didn't admit it, conservatives of the last two decades based their educational policies on the assumption of Black and other minority group inferiority. With the publication of *The Bell Curve*, the dirty little secret is now out. The right-wing can no longer deny the racism that grounds their policies. Though they had not read Herrnstein and Murray, the authors of *Thirteen Questions* were responding to the right-wing educational policies of the conservative Reagan and Bush administrations and the neo-liberal Clinton administration's continuation of such programs.

In this context, the authors of this volume address troubling questions that beset educators of the mid-1990s and all ages:

Upon what criteria do we base our decisions about what type of society our schools should work to create? How do we decide what we need to know or not to know? What is the nature of the process that certifies certain information as valuable school knowledge? How do we apply the knowledge gained in schools to our own lives and the larger society? In order to tell coherent, convincing stories about our lives as educators and to formulate answers to these questions we must develop a system of meaning. For our story to be compelling, the system of meaning must be just, optimistic, empathetic, and democratic.

Making Sense of Education: Developing a System of Meaning

Living in an era with no name, in a "liberal" nation-state with an increasingly anti-liberal population, in a "democratic" society with an electorate uninterested in politics, Americans have no set of precepts by which to consider their institutions. America's late twentieth century failure of vision has opened the way for the unlikely return of the philosophy of the free market. As a result, social policy and even educational policy are debated in terms of how they fit with the needs of the market. Social and moral understandings are replaced by a failed economic theory that requires a radical constraint of our political and social choices. Compassion for the poor, the market lets us know, is wrong-headed because any interference with the labor market will always result in unfortunate economic and social consequences. Moral issues in this context are always secondary to the needs of the market deity. Selfishness, not generosity, makes the world go 'round in the conservative universe.

When contemporary men and women are asked what they do for a living, most will describe their everyday chores. Rarely do they discuss the larger purpose of their job or its relation to the objectives of the bigger enterprise of which they are a part. Any social or education reform demands the creation of a guiding vision, a purpose that helps individuals make meaning. Indeed, the malformations of Western culture will never be addressed until a vision is formulated. Students drift through school with little understanding of the meaning of education that goes beyond "its in the curriculum" or "look in the textbook." Teacher education often ignores questions of educational meaning, focusing its attention on techniques of delivering information.

As we attempt to make educational meaning and raise questions of school purpose, we are working to construct a system of meaning with social goals that propel our larger vision. As dramatic as it may seem, many argue that not only does educational reform rest on the creation of a system of meaning, but human survival itself may be at stake. Short-term, technicist thinking has allowed the world's eco-system to be threatened, justified the spending of unfathomable monies on weapons, and ignored the needs of the poor and dispossessed. Education, operating with the blinders of such thinking, has accepted and even promoted such cognitive pathology. The idea that school may need to help students make meaning in a time of informational chaos has never been high on education's list of priorities. A critical system of meaning can be used to help us define school purpose, the nature of education and what it means to be a smart learner and teacher.

Our critical system of meaning helps us function in the midst of uncertainty. Grounded on feminist notions of passionate knowing, African American epistemologies, subjugated knowledges (ways of knowing that have been traditionally excluded from the conversation of mainstream educators), the ethics of liberation theology, critical theory, and progressive concerns with justice, liberty, and equality, our system of meaning grounds a critical pedagogy. Starting with our understanding of critical theory, we come to understand the ways that our consciousness has been shaped by history. A critical education, for example will always be mindful of how a student's social and historical context will help shape her or his view of schooling and the world. At the same time, our critical system of meaning draws upon feminist theory to analyze the personal—how our private selves have been shaped by history. Guided by feminist impulses, critical educators expose buried parts of the self in the attempt to overcome impediments to self-direction.

How do students and teachers come to construct their views of reality? critical educators ask. Led by the critical system of meaning, such educators come to understand a socially constructed world, focusing on the forces that shape individual perspectives. Why are some constructions of educational reality embraced and officially legitimated by the dominant culture, they ask, while others are repressed (McLaren, 1989, p. 169; Lincoln and Guba, 1985, p. 78). Thus, educators inspired by a critical system of meaning seek a new angle, a unique insight into social and educational reality. They come to understand the way power regulates discourses. Discursive practices are defined as a set of tacit rules that regulate what can and cannot be said, who can speak with blessing of authority and who must listen, whose social and educational constructions are scientific and valid and those whose are unscientific and unimportant. In the everyday world of teachers, legitimized discourses insidiously tell teachers what books may be read by students, what instructional methods may be utilized, and what belief systems, definitions of school, work, and citizenship, and success may be taught.

With the help of their critical system of meaning, critical teachers come to understand how schools identify, often unconsciously, conceptions of what it means to be educated in the terms of upper middle-class white culture; expressions of working class or non-white culture may be viewed as uneducated and inferior. Critical teachers come to understand that the culture of the school forces students to sever identification with their minority group or working class backgrounds in the name of school success. Thus, the school privileges particular practices and certain methods of discerning truth. In this context, Michel Foucault argues that truth is not relative (i.e., all world views embraced by different teachers, cultures, and individuals are of equal worth), but is relational (constructions considered true are contingent on the power relations and historical context in which they are formulated and acted upon). The question that grounds our attempt to formulate a system of meaning on which to base our critical education asks: If what we designate as truth is relational and not certain, then what set of assumptions can we use to guide our vision of what education will become? (McLaren, 1989, pp. 167-82).

This is precisely why the development of a critical system of meaning is so important. It is why liberation theology is so important to such development. With its roots deep in the Latin American struggle against poverty and colonialism, liberation theology facilitates the formulation of an ethical starting line to rethink education. Liberation theology makes no apology for its identification with the perspective of those who are excluded and subjugated. Proclaiming their solidarity with the marginalized, liberation theologians work alongside them in their attempt to expose the existing social order as oppressive and unethical. All aspects of a critical system of meaning and the education that grows out of it rest on this notion of identification with the perspective of the oppressed. Accordingly, one of the main goals of a critical education is to reveal the ways that mainstream schooling and the economic order serve to perpetuate the hopelessness of the subjugated (Welch, 1985, p. 31). On the basis of this knowledge, of the dangerous memory of the oppressed, economic and educational strategies for overcoming such oppression can be grounded.

There is no doubt that our critical system of meaning and the education it fosters will elicit charges of educational politicization, of tainted, subjective teaching. Critical pedagogy asserts that such forms of pious pseudo-objectivity must be confronted. If critical teachers cave in to such objectivist critics, the possibility of taking a moral stand in education, of seeing education as something more than a technical act, will be destroyed. As objectivist critics argue that we must keep politics out of education, they misrepresent the basic tenets of a critical education. Such critics miss the point that inquiry is never neutral—alas, when we attempt to remain neutral, like many German churches in the Third Reich, we support the prevailing power structure. Why is it, critical educators ask, that teaching which supports existing arrangements is objective while teaching which challenges the status quo is biased. Asserting a position is not the same as imposing a position on students. Critical educators understand that their students and colleagues have the right to reject everything they assert.

Along with other advocates of critical pedagogy, we believe that uncritical, mainstream teachers are just as value-laden in their teaching as any critical educator. To assume a position that refuses to seek the structural sources of human suffering and exploitation is to support oppression and the power relations that sustain it. The arguments of objectivist teachers that any teaching grounded on explicit value assumptions is subjective to the point of worthlessness is similar to the nineteenth century ruling class idea that engaging in social criticism violated a "gentlemanly" code of civility. It is similar to a twentieth century notion of positive thinking (e.g., Dale Carnegie and Zig Ziglar) that views overt oppositional behavior as a form of negativity that is not only politically wrong but distasteful as well. Indeed, the difference between teaching that subscribes to a critical system of meaning and traditional objectivist teaching rests on the critical teachers' willingness to reveal their allegiances, to admit their solidarities and value structures, and to encourage analysis of the ways such orientations affect their teaching.

The critical system of meaning helps create a consciousness that frees us from the oppression of power's shaping of our consciousness. Critical theorists have traditionally referred to this freeing process as emancipation or empowerment. Emancipation always involves confrontation with the forces that have shaped our consciousness. Such a confrontation allows us to glimpse who we want to be, as we struggle to understand how we have come to see the world. In our emancipatory journey toward self-direction, our interactions with a critical system of meaning alerts us to the complexity of the task. Critical teachers come to understand that human identity is such a chaotic knot of intertwined forces that no social agent can ever completely disentangle them. Using Michel Foucault's concept of genealogy, we trace the formation of our subjectivities. We begin to see ourselves at various points in the web of reality, ever-confined by our placement, but liberated by our appreciation of our predicament. Thus, we begin to understand and disengage ourselves from the meta-narratives (the guiding stories of our culture) that have laid the basis for the dominant way of seeing. Our ability to see from a variety of perspectives forms the basis of a long-running meta-dialogue with ourselves. This inner conversation leads to a perpetual redefinition of our images of both self and world.

"Don't Bother Me With Your Damn Theory": Educational Theory as Meaning Making, As a Way of Seeing

Another way of considering this notion of meaning making of constructing an educational vision involves the notion of theory and teacher theorizing. Over the decades, teachers have come to resent education professors in their "ivory tower" offices making pronouncements on what teachers should do in classrooms. "That sounds good in *theory*, but . . ." has been repeated in thousands of schools by thousands of teachers. In our opinion, teachers had every right to feel this way: their resentment of the outside expert dictating what they should do is justified. Previous education theory used rigorous scientific investigation to produce a body of data about "regularities" in educational practice. This set of laws formed the foundation for the validated ways teachers should function in their classrooms. Theory in this modernist sense highlighted the unimportance of teachers in the educational workplace: teacher experience is irrelevant, the generalizations produced by experts are what really matter.

Democratic progressive educators reject this technical view of educational theory. In its place they substitute a different way of seeing the world, a different view of what constitutes educational knowledge. Theory from this new perspective is not a set of official laws—on the contrary, it is a filter through which men and women view information and the world around them; indeed, theorizing is an act of meaning making. Henry Giroux argues that theory allows teachers "to see what they are seeing" (Giroux, 1988, p. 47). In this reconceptualized sense theory helps us formulate questions about the world, providing in the process conceptual tools that allow us to think about the way knowledge is legitimized. As one studies the thirteen questions addressed in this book, he or she becomes aware that theory provides us with conceptual lenses to make meaning, it helps us understand what possible actions are needed to bring about social and educational justice at a particular time and place. It is important to note that our reconceptualized notion of theory does not dictate practice. It does not provide a set of universal principles or a blueprint for educational activity. Sometimes this characteristic frustrates practitioners who are accustomed to officials handing them a list of strategies and goals they can apply on Monday morning. Our reconceptualized notion of theory respects teachers' abilities to organize and teacher their classes in whatever manner they deem appropriate.

If teachers fail to develop their theoretical insights, their ability to distinguish and help their students distinguish between "truth" and "social construction" will be undermined. Such differentiation involves the ability to think about thinking. In such a process all "facts" must be questioned; such questioning means that students and teachers must explore the origin of what is known. How do issues of power figure in its production? Whose interests benefit from the dispersion of such information? In this book, Magda Lewis and Donaldo Macedo engage these questions, as they blend theory with a critical system of meaning.

What is Critical Theory?: Understanding How Our Consciousness is Constructed

The theoretical tradition that grounds our view of education comes from the critical theory emerging from the Frankfurt School of Social Research in Germany in the 1920s. Seeing the world from the vantage point of post-World War I Germany with its economic depression, inflation, and unemployment, the critical theorists (Max Horkheimer, Theodor Adorno, Walter Benjamin, Leo Lowenthal, and Herbert Marcuse) focused on power and domination within an industrialized age. Critical theory is especially concerned with how domination takes place, the way human relations are shaped in the workplace, the schools, and everyday life. Critical theorists want to promote an individual's consciousness of himself or herself as a social being. An individual who has gained such a consciousness understands how and why her or his political opinions, student/teacher role, religious beliefs, gender role, and racial self-image is shaped by dominant perspectives,

Critical theory, thus, promotes self-reflection that results in changes of perspective. Men and women come to know themselves by bringing to consciousness the process by which their viewpoints were formed. Strategies used to confront individual and social pathologies can be negotiated once self-reflection takes place. Critical theory is quick to point out such strategies do not take the form of rules and precise regulations. Instead, a framework of principles is developed around which possible actions can be discussed and analyzed. Teachers who are conversant with critical theory are never certain of the exact path of action they will take as a result of their analysis. This can be quite frustrating to those raised in the tradition that is accustomed to a specific set of procedures designed to direct their actions. Critical pedagogy is the term used to describe what emerges when critical theory encounters education. Like critical theory in general, critical pedagogy refuses to delineate a specific set of teaching procedures. Critical pedagogues, Peter McLaren maintains, confront the ways of seeing that dominate traditional liberal and conservative critiques of schooling (McLaren, 1994, p. 167). Moving beyond these analytical forms, critical pedagogy helps students and teachers understand how schools work by exposing student sorting processes and the ways that power influences the curriculum.

Advocates of a critical pedagogy make no pretense of neutrality. Unlike many educational approaches, critical theorists expose their values and openly work to achieve them. For example, critical pedagogy is dedicated to the notion of egalitarianism and the elimination of human suffering. Critical teachers are unafraid to ask questions such as what is the relationship between social inequality and the suffering that accompanies it and the schooling process. The concerns raised by such a question shapes many of the everyday activities of critical teachers.

Working in solidarity with subordinate and marginalized groups, critical teachers attempt to expose the subtle and often hidden educational processes that privilege the already affluent and undermine the efforts of the poor.

Close Encounters With Critical Pedagogy:
The Smell of Our Students' Fear

Our education students over the years have had little academic experience to prepare them for their initial encounter with critical pedagogy. When they first hear us talk about it and read about it, they find it mysterious and frightening. It doesn't make sense because they have been taught that all education is a positive force in all students' lives. The idea that education can be deployed in ways that actually undermine students' efforts to gain socio-economic mobility and control over their lives runs counter to the lessons of their Sunday School teachers, scout leaders, and Mr. Rogers. Bart Simpson may be one of the few voices that disagrees with this conventional wisdom— and their junior high school teachers warned them about him.

They typically move through a relatively similar process in their response to the critical message. At first our students are confused and bewildered by its unfamiliar language and its unexpected assertions about the effects of schooling. Secondly, they begin to recognize and identify in themselves our descriptions of particular learned student behaviors such as note-taking geared around isolated facts (factoids) involving names, dates, and firsts (the first high school was founded in Kalamazoo, etc. . .). At the same time, students begin to realize that education's concern with isolated facts is often accompanied by school experiences having little to do with larger conceptual understandings, relation of data memorized to one's everyday experience, or the application of the learned facts to the lived world. Indeed, they begin to realize that too much of their school experience in elementary, high school, and even college revolved around rote memorization and their ability to follow directions without deviation. Finally, students become involved with the development of a contextualized understanding of the relationship between larger social phenomena and educational practice. It is at this point, that students begin to understand the connection between mainstream social assumptions and their view of themselves as future teachers. By this time, students begin to gain comfort with the new critical language and class time is filled with student stories illustrating the ways unexamined social and educational assumptions have shaped their consciousness. It is a time of thoughtful analysis when the mature realization hits home: sophisticated thinking and dynamic analysis are not always rewarded in the world of education.

References

Brosio, R. (1994). *A Radical Democratic Critique of Capitalist Education*, New York: Peter Lang.

Giroux, H. (1988). *Schooling and the Struggle for Public Life*. Minneapolis: University of Minnesota Press.

Herrnstein, R. and C. Murray (1994). *The Bell Curve: Intellignece and Class Structure in American Life*. New York: The Free Press.

Lincoln, Y. And E. Guba (1985). *Naturalistic Inquiry*. Beverly Hills, California: Sage Publications.

McLaren, P. (1994). "Multiculturalism and the postmodern critique: Toward a pedagogy of resistance and transformation," in H. Giroux and P. McLaren, *Between Borders: Pedagogy and the Politics of Cultural Studies*. New York: Longman.

Welch, S. (1985). *Communities of Resistance and Solidarity*. Maryknoll, New York: Orbis Books.

Chapter I

The Curriculum: What are the basics and are we teaching them?

Madeleine R. Grumet

William F. Pinar

Madeleine R. Grumet

Often we imagine that in other times this question—"The Curriculum: What are the basics and are we teaching them"—would never have to be asked. If the basics were basic, we imagine, they would be felt in the pulse of the community. They would be measured in the gait of its people and weighed in the lightness of sorrow. The basics are drawn from a fantasy of communion, and we project this wish on to history, mistaking the rounded edges of the past for a perfect circle of consensus. When the fantasy shifts location from historical sentimentality to a current curriculum, it becomes an agenda of control imposed on a community whose diversity splinters the steady rhythms of shared lives. Rather than describing an existing consensus, the basics are deployed to create an arbitrary compact. They function as forms of control.

The very word, BASIC, compels selection. It demands the discrimination that ranks some issues as essential and others as not. Here's the BASIC thing to remember, we say, wielding the giant spotlight of our attention, and suddenly all else falls into darkness. I, myself, have always been pretty suspicious of that spotlight, always straining to see what lives in its shadow, always hoping that whoever directs its beam will be distracted and turn too quickly, letting the light pour into the world we weren't supposed to see.

As I struggle to write about "the basics," I too try to evade the spotlight of selection. I dip and weave and dart into the shadow whenever I can. I am both proud of and a little embarrassed by this fancy choreography of mine. Elder statesmen have taken me aside to caution me that such an elliptical style will never sell in Peoria. Metaphor muddies the waters they say. Actually, they don't say it that way, that's the way I would say what they say when they say, "Madeleine, why can't you just say it simply?" Well, it's just that simply always seems like such a lie.

I am not the only one to be so suspicious. During the last few decades scholars have adopted a structuralist perspective to avoid the lie of simplicity. Rather than reducing the essential to a few items, points, methods, structuralism asserts that all thought and culture is part of a system which incorporates many elements linked in complex relationships to each other. While any particular idea in the structure is not considered essential, the design or relationships that characterize the system is.

Contemporary literary and social criticism, sometimes called postmodernism, disdain structuralism's assertions of systemic coherence. Postmodern criticism distrusts attributions to a single system or to a single author, or a main idea, portraying this focus as arbitrary and discriminatory as it directs our attention toward some values and away from others. Postmodern criticism peers over the spotlight of consensus and certainty to catch glimpses of dispute and doubt; beyond an identifiable origin for thought it discerns a diffuse history of half truths, borrowed phrases and collective fantasies.

I was uncomfortable with structuralism's overarching systems, but I am also uncomfortable with post-structuralism's contempt for identity. Identity is lived before it is thought, and even though thought may help us to press agiainst the borders of our habits and personalities, it is out of these lived and situated intuitions that we make love, war and all decisions that are later described as our values.

We don't need to go to school to learn these basics. They are threaded through body-knowledge, and no amount of resolve can make them disappear. What is basic to education is neither the system that surrounds us nor the situation of each individual's lived experience. What is basic to education is the relation between the two.

THE BASICS in all their generic and reductive splendor are meaningless to me when promulgated without reference to persons, places or times. Basic to whom? For what? When?

Relation is basic to education. But ironically, it is relation that is most often elided when we are asked to list the basics. In its place we get the poles that relation has failed to connect: either literacy, or numeracy; either critical thinking or values; either the great books or multicultural tolerance. These pairs join others that have bifurcated thought about education for centuries: the individual vs. the community; mind vs. body; cognition vs. affect; pure science vs. applied science; public vs. private.

When we say that we are educating someone, we are introducing that person, young or old, to ways of being and acting in the world that are new to his or her experience. And it is the relation between that person's experience in the world and the new material that differentiates education from training, indoctrination, or a mere display of whatever is new or exotic.

This relation of what we know to what we don't know is lodged in the etymology of the word basic, which brings us back to its base, literally a stepping stone. But in our current usage of the word, we have kept the stone and lost the step. Sadly, the history of language is too often a collapse of words for action into words for things. The base of basic is a springboard for action. It is the provision that supports the flexed ankle, the bent knee. It is the necessary condition for movement. Think about your body as you move from one step to another. The steps are static. The movement is in you as you shift your weight between them. What is basic is what goes on in the middle.

We live in the middle. When educaiton forsakes the middle for the ends, or the beginnings it is deadly. Fascinated with the ends, we have celebrated ancestor worship, proclaiming the texts of dead men to be our standards for human experience. Drawn to the beginnings, we have denied the capacity of people to be active agents in the development of their own character, reducing them to biological, genetic, or social determinants. One can talk about the basics of developmental psychology or great literature, because they are, after all, things: collections of words, repeated, cited and entombed in the Library of Congress. But educaiton is about a human being making sense of her life in the world, and when we confuse her movement with the stops on her itinerary, or worse with someone else's travel memoirs, we obstruct it.

Because we have been fascinated with the ends of education and not the middle we have not been teaching the basics. We have reduced the elementary school curriculum to a developmental mythology, draining the texture and wonder of the world from the books we give young children to read and from the school day stuffed with deadly age-appropriate routines. We have compensated for the emptiness of the elementary school curriculum by dedicating secondary and higher education to ancestor worship, oblivious to the world that students actually live in and care about.

In our anxiety to protect, promote and produce our children, we regularly leave out the second step. We wedge them into the base, calling it a firm foundation, and sink them into the cement of its assumptions. We prohibit their movement by providing no other stepping stones. They will move anyway. They will zone out, tune out, freak out, drop out.

Take black holes, for instance. I have sat in the back of classrooms where students read aloud from science textbooks describing black holes as if they were pot holes. Only someone steeped in the theory of eternal return could pay attention to that text without terror. Neither text nor teacher acknowledged or questioned the horror of the relentless destruction, the great cavernous suction that the text described. I looked around the classroom. The only terrified person in it was me. The seventh graders, even those taking notes, seemed isolated from the text, from the world and from the universe that it described. Black holes were in the assigned chapter with five questions at the end of it to be done for homework. The questions merely mimicked the chapter prose, so they could be answered without having to even imagine a black hole, let alone worry about one. All the kids had to do was scan the pages to find the black hole paragraph and copy out the appropriate sentences for answers. The really savvy kids had learned to scan the questions before reading the chapter, marking the answer paragraphs as they found them, thus making a reading that dipped below the surface of letter recognition unnecessary.

Lake Jack Webb, this lesson sought "the facts ma'am, just the facts." All the details, associations, asides that complicate the testimony are scoured from this curriculum as they were from *Dragnet's* macho inquiry. And in the name of the basics, relation, feeling, fantasy, anxiety, aggression, association, memory, irony are all banished. Now the problem is that there is little that we can truly think about that is not hooked to us by these and other thoughts and feelings. When we bypass these routes to knowledge, we bypass the knowing, the thing to be known, the world.

Our relationships to the world are rooted in our relationships to the people who care for us. Their interest in us is necessary to our capacity to be interested in the world that interests them. All of our cognitive manipulations, phonics or miscue analysis, schema presentation or hands-on mathematics and science are irrelevant unless we surround children with adults who care about them. What is basic to the elementary school curriculum is the space and time and presence that make these relationships possible. Small classes. Family groupings. Duration, staying with a group of teachers for a few years, being known, recognized, loved.

In later years what is basic can not be reduced to the Great Books or American History, to world geography or geology. It is the relation of these histories of human action and interpretation to the lives of the children studying them that is essential. Those connections are not merely motivators, clever intros to trick a group of students into interest. Those connections are the source of the questions that support research, of the desires that seek expression, of the choices that constitute values. What is basic is not a certain set of texts, or principles or algorithms, but the conversation that makes sense of these things. Curriculum is that conversation. It is the process of making sense with a group of people of the systems that shape and organize the world that we can think about together.

The spotlight of the curriculum is necessarily arbitrary or, at least, conventional. The expectation that everyone will turn to page 87, work on question 4 or go to the library to research a social studies project serves to remind us that knowledge is a social project, something we do in common with other people. Even if the text we find on page 87 is the Ten Commandments, or the task posed in question 4 reveals the law of conservation, what is basic to curriculum is the opportunity to consider the opposites and alternatives to these theses. Each proposition about the world that constitutes the body of knowledge is asserted by suppressing its opposite. The function of curriculum is to nest that propostion in the network of its alternatives and opposites; that is why curriculum is never the text, or the topic, never the method or the syllabus. Curriculum is the act of making sense of these things and that requires understanding the ways that they do and do not stand for our experience.

Well, for someone hesitant to expound on the basics, I do seem to have found my footing. The base of these assertions is located in the hundreds of narratives written by people in answer to the question: What is educational experience? The stories written in response to that question are always about connection. They are stories about the separation from loved ones, or about being recognized by a teacher or by other students. They are stories of travel, when lonely presence in a new place reveals the law of relation that supports human identity and community.

This short story was written by a woman who came to William Smith College as an adult student. Her answer to the question, What is educational experience? is this account of the connection she made between learning letters and understanding the relation of intellectual and lived experience.

> I remember sitting in Sr. Marie Therese's kindergarten class sometime in November when I was five years old. I was sitting at a brand new blonde wood table with shiny formica top, cold to the touch. The table was near the window, the glare of which reflected all around my work book. My book was open and the assignment was to do rows and rows of letters. This day was for the letter V.
>
> I was about halfway down the page of V's when something reflecting on the table caught my eye. It looked like lots of flying V's. I looked around and saw in the sky migrating geese, and they did look like V's. They even flew together forming one big V. I was amazed. I never say anything like this before. Those geese flew away and as I looked around for more I saw the upside down skinny V the church steeple made against the sky, and the fatter also inverted V's of every roof of every house. Every branch of every tree seemed to make V's. The street corner where Mr. Strang, the crossing guard, stood was the bottom point of the biggest V in the whole world.
>
> I laughed out loud to think what Mr. Strang would say if I told him he worked on the world's biggest V. Sister heard me laughing and called me up to her desk. She wanted to know what was funny. I told her, everything. About my page of V's, the geese, Mr. Strang; and how everything seemed to have a V in it. She smiled, said I was being silly, patted my head and told me to go sit back down and finish my work.
>
> I was feeling so happy, so accomplished, that her disinterest didn't faze me. I was boldly confident in my discovery, and actually felt she was missing out on a biggy. For my last row of V's on the page I made them flying away geese with little feet hanging down. This was my first

recollection of drawing from real life. It, drawing, was and still is an important part of my life.

The junctions crossed in this narrative link text, community, nature and school. What is formal and abstract, the letter V, becomes intertwined with a system of meanings tied to this child's world. Like the migrating geese, that understanding will carry her to distant places without undermining her ability to come home again. With little feet hanging down, these birds have landing gear intact. Sister Marie Therese smiles, and pats Mary's head but she doesn't celebrate her discovery of relation, expressed in her insight and drawing. I don't know if Mary ever told Mr. Strang, the crossing guard, but I do know that after twenty years, Mary told the story again, this time to me, when she was studying to be a a teacher. That was years ago, and I am still celebrating.

William F. Pinar

Such a question is inextricably linked with questions of national and private identity, themselves intersecting issues. The conservatives of the 1980's have insisted that **their** identities are basic. Predictably they have listed what they were taught and what they have learned as what everybody must be taught, what everybody must learn. We Americans are not—historically, the contemporary period, or in the future—fundamentally European-American men. Important as European-American men have been to the development of the American character, they represent a fragment of that character. To characterize their achievements, which to an immeasurable extent **are** also the achievements of those who have historically served them—women, homosexuals, African Americans, Asian Americans, Hispanic Americans (and those whose land they occupied, Native American), as "basic" to knowledge, to what we shall attempt to pass to the generations who will outlive us, is mistaken. A Eurocentric and patriarachal curriculum is not basic; historically and in the present period, not to say the future, it is marginal. In what follows I focus upon African Americans to illustrate the more general relationship between identity and curriculum.

Curriculum and Identity

"We are what we know." We are, however, also what we do not know. If what we know about ourselves—history, our culture, our national identity—is deformed by absences, denials, and incompleteness, then our identity—both as individuals and as Americans—is fractured. This fractured self is a repressed self. Such a self lacks access both to itself and to the world. Repressed, the self's capacity for intelligence, for informed action, even for simple functional competence, is impaired. Its sense of history, gender, and politics is incomplete and distorted.

Public debate over a "common" or core curriculum reveals an explicit racial aspect. The exchange at a 1989 conference, sponsored by the conservative research and education policy center founded by former Education Secretary William Bennett and *The Closing of the American Mind* author Allan Bloom, at the Madison Center, is illustrative. The Center's president, John Agresto, characterized the conference as "response to the academy's current trivialization of liberal education and the continuing attacks on the canons of traditional collegiate instruction. "Under the cover of pluralism is" criticizes Agresto, "the dismissal of the past" (O'Brien, 1989). In opposition, Houston Baker, noted literary critic and professor of English at the University of Pennsylvania, charged that the continued curricular emphasis upon western civilization constitutes "A willfull ignorance and aggression toward Blacks" (O'Brien, 1989). Regarding the so-called "great books" curriculum of St. John's College (Maryland), Baker commented: "The Great Books won't save us but rap may because it might finally allow us to recognize that the world is no longer white and one might even say no longer bookish." Jonathon Culler, the famous post-structuralist literary critic and professor of English at Cornell University, cited a 1988 study of that literature taught in high schools conducted by the center for the Teaching and Learning of Literature at the State University of New York at Albany. Albany researchers found that 27 books were required in more than 30 percent of the schools surveyed. Culler commented: " I find it scandalous that long after the civil rights movement, there are no books by Black authors in the top 27, and books by and about women are so poorly represented" (O'Brien, 1989).

Current debates regarding the "canon"—about what is basic to the curriculum—can be linked with questions of self and identity. Such an understanding shifts the curricular debate from preoccupations with equity or with multiculturalism to debates regarding the relationship between knowledge and ourselves. The Eurocentric and patriarchal character of school curriculum functions not only to deny "role models" to non-European-American male students, it denies self-understanding to "white boys" as well. The American self is not exclusively or even primarily an European American male self. Fundamentally, it is African American, Asian American, Hispanic American, Native American, female, homosexual self. To a still unacknowledged extent, the American nation was built and is occupied culturally by African Americans, Asian Americans, Hispanic Americans, by woman, and by homosexuals. The presence of these persons and the cultural traditions they represent and embody informs every element of American life. For European American male students to understand who they are, they must understand that their existence (and identity) is predicted upon, inter-related to, and constituted in fundamental ways by African Americans, Asian Americans, Hispanic Americans Native Americans, by women, and by homosexuals.

The American self-denied and repressed "acts out" repression via imperialism in foreign policy and political and economic repression domestically as it attempts to maintain the denial. The refusal—sometimes unconscious, sometimes not—to incorporate, for instance, African American knowledge into the mainstream curriculum can be understood as a psychoanalytic as well as political process of repression. Understanding curriculum as the revelation and construction of identity implies understanding education as a form of social psychoanalysis. The American identity is constructed partly by denial, by maintaining fictions. It is not exclusively or even primarily European or male. That delusion represents a fantasy, a flight from truth.

The absence of African American knowledge (again the argument applies to the other traditions and knowledges) in many American schools' curriculum is not simple oversight. Its absence represents an academic instance of racism, or in Baker's apt phrase, "willful ignorance and agreesion toward Blacks." Just as African Americans have been denied their civil rights in society generally, they have been denied access to their history and culture in school. Not only African Americans have been denied, however. Institutional racism deforms white students as well. By refusing to understand curriculum as a racial text, students misunderstand who they are as racialized, gendered, historical, political creatures. Such deformity occurs—for most "whites"—almost "unconsciously". Many European American students and their parents—and many curriculum specialists —would deny that curriculum is about identity. Such denial is done "innocently;" it represents an instance of repression in its psychoanalytic sense. Socially, psychological repression expresses itself as political repression.

Repression impairs intelligence, as it siphons off energy from, for instance, problem-solving to maintain the repression. Further, repression implies that information is limited, as well as distorting that information which is available. The contemporary crisis of American education is complex in its nature and causes; it is not reducible to one factor or one set of factors, such as poorly prepared teachers, out-of-date curriculum, malnourished students, developmentally and/or culturally inappropriate examinations and other school practices. One overlooked factor is repression, the repression of African Americans in American society, the repression of women, the repression of other marginalized groups, and the repression of non-European knowledge. Such repression is evident in the schools in several ways, including funding inequities, tracking, teaching practices, and curriculum that is Eurocentric and unrelated to the lived experience of students.

Freudian imagery of the self is provocative here. During the decades of the 1980's the businessman represented the American prototype. Lee Iaccoca, Donald Trump, Michael Milken: white, male, savvy, shrewd, calculating, devoted to the bottom line. If this prototype represented the American ego: realistic, adaptive, adjusting in self-profiting ways to "reality" then African Americans represented the "id pleasure seeking, unpredictable, accomplished in athletics and the arts. American culture projected African Americans as the "id," and in classical Freudian style, maintained relative repression of the "pleasure principle" so that—presumably—ego stability and hegemony could be maintained. Those elements of American life could be said to represent the "superego", fundamentalist religious groups, were permitted by the "business" ego to grow in size and influence. Those groups marginal to this version of the "ego"—African American, other marginalized ethnic groups, women, children, gays—were undermined, via public policy and in political practice.

Christopher Lasch has argued that the conservative political prescription for schools and society during the 1980's can be characterized as superego in nature. Illustrative of this "superego" voice are slogans such as "more homework," "just say no," "work harder." Conservatives insisted that the problem with American society was simple laziness (not their own of course), and in this simpleminded analysis African Americans were assigned a major blameworthy role. True enough, liberals continue to call for rational deliberation, incorporating aspects of the unconscious (African Americans in the parallel) into the conscious ego (mainstream society), but in controlled and planned ways (the liberal conceptualization of an orderly, incremental civil rights movement). My point is that the question of school curriculum is also a question about the self, the American self. Understanding curriculum as a racial text means understanding America as fundamentally a racialized and gendered place, as fundamentally an African American place, and the American identity as inescapably African Americans as well as European, Hispanic/Latino, Native American, Asian American, female and homosexual. African Americans are ego and super-ego as well as id. Debates over the debates over the constitution of the American self.

European Americans and African Americans are two-sided of the same cultural coin, two interrelated narratives in the American story. The former cannot hope to understand themselves unless they are knowledgeable and knowing of the latter, and vice-versa. The sequestered suburban white student is uninformed unless he or she comes to understand how, culturally, he or she is also African American. As James Baldwin has pointed out, "white" does not exist apart from "black." The two co-exist, intermingle, and the repression of this knowledge deforms us all, especially those who are white and male. All Americans are racialized, gendered beings; knowledge of who we have been, who we are, and who we will become is a text; curriculum—our construction and reconstruction of this knowledge—is indeed a racialized, gendered text.

During the past decade much has been made of the failure of public-school students to learn even the most elementary and necessary facts regarding their history, geography, and culture. Cultural literacy is a non-controversial requirements for any citizenry. What becomes controversial is the composition of such literacy. In the popular press voices express views of cultural literacy that are informed by, primarily, Eurocentric and patriarchal knowledge systems. Without question American students must know and understand the European antecedents of contemporary American culture. However, this knowledge ought not to be used as a defense against "otherness," a denial of our cultural unconscious.

Understanding curriculum as a text of identity is especially urgent in the present period of neo-conservatism during which racial and gender attacks and racial and gender antagonism have increased (Omni and Winant, 1986; *Chronicle of Higher Education*, 1990). In the November, 1990 election, David Duke's white supremacy candidacy for the U.S. Senate brought him 60% of the white vote in Louisiana. The military adventure in the Persian Gulf masks the continued deterioration of the American cultural "infrastructure." The hour is late; Baldwin predicts it is "the fire next time."

Conclusion

Curriculum is "cultural capital," and under current—politically conservative—conditions, African American culture is "black-market currency." Because knowledge of American culture is characterized by distortions, repressions, and silences—what holds true for the South holds true in regional different ways for the nation—American identity is deformed. Estranged from African Americans, European American men are estranged from themselves. Being repressed unfortunately, also means being stupid, and in order to realize our national intelligence we need to remember—in social psychoanalytic fashion—those denied and repressed elements of who we are. This means, in part, incorporating African American experience in the school curriculum, not marginalized as "black studies" (although also institutionalized in that form as space for separatist, intellectually autonomous research and action) but integrated throughout the curriculum.

Organizationally a next step might include the establishment of an American cultures requirement in the general education of elementary, secondary as well as university students. The University of California's Center for the Teaching and Study of American Cultures (opened May 11, 1990) will create courses that will fulfill the American Cultures requirement at the University of California, a requirement approved by Berkeley faculty in April 1989. The requirements must explore at least three of five ethnic groups: African Americans. American Indians, Asian Americans, Chicanos/Latinos and European Americans (*San Francisco Chronicle*. May 11, 1990, p. A6). Every university ought to enact such a requirement, as one initiative to challenge intellectual repression. However, this information must not await the college experience. Beginning in elementary school and continuing throughout secondary school courses in American cultures ought to be required. Such courses will hardly guarantee the end of racism; indeed what we know about repression suggests that "backlash" will occur periodically.

Curricular integration in the public schools is underway, of course. For instance, reports of the "infusion of African and African American knowledge in the school curriculum will be made, among other places at the second national conference on this topic. Among the sponsors if this meeting are American Airlines and a Georgia utilities company, surely a sign that the effort has begun to enter the rhetorical mainstream. Entering the curricular mainstream on a mass scale will prove to be, I suspect, another matter.

Obviously, these are complicated issues. Debates over what is basic to the curriculum are also debates over identity. Construed as questions concerning who we are, history and culture make it clear that we are—in a fundamental sense—African American, Asian American, Hispanic American, Native American, female and homosexuals. It is not only African Americans who are deprived when their history is underemphasized, it is European—and other American as well. It is in our own self interest—read European American self interest—to incorporate an expanded and more accurate concept of who we are as individuals and as civic creatures. Educationally, this requires understanding curriculum as a text of identity, and in so doing, we begin to understand ourselves.

(A version of this paper appears as the introduction to *Understanding Curriculum as a Racial Text*, edited by Louis A. Castenell, Jr., and William F. Pinar, State University of New York Press, 1993).

References

Lasch, Christopher (1984). *The minimal self.* New York: Norton.

O'Brien, E. (1989). "Debates over curriculum expansion continues." *Black Issues in Higher Education,* 6-18 (November 23, 1989), 1-26.

Chapter II

Power and Education: Who decides the forms schools have taken, and who should decide?

Magda Lewis

Donaldo Macedo

Magda Lewis

When first asked to write a paper on the topic of power and education I wasn't sure where to begin. For those of us teaching and writing from the perspective of critical/feminist pedagogy the answer to the question of who decides educational forms seems obvious. It suggests the promise of a short discussion. *If we are not men, if we are not white, if we are not economically advantaged, if we survive by the labour of our hands, if we are not heterosexual, and if we do not embody and display the valued assets of the privilege of Euro-American culture*, the school curriculum and schooling experience fling us to the margins. Nowhere in the curriculum do we see even a vague glimpse of a reflection of ourselves, of our present realities or of our future dreams. "Typically," says Alison Dewar (1987), "the stories we tell in schools, colleges and universities are ones that reflect the past, present, and future of powerful groups in society. The knowledge we teach in our educational system has a white, middle class, androcentric bias. More importantly, this bias is not presented as one possible version of reality, but more often is taught as the only legitimate and therefore, representative version of reality" (p. 265).

While any number of studies might show this to be the case my knowledge of it comes more directly through the body—my body—overtly contained within the academy by the ideological frames of allowable knowledge. The body of knowledge that is the curriculum and the body experience of being schooled—learning to be still and quiet—are not separable from each other in the process of education. However else we understand the world; indeed however we might wish to intellectualize and thereby hide the lived effect of the realities we know we have lived, the concrete experiences of inclusion or of marginalization are the negotiated memories which we carry and which become the educational moments through which we come to explain the world to ourselves.

As form, education through schooling both offers and requires the consent to a contained agenda. For students marginalized through their gender, class, race, ethnicity, culture and sexuality, questions of the relationship between education and power have substantively to do with how they are encouraged to embrace forms of schooling that systematically require them to deny who they are; that measure their performance in school by how well they succeed in negating themselves; that leave those parts of their lives that do not fit inside the dominant molding forms to pour and splash over the edges of what's acceptable and allowable.

In this paper I shall draw on my own history in order to tell this side of the schooling experience. This is not an easy thing to do. To begin I need to say that for me this telling of my own educational experiences presents itself as a paradox. The social and cultural implications associated with being a female university professor implores me to keep silent by making unspeakable the realities I know I have lived. Yet who I am is not only constructed by who I have become but as well by the memories of those parts of my life that I have been asked to leave as unformed/unframed pools both uncontained as well as unaccounted for inside the forms that articulate education and schooling. I use my experiences not as a form of catharsis but as a series of metaphors that reveals for me in graphic and lived ways the relationship between education, form and power.

In the context of education the question of how ideas, knowledge and conceptualizations arise brings to the fore exactly the problems to which critical/feminist critique has pointed. Schooling practices support a particular set of ideological beliefs surrounding the work of intellectual production: that as intellectuals we do our work apart from how, where and with whom we live our personal and intellectual lives; that in order to this work in its most pure and therefore desirable form we need to disassociate ourselves from the lived "trivialities" of our everyday lives; that the best text is that which silences what Susan Sontag (1987), referencing Roland Barthes, calls "the most delicate mechanisms of social exchange" (p. 459).

Yet at the level of every day life where is that moment when a seemingly insignificant individual event becomes a moment of possibility, a speakable/revolutionary moment, or conversely a moment of closure and loss? What is the measure of significance of these everyday relationships and events? It seems to me, that valorized academic practices steeped, as they are, in notions of "objectivity" and "independent" work, guarantee that what ought to be considered most important is trivialized into insignificance and what is elevated to truth is generated mostly out of irrelevance. It also mystifies the reality of how knowledge is produced, by whom and under what conditions.

By definition social life is collective and interdependent. Historically we enter and live out social relations unequally. Whether or not we choose to acknowledge it, the knowledge we derive from our experiences is a consequence of these social/ historical realities lived in minute detail. That dominant social, cultural groups claim the privilege of being able to renege ownership of the knowledge they derive from their experience and call it universal, speaks more about their power than about the "truths" they claim to have uncovered.

The stories I learned in school had a remarkable singularity about them—a single voicedness where debates, if they took place at all, questioned only the details without remotely touching the foundations of the basic paradigms upon which the stories were premised. Throughout the seventeen years of formal education that preceded my graduate studies I had not studied the history, culture and political realities of women, of the labouring classes, of racial and ethnic minorities, of gays and lesbians. This is all the more remarkable when I consider that my area of study was the great thinkers of Western intellectual tradition. A couple of years ago I revisited my undergraduate philosophy texts still sitting—now somewhat sundrained—on my book shelves, only to discover to my dismay that there was not a single volume among them written by a woman. Nor had any of them been written by anyone who could be identified as an author of colour. To my recollection issues of ethnic and cultural difference were never discussed. There were no voices from the labour movement. Nor indeed was it made remotely possible for me to learn from those texts a discourse beyond the massive assumptions and prescriptions of heterosexuality.

All of this might be astonishing enough. Given the language of educational rhetoric that claims for itself ideologies and practices that embrace notions of freedom, democracy and equality, the distinctly one sidedness of the story I learned in school seems a curious oversight—even more so since I earned my pre-graduate education in the heady reformist days of the sixties and early seventies. However, on looking back, what seems even more astounding than that these should have been the books from which I was asked to absorb the knowledge of the culture which promised me equality of possibility, was that at the time I read these books I had not even registered the deeply exclusionary practices that they both created and made to seem natural. Not to have noticed my own violation speaks of a process more deeply violating that I could have imagined at the time. This experience is what I have since come to call the double-cross-reversal: the privilege of the dominant to talk at great length about that which is not and to stay silent about and ignore that which is. In this reversal, for socially subordinate groups, possibility is defined through denial, freedom is reinterpreted through constraint, violence is justified as protection, and in schools, contrary to the belief that it is a place where knowledge is shared, knowledge withheld articulates the curriculum. More recently this awareness has brought me to rethink my own educational experiences and to use them as the ground from which to explore the question of 'education and power'.

Over sixty years ago Virginia Woolf (1929) pointed out that in education we do not come together equally. She was neither the first nor the last to make this point. However, she makes it exquisitely. The stories I carry with me about my own educational experiences arise from my own locus of desire—to sing, to dance—to speak—simple acts of possibility. Yet history has shown us that such possibilities are never simple. We carry the baggage of our history and it makes us *shy*:

> and the shyness of the poor is another mystery. I myself in the midst of it can't explain it. Perhaps it is neither a form of cowardice nor of heroism. It may be lack of arrogance (The School Boys of Barbiana, 1971, p. 4).

At one level we are made shy by our collective history and experience of marginalization. But at another level—at a level that is lived more closely—at a level that is less easy to distance—we are made shy by our personal histories; those strands of experience that weave the patterns of our lives. Our social identities are cross cut not only by who we are but, as well, by the ceaseless reinforcement of who we are not. And in this schools play a major part.

I remember some considerable years ago arriving as a grade nine student in a new high school. As for many students, for me, the transition between elementary and high school signalled the possibility for new beginnings. I was excited at the idea of what I thought I was about to learn. And I was excited about where I believed this learning was going to take me. In looking ahead I was determined to leave behind what as a child I had learned to live as the silencing vestiges of my ethnic/immigrant background often experienced as a deeply carried "shyness"—an unwillingness to demand that I be noticed.

As a child and then as a young adult I had learned early that the self embraced project of my education required the abandonment of the cultural/social practices I had carried with me across two continents to this new place I was to call home. Along with a new language, I had learned to pack a lunch I no longer needed to sneak unseen out of a brown paper bag for fear of being associated with the cultural oddities of taste and cuisine that it carried. One of the legacies of my education is, for the most part, the loss of this culture that is no longer an identifiable aspect of who I am. Except for a slight 'lilt' in my enunciation, noticed only by those with a 'good ear' and often mistaken for regional exoticism, there is nothing about me that would signal the cultural shifts of perspective I was required to accomplish as a child of nine. Lost in this imposed yet self embraced transition from Other to Acceptable were the familial practices wrapped inside the external specificity of the culture of my childhood that embraced it and were embraced by it—there are still words of endearment I can speak only in the language of my childhood for them to have any significance deeper than the dictionary meanings they carry.

Never acknowledged as a loss, the shedding of the skin of my ethnicity was supposed to be painless—and I told myself that it was. It was only much later that I understood that even the possibility of this self imposed pain was made available to me only because I was white in a deeply racist culture. It was a privilege

I could not have appropriated had I been a black child or a child whose visible ethnicity makes them even more invisible in the curriculum and schooling experience that I was made. My brother and I learned to mimic and then laugh at the culture of the children we both struggled not to be. We internalized the violation of our negation to ease the pain of our loss. I still take delight in the richness of the nuances of a language I now speak, read and write with hesitation and uncertainty. Yet, as a child in a school system obsessed with the devaluation and marginalization of multiple language speakers/multiple culture carriers—where the ability to speak more than one language was seen to be an intellectual liability rather than a richly useful asset—my struggle to leave behind the culture/language of my childhood created in me an equal and opposite obsession to get the new language right as it simultaneously and, I believe deliberately, alienated me from those, like my parents, who could not. Gradually my syntax and accent gave me away less and less.

Questions of ethnicity long since suppressed I was ready to create new possibilities for myself. Yet, on the particular day which I remember so vividly, my experience of Other was rearticulated across what I eventually came to learn were a new set of parameters, that of gender. Having been cajoled out of the stuffiness of the library into the warm sunshine of that bright September day I set about to find a quiet place in which to spin my dreams about my future. My arms loaded with books and my mind preoccupied I proceeded to cross what appeared to me to be a large lovely green space. Suddenly I saw a cluster of young men charging toward me. In panic and with knees weak with terror I realized I was standing in the middle of the football field. Not knowing which way I should go—and in reality having nowhere to go—I stood transfixed and bewildered. In retrospect I should have known: in most high schools (certainly and of those I went to) the only available green space was, by priority, given over to the playing of football, an activity that not only eliminated many of the young men but all of the young women. As they mowed me down I realized I had trespassed into a space not intended for me. My presence in that space, not unnoticed by this advancing steam roller, had no effect on their will, desire or inclination to stop short of what to me was a potential disaster. The game was all.

It is because of the way this story has stayed with me for well over twenty years, that I now choose to read it as a metaphor not only for the experience of girls in school, not only for all marginal cultural/social groups in a society that is marked so massively and unmistakably by the privilege of domination but for the condition of the world itself scored profoundly by the horrors of unprecedented military weaponry, constant political tensions and a global awareness of pain, cruelty and injustice that tries our sanity daily. As I write these words following the war in the Persian Gulf, the world is caught in the aftermath, yet still ongoing brutality, of the evil phallic posturing of insane men who have learned the lessons of their unexamined privilege well: the ritualized game of exclusion, violation and obliteration of the many for the narcissistic pleasure of their own power to destroy.

With this experience lodged firmly in my subconscious, because it is only recently that I have been able to understand the psychological/emotional import that the incident had on how I formulated the possibilities of my own schooling and future, I proceeded through the various levels of credentialization in the increasingly marginalizing world of academia. That this world is also increasingly masculinized and male centered is not beside the point. And while I found myself again and again back in the middle of that metaphorical football field, picking myself up, looking still and again for that quiet place where I could spin my dreams, I found that increasingly the mowing down was less arbitrary and while more subtle and sophisticated certainly more profound.

Proceeding through high school, ten university and finally graduate school, as a woman in the academy I found myself repeatedly faced with the production of the demonstration of my knowledgability and skill with words in an environment where both what I knew and the words through which I understood this knowledge hovered on the margins outside the pale of masculine homosociality catching only partial and momentary glances, as bodies shift, of the fire that burns at the centre of male academic practices and camaraderie. Mary Daly's (1978) remarkable exposition of social practices that rivet patriarchal power into place (witchburnings, suttees, footbinding, genital mutilation, modern gynecological practices, and the socially sanctioned and institutionalized violence against women world wide) would suggest that the fuel for this fire is to be found in the bodies of women.

Like a seductive lover, my education both offered and simultaneously withheld the promise of a future I could embrace. Moving closer the tips of my fingers warmed. Simultaneously I caught the sideways glances that were sometimes bewildered by, sometimes hostile to, yet sometimes grateful for my presence. No longer marginalized through my ethnicity it was now as a woman that I became aware of my signification as the Other—a body that did not conform to the straight lines of the masculine body of knowledge that makes acceptable discourse and self presentation. Bewildered by the ambiguities of my place around the warming fire, bruised by my inability to decode these contradictory discourses my immediate inclination, almost intuitive . . . (and what is intuition beyond a profound sensitivity to lived realities) . . . my intuition was to pull back into a terrain that I knew. As my eyes began to focus and adjust to what the light at the centre had made to appear as a black void, I caught the movement of the other bodies in the shadows. Having stayed focused in this direction long enough, what had been made to appear as darkness and formlessness has begun to present itself with the clarity of a moonlit winter night.

Transforming experience into metaphor has enabled me to "render visible the visible" (Bersianik, 1986, p. 48). It has allowed me to break the code of silence enforced by the mandates of objectivity and finally speak what through my experience I had always known: *if we are not men, if we are not white, if we are not economically advantaged, if we survive by the labour of our hands, if we are not heterosexual, and if we do not embody and display the valued assets of the privilege of Euro-American culture,* schools are not the sites of possibility which the rhetoric of educational discourse wishes to portray. What I learned in school was that successful forms of self violation are rewarded with credentials; that the study of the accomplishments of great men simultane-

ously hides the life realities of those whose labour—often gratu-
itous—were/are required to reproduce the world in which some
men (very specific men) could become great; and finally that
educational rhetoric conforms to the mandates of the double-
cross-reversal, offering a great deal of information about that
which is not, and withholding information about that which is.

Now I sit on the other side of the classroom divide. The
stories my students tell me about their educational experiences
are not unlike those I already know all too well. Women speak
of unconscionable sexism while those in power co-opt the
language of the powerless. Women's struggle for equality and
inclusion, and our attempts to gain public acknowledgement of
our violation and marginalization are countered by claims of
reverse sexism, preferential treatment of women and the silencing and intimidation of those who have never known what it
means to be truly without voice, as women are, not because we
cannot speak but because we are not heard and not being
heard we cease to speak. Women repeatedly tell me of their
conscious decision to stop speaking in classrooms where sexism
is a non-negotiable dynamic of the curriculum and classroom
practice. Some women tell me of not having spoken in class for
years. Economic marginality continues to limit students' access
to education. The division between mental and manual labour
continues to suppress what counts as acceptable knowledge.
Many students who carry the weighted baggage of their
racial/ethnic identity slow and eventually step to the sidelines
in the race for academic success. And questions of sexual identity never enter the classroom even as we turn a blind eye to the
violations of homophobia that hold many students physically,
emotionally and psychologically hostage to their peers.

This is not to say that there are not courageous teachers who
struggle to maintain programmes and create curriculum against
the will of those whose interests are not served by students who
know too much. These teachers know all too well that the question posed in the title of this article can only be rhetorical. We
know who should decide the forms schools should take: those
for whom schools are ostensibly intended inclusive of all of the
multiple identities of individuals and social groups. Yet we also
know who does articulate educational forms and re/forms. In

this context, the challenge of critical/feminist pedagogy is to find that vacuous space between rhetoric and practice; between the language of democracy, freedom, possibility and justice and the actuality of constraint, denial of voice and containment of possibility, and claim that space—like a crack in the pavement where a flower might grow—as a place from which to listen and speakin order to enact with our students transformative practices in the classroom.

References

Bersianik, L. (1986). "Aristotle's lantern: an essay on criticism." In S. Neuman and S. Kamboureli (eds.). *Amazing Space: Writing Canadian Women Writing*. Edmonton: Lonspoon Press.

Daly, M. (1978). *Gyn/Ecology: The metaethics of Radical Feminism*. Boston: The Beacon Press.

Dewar, A. (1987). "Knowledge and gender in physical education." In J. Gaskel land A. McLaren (eds.). *Women and Education: A Canadian Perspective*. Calgary: Detselig Enterprises Limited.

Sontag, S. (Ed.). (1987). *A Barthes Reader*. New York: Hill and Wang.

The School Boys of Barbiana. (1971). *Letter to a Teacher*. Trans. by N. Rossi and T. Cole. New York: Vintage Books.

Woolf, V. (1929). *A Room of One's Own*. London: The Hogarth Press.

Donaldo Macedo

The Liberal Grip:
An Entrapment Pedagogy

Because the issue of who controls school is rarely raised in the US educational debate, the politics of "which content gets taught, to whom, in favor of what, of whom, against what, against whom"[1] is seldom critically understood. Such an understanding requires not only a thorough analysis of the structure of schooling and the ideology that informs it, but it also necessitates a critical understanding of the interdependence between schooling and the socio-cultural and political reality of the society within which schools exist. This is not an easy task in the United States, particularly because of the myth that schools are very much kept independent of society and dislodged from the political reality that shapes them historically. By and large, schools in the United States were not viewed as having an organic relationship with the community at large. As Peter Negroni, the superintendent of the Holyoke Public Schools in Massachusetts argues, "Americans have not made the connection between an effective quality of life in the community and the quality of public schooling in the community. The complete and total interdependence of community, schooling and democracy must be recognized by America as part of reform efforts."[2]

Unfortunately, absent from the present school reform debate is the language of democracy that points to the organic interrelationship between schooling and the community so as to understand "the primacy of the ethical, social, and civic in public life."[3] Is it ethical to take precious funding from the Brockton Public Schools in Massachusetts that is on the verge of bankruptcy and give it to the more affluent neighboring Avon Public Schools? Where in Bush's America 2000 do you find references to educational equity, social justice and liberatory education? On the contrary, America 2000 embraces a corporate ideology that promotes individualism, privatization and competition as seen below:

1. every child will start school ready to learn;
2. the high school graduation rate will increase to 90 percent;
3. competency will be demonstrated in five core subjects in grades 4, 8, and 12;
4. American students will be ranked first in the world in both math and sciences;
5. every American adult will be a literate and responsible citizen;
6. every school will be liberated from drugs and violence.[4]

What Bush failed to articulate is that drugs and violence in schools are directly linked to the "savage inequalities" in the society that generates despair of poverty, loss of dignity, dehumanization, and hopelessness. It would make immensely more sense if Bush's America 2000 proposed to also liberate subordinate students from the yoke of poverty, social injustices, racism, sexism and other discriminatory practices that characterize their reality.

In contrast to the United States market notion of school reform that has "virtually replaced citizens or even person as the principal mode of reference to human beings,"[5] Paulo Freire put into motion an educational transformation plan whose major goal was:

1. democratization and access;
2. democratization of administration;
3. new quality of teaching;
4. youth and adult education;

Paulo Freire's notion of educational transformation involves the democratization of the pedagogical and educational power so that students, staff, teachers, educational specialists, and parents come together to develop a plan that is grassroots generated, accepting the tension and contradictions that are always present in all participatory efforts, thereby searching for a democratic substantivity.[6]

This search for democratic substantivity is evidenced in the transformation of the curriculum in which when one "necessarily [teaches] the content, one teaches also how to think critically."[7] Thus, the transformation of the curriculum required rigorous analysis that led to "the identification of significant contexts from which the generative themes are developed."[8] As exemplified below.

— Work and leisure: road to security.
— It is possible to live without violence.
— School and the interaction of humans in the occupation of space.
— Work and life. How does one construct relationships?
— Citizenship: how to achieve and how to keep it.
— Community: conviviality, consciousness and transformation.
— Neighborhood.
— Access, occupation, and appropriation of space by humans.

In emphasizing and prioritizing the democratization of schools, Paulo Freire had to decentralize power so as to divest school administrators of excessive power while creating structures where teachers, students, parents, school staff, and the community can empower themselves so as to participate and contribute in the school transformation process. As Paulo Freire correctly argues:

> In a really progressive, democratic, and non-authoritarian way, one does not change the "face" of schools through the central office. One cannot decree that, from today on, the schools will be competent, serious, and joyful. One cannot democratize schools authoritarianly.[9]

Compare the goal to democratize schools in a country that is just beginning to experience democracy after decades of a cruel military dictatorship fully supported by the United States with the proposals put forth by our educational leaders. For example, take Chester Finn's argument "against local control, and giving power to professional educators and lay governing boards."[10] Or Chubb and Moe's contention that "public schools have been pulled in too many directions by the 'excess' of democratic demands."[11] In other words, the teaching of students about "multiculturalism, environmentalism, and a thousand other world-saving crusades . . . issues for which neither [students] nor teachers have even the rudiments of competence."[12] While Paulo Freire was trying to democratize schools by diverting the central administration of excessive power, and proposing that even principals be democratically elected by their respective schools, in Massachusetts, the birth place of democratic public schooling, Governor Weld instituted draconian educational cuts while proposing the privatization of schools via school choice. In Boston, the birth place of the first public school in the United States, Mayor Ray Flynn moved aggressively to dismantle the elected school committee and replaced it with his appointed members.

In a short two and a half years, the retention rate in the Sao Paulo schools went up to 81%, the best result obtained in the last decade. Under Freire's administration, community councils were created with real democratic power to negotiate school issues that ranged from curricular reform to school renovation. Teacher's salaries were increased dramatically and on-going teacher preparation was initiated. More than ninety social movements, including the Unions, signed a pact with the Educational Bureau to work toward the total eradication of illiteracy in Sao Paulo. This is in marked contrast with the Boston Compact, formed mostly by business leaders.

The democratic spirit of Freire's administration alerted the society that "we should not call on the people to come to the school to receive instruction, recipes, threats, reprehension and punishment, but to participate collectively in the construction of knowledge, that goes beyond the knowledge made by pure experience, that takes into consideration its needs and turns it into a tool of struggle, making it possible for them to become subjects of their own history. The people's participation in the creation of culture ruptures with the tradition that considers that only the elites are competent and knowledgeable about the needs and interests of the entire society."[13]

This call for collective participation differs significantly from the plan proposed by Benno Schmidt Jr., who left Yale to head the first for profit schools in the nation. Schmidt argues that "if restrictive union contracts are a burden for many school districts, Project Edison would go one better than merely hiring nonunion workers: it would get people to work for free."[14] Schmidt's notion of collective participation is that "children and parent will be volunteers, if you will, taking on much more of the burden" of running schools. He equates his plan to Japan where "kids cook the meals, run the cafeteria, take care of the upkeep of the schools. Imagine a model where children are partners in the education effort."[15] Unlike Freire's concept of collective participation, Schmidt's view of educational partnership is stripped of any and democratic intellectual substance to the extent that it relegates collective participation to only utilitarian chores, a splendid curriculum to adapt poor kids to the flip-hamburgernization economy.

A democratic society that acquiesces its public responsibility is a democracy in crisis. A society that equates for profit privatization with democracy is a society with confused priorities. A democratic society that falsely believes, in view of the S&L debacle and the Wall Street scandals, for example, that quality, productivity, honesty, and efficiency can be achieved only through for profit privatization is a society characterized by a bankruptcy of ideas. If we follow the line of argument that "private" is best, we should once again consider Jack Beaty's question: "would we set up a private Pentagon to improve our public defense establishment?"[16] Would private is best-logic eradicate the on-going problems in the military that range from rampant sexual harassment, as exemplified by the Tailhook scandal, payment of over six hundred dollars for a toilet seat to billions for planes that don't fly and Pentagon officials turn consultants through the revolving door effect.

Most Americans would find the privatization of the Pentagon an utter absurdity claiming a national priority for a strong defense. I contend that the safeguarding of our democracy rests much more on the creation of an educated smart citizenry than on the creation of smart bombs.

School choice as a reform discourse places the educational debate outside the social reality that generates discrimination, racism, sexism and economic inequality. Thus, the present educational reform fails to address the interrelationship between schools and the sociocultural reality within which schools exist. Hence, it becomes extremely difficult to change schools without changing the society that created undemocratic schools characterized by cruel and stark inequalities.

In order to transform schools into democratic sites, we must, first and foremost, analyze and understand the structural and causal realities that produced undemocratic and unequal schools in the first place. It is thus imperative to analyze and describe the social and historical conditions of the United States so as to, on the one hand, explain the ideology that produced undemocratic schools and is presently reproducing education inequalities through systemic hidden mechanisms. On the other hand, educators need to also understand the students' cultural production, including their resistance, and develop pedagogies that speak to the reality of the culture produced by students.

In this paper, I will analyze how different and contradictory ideologies are played out so as to reproduce power asymmetries along the lines of race, gender, ethnicity, and language. I will argue that the present ambiguity in the contemporary school reform debate is directly linked to both conservative and liberal ideologies that shape and maintain the "savage inequalities" of schools. In other words, the reform is being carried out by those players who have been and are part of the problem they are trying to solve. That is, given the complexity of our rapidly changing multicultural society, reform represents only a cosmetic change, leaving the inherent ideology that informs education unproblematic and unchanged. In reality, what we really need is not reform, what we need is transformation.

Liberalism and the Pedagogy of Entrapment

The present school reform in the United States can be best characterized by conservative forces that aggressively want to maintain the status quo from which they have benefited greatly, and by liberal forces that recognize that certain changes are needed so long as they consist of the gradual incorporation of subordinate social and cultural groups into the structural reality of schools. However, the proposed incorporation of these groups should never interrogate the asymmetrical power relations that give white liberals their privilege. Thus, many white liberals willingly call and work for curriculum diversity but are reluctant to confront issues of inequality, power, ethics, race, and ethnicity that could lead to the transformation of schools so as to make them more democratic, less racist, more humane, and less discriminatory.

What is rarely discussed in the present school reform debate is the total integration of diverse racial and cultural groups, leading to their active presence within the school reality so as to transcend what Lani Guinier correctly calls "the triumph of tokenism." A total integration of diverse subordinate groups into an active democratic participation in schools, can begin to create structures that will lead to a total de-colonization of the subordinate groups so they can move from their object position in the margin to a subject position at the core of the school life. This, obviously, implies not a curriculum diversity for inequality in the form of "triumphant tokenism" but a process that makes diversity the very core of the school reality. A total integration of subordinate students would also imply moving beyond reforms based on choice. It would require not only a total transformation of schools but also the transformation of those social and political forces that shape and maintain the present "savage inequalities." A true transformation of schools would require a political and historical project that consciously transcended the educational system created and maintained by the dominant group for its own benefit.

A total transformation of schools informed by a truly cultural democracy cannot remain paralyzed by the liberal abstraction of cultural diversity and pluralism. School transformation must speak directly to the undemocratic nature of schools which is part and parcel of a colonial legacy. Educators must realize that beneath the democratic veil of schools lies a colonial historical will that has bequeathed us the rampant social inequality along the lines of race, class, gender, language, and ethnicity. Once educators become cognizant of the colonial ideology that still informs our schools, they can begin to create pedagogical structures that will lead to a total de-colonization so as to achieve democratization.

It is the colonizer, paternalistic attitude that led a white middle-class professor to pronounce publicly, at a major conference, that community people don't need to go to college because they know so much more than do members of the university community thus there is little that the university can teach them. While making such public statements this professor was busily moving from the inner-city to an affluent suburb making sure that her children attend better schools. A similar attitude emerged in a recent meeting to develop a community-university relationship grant proposal. During the meeting, a liberal white professor rightly protested the absence of community members in the committee. However, in attempting to valorize the community knowledge base, she rapidly fell into a romantic paternalism by stating that the community people knew much more than the university professors and that they should be invited to come to teach us rather than we teaching them. This position not only discourages community members from having access to the cultural capital from which these professors have benefited greatly but it also disfigures the reality context which makes the university cultural capital indispensable for any type of real empowerment. It also smacks of a false generosity of paternalism which Freire aggressively opposes: "The pedagogy of the oppressed animated by authentic humanism (and not humanitarianism) generously presents itself as a pedagogy of man. Pedagogy which begins with the egoistic interests of the oppressors (an egoism cloaked in the false generosity of paternalism) and makes of the oppressed the objects of its humanitarianism, itself maintains and embodies oppression. It is an instrument of dehumanization." [17] The paternalistic pedagogical attitude represents a liberal middle-class narcissism that gives rise to pseudo-critical educators who are part of and responsible for the same social order they claim to renounce.

This is not surprising since liberalism, as a school of thought and as ideology, always prioritized the right to private property ownership while relegating human freedom and other rights to "mere epiphenomenon or derivatives" [18] A rigorous analysis of thinkers such as Thomas Hobbes and John Locke will clearly show that the real essence of liberalism is the right to own private property. The right to private property ownership could only be preserved through auto-conservation. This led Linbomir Tadic to pose the following question: "isn't conservatism a more determinant characteristic for liberalism than the tendency toward freedom?"[19] He concludes that due to this insipid ambiguity, liberalism is always positioned ideologically between revolution and reactionarism. In other words, liberalism vacillates between two opposing poles.

It is this liberal position of vacillation that, on the one hand, propels many individuals to denounce all forms of oppression and even side with the oppressed through a form of romanticism as demonstrated by my colleague's blind celebration of the subordinate community knowledge base. On the other hand, the intrinsic liberal value to conserve one's position of privilege (either from acquired property or other cultural capital specific to one's privileged class), forces them to always make sure that their children go to the best schools as a means to acquire the necessary cultural capital that will guarantee the children the same privileges enjoyed by their parents.

It is for this reason that many liberals prefer to go to Australia to study the causes of illiteracy among Aborigines rather than attempting to analyze the oppressive structures in the United States that have generated an unacceptably high level of illiteracy (and poverty) among the diverse subordinate racial and cultural groups. In distant and remote areas of the world, these liberals are able to safely display their presumed benevolence toward the oppressive conditions of a particular subordinate cultural group without having to accept that, because of their privileged position, they are part of a social order that created the very reality of oppression they want to study. Studying and anthropologizing subordinate cultural groups in remote areas of the world, as well as in the United States position many liberals as tourists that can "become enamored and perhaps interested in the [groups] for a time."[20] but always shielding themselves from the reality that created those conditions they wanted to study in the first place.

The position of many liberals in the United States is similar to that of the leftist colonialists who, in not wanting to commit cultural privilege suicide, found themselves in an ever-present contradiction. This contradiction surfaces often when many liberals feel threatened by the legitimacy of the subordinate group's struggle—a struggle that not only may not include them but also demand that their liberal treatment of oppression as abstract ideas must be translated into concrete political action. An example that comes to mind is when I was discussing some of these issues with graduate students at Harvard, a middle-class white woman impatiently asked me if I was suggesting that she give up her job. I responded that the answer was complex but that, in some instances, giving up one's job may be necessary. I pointed out to her that as a middle-class white Harvard graduate student she had immensely more opportunities in securing jobs than many minority women with whom she worked in the community. Her continued occupation of leadership position in a subordinate community meant that a minority woman would not occupy that position. I gave as an example the student Literacy Corps Tutor Training Program that was designed to train tutors to provide literacy in various communities. In this program, over eighty-six percent of coordinators are middle-class white women. That means that if they become eternal in their coordinatorship positions, almost ninety percent of minority women and men would not have the chance to occupy such leadership positions. I also called to her attention, that minority women have infinitely less opportunity outside their racial context to compete for leadership positions.

As the discussion became a little tense, another white-middle class student cited an episode that helped us come to a closure. She told us that a female friend of her had given up a successful career in business to work in the community with battered mothers. Enthusiastic in her altruism, she went into a community center where she explained to one of the center staff how much more rewarding it would be to work helping people in need than just making money. The African-American staff member responded: "M'am, if you really want to help us, go back to your white folks and tell them to keep the wall of racism from crushing us." This metaphor brought home a point I was not able to make during the discussion. That is, the issue is not to give up or not give up a job. The real issue is to understand one's privileged position in the process of helping so as not to, on the one hand, turn help into a type of missionary paternalism and, on the other hand, limit the possibilities for the creation of structures that lead to real empowerment. The metaphor also points to white teachers' responsibility to attack oppression at its very source, which is often white racist supremacy. Otherwise, the romanticism to "empower" subordinate students lead to insidious paternalism that provoked a Nigerian undergraduate student enrolled in a literacy tutor training program to tell her white teacher while they were discussing issues of oppression: "I am tired of the oppressor always reminding the oppressed of their condition."

Control Change so as Not to Change

A fundamental question that is rarely raised is how can schools of education provide leadership in the process of educational reform since they are, by and large, responsible for the creation of what Senge accurately calls a school culture which is "subject to crippling learning disabilities?" We need to ask the following:

— Can schools of education that function as a cultural reproduction model create pedagogical spaces to prepare teachers who will be agents of change and who will be committed to education for liberation?

— How can schools of education reconcile their technicist and often undemocratic approach to teacher preparation with the urgency to democratize schools?

— How can schools of education that have been accomplices to racial, cultural, gender and ethnic discrimination create the necessary pedagogical spaces that will lead to cultural democracy?

The paradox is that while many schools of education have been "crippled with learning disabilities," they are expected to play a major role in the reform of schools. In most instances, schools of education represent the most conservative sector of university life bent on reproducing values designed to maintain the status quo while de-skilling teachers through a labyrinth of how-to methods courses devoid of any substantive content. When content is incorporated into courses, it consists of secondary sources usually presented as translations from primary sources. Often, the content ignores subordinate students' culture production and the antagonistic relations generated by the discriminating school practices and the subsequent resistance of students to "savage inequalities." Schools of education cannot succeed in preparing future teachers for leadership positions and to be agents of change if they continue to advocate the consumption of neatly packaged instructional programs that are presented as the panacea to difficulties students face in the acquisition of pre-packaged knowledge. Schools of education cannot point teachers to a truly cultural democracy if they fail to prepare teachers to both analyze and understand how subordinate cultures are produced in the classrooms and society at large. Teachers need also to understand the antagonistic relationships between subordinate cultures and the dominant values of the curriculum. Take, for example, the resistance to speaking the required standard dialect of the curriculum. The dominant curriculum is designed primarily to reproduce the inequality of social classes, while it mostly benefits the interests of the dominant class. Teachers need to capitalize on the antagonistic cultural elements produced in subordinate students' acts of resistance, and create a pedagogy that would enable students to comprehend their world so they read it and act upon it and, if necessary, transform it. That is, teachers need to understand how to use students' resistances and world as a platform from which they can transcend the mechanistic nature of education imposed upon them by the dominant ideology. The de-skilling of teachers is:

> . . . further complicated by the fact that schools are presently organized around an industrial model rather than an informational model. Schools are traditionally organized to produce young people who are capable of working in isolation and taking directions . . . The role of the schools today is such that it attempts to extinguish the natural desire of people to gather, be inquisitive and interact.[21]

Because many schools of education train teachers to become technicists who walk un-reflexively through a labyrinth of procedures and approaches, they are, in some cases, either unwilling or unable to prepare teachers to become intellectuals able to assume leadership through independent thought and actions.

With rare exception, schools of education generally do not offer pedagogical spaces where future teachers can engage in the development of a critical attitude informed by a praxis that involves both reflection and political action. It is thus, not surprising, that the present school reform movement remains at the cosmetic level dislodged from the structural reality that necessitated the call for reform in the first place. In noting that "[t]oo often meaningless changes are defined as transformation"[22], Peter Negroni cautions us that:

> One cannot simply rearrange the chairs in a classroom into a circle and proclaim that this will help instruction. In America's public schools, historically, children have been asked to sit one behind the other and told to be still, be quiet and never to talk to each other. If the change constitutes putting the children in a circle and telling them to be still, be quiet and never talk to each other, little has been done to change the results.[23]

The above quote captures the drama of the present school reform debate, not only through the trivializing of reform itself, in the form of cosmetic changes, but also through the refusal of most educators to unveil the hidden ideology of racism and sexism that serves to devalue and dis-confirm the lived-experiences, culture, history and language of subordinated students. The unwillingness to unpack the schools' hidden ideology has given rise to a plethora of methods and approaches presented as panaceas that are destined to failure and substitution by similar, faddish "teacher-proof" methods. Regardless of how progressive these methods may be, unless they are supported by the school ideology, they will inevitably fail. Methods can only be effective if teachers who adopt them understand fully both the methods' limits and possibilities in relation to the restrictions set by the school ideology. It is of paramount importance that teachers understand that the adoption of a progressive methodology will not necessarily succeed if the dominant ideology within the school reality is diametrically opposed to the prinicples and values of the chosen progressive methodology. That is why Paulo Freire often cautions educators against the uncritical importation or exportation of methodologies. He argues that the success of any educational transformation goes hand in hand with societal transformations as well. A society that remains racist, undemocratic and discriminatory will not tolerate the transformation of schools and their democratization.

Notes

1　Freire, P. *Pedagogy of the City.* New York: Continuum Publishing Co., 1993, p. 40

2　Negroni, P. "The Transformation of America's Public Schools." Unpublished article, p. 12

3　Giroux, A.H. *Living Dangerously: Multiculturalism and the Politics of Difference.* (New York: Peter Lang, 1993), p. 128

4　*America 2000: An Education Strategy.* (Washington, D.C.: US Department of Education, 1991), p. 4

5　Kilianski, S.E. New *York Times,* July 15, 1992, p. A20 [**Name of Article**]

6　Cited in Moacir Gadotti, *Convite a Leitura de Paulo Freire.* (Sao Paulo: Editora Scipione, 1989), p. 32

7　Freire, P. *Pedagogy of the City.* (New York: Continuum Publishing Co., 1993), p 19

8　Saul, A.M. in Freire, P. *Pedagogy of the City.* (New York: Continuum Publishing Co., 1993), p 150

9　Freire, P. *Pedagogy of the City.* (New York: Continuum Publishing Co., 1993), pp. 19-20

10　Giroux, A.H. *Living Dangerously: Multiculturalism and the Politics of Difference.* (New York: Peter Lang, 1993), p.131

11　Ibid., p. 131

12　Ibid., p. 131

13　Freire, P. *Pedagogy of the City.* (New York: Continuum Publishing Co., 1993), p 20

14　Hemp, P. "From Whittle, a $2.3B Education Plan", *The Boston Globe,* August 30, 1992, p. 25

15　Ibid., p. 25

16　Beaty, J. "The Bankruptcy of Conservatism", *Boston Globe,* August 14, 1992.

17 Freire, P. *Pedagogy of the Oppressed.* (New York: Continuum Publication Co., 1990), p. 30

18 Markovic, M., Tadic, L., Galic, D. *Liberalismo y Socialismo: Teoria y Praxis.* (Mexico: Editorial Grijalbo, S.A. 1977), p. 19

19 Ibid. p. 17

20 Memmi, A. *The Colonizer and the Colonized.* (Boston: Beacon Press, 1991), p. 26

21 Negroni, P. "The Transformation of America's Public Schools." Unpublished article p. 9

22 Ibid., p. 10

23 Ibid., p. 10

Chapter III

Teachers Under Suspicion: Is it true that teachers aren't as good as they used to be?

Shirley R. Steinberg

Deborah P. Britzman

Shirley R. Steinberg

I remember myself as a skinny, freckled, unpopular freshman at West High. My hair was curly in an age where straight hair was essential. I asked too many questions, interrupted in class. My friends were equally awkward and I knew early that my looks and aggressive manner would be my badge of inadmission to the "cool" group. Teachers didn't like me much, I asked the wrong questions, argued and made asides to no one in particular. By the ninth grade, the citizenship spaces on my report cards had been filled with: "behavior problem", "Shirley has potential but refuses to use it," "egocentric," "interrupts in class," "talkative," "a disturbance," . . . ad nauseum.

Martha Gatsinaris was my ninth grade English teacher. Young, vibrant, an excellent dresser, Mrs. "G" knew *everything*, especially about books. I was a closet reader and felt most of my school-mandated reading was a real drag. My previous teachers had used anthologies or condensed books and Mrs. G taught from the *real* novels.

Our first book was *Nigger of the Narcissus* by Joseph Conrad. In l965 the risk of teaching a book with that title was not lost on our class. Parents complained, yet we combed through that novel for months. Mrs. G facilitated us to reveal literary symbols and sociological concepts throughout the novel. (In those days, however I just thought she was an "out-of-sight" teacher). Our lives were filled with the dangers and dreams of James Waite and other characters—our vocabulary was from the book, our in-class journals integrated our lives with those of the characters and when we approached Mrs. G to write and produce a play in lieu of a final exam, our theatrics melded our world with Conrad's masterpiece.

Mrs. G was the teacher who we stopped by to see in the morning, her room was our lunchroom, we erased boards after school and collected books. She invited our class to her home to have a "real" Greek dinner and her husband taught us Greek dancing.

Mrs. G had a way of tolerating my interruptions, accomodating and answering my questions to the point that by mid-year, someone noticed that I wasn't interrupting anymore, that the whole class listened to my comments—they didn't laugh and I no longer heard them whisper or saw them roll their eyes when I spoke.

The year I finished ninth grade, I was established as an important part of the speech and drama club,; people actually were interested in my opinion (without my forcing them), and I looked forward to my final three years of high school. My physical appearance hadn't changed much (in a year of bra-burning, I still wasn't wearing one), but I felt good about who I was.

Two years later, I left West High, and one summer day, Mrs. G drove three hours with my best friend to spend the day. As she left, she handed me a copy of *Tristan und Isolde*, and told me to never stop asking questions, to read everything, to be critical and never stop being myself.

Twenty-six years later, I tried to find Mrs. G, to tell her that I too, was an English teacher . . . to thank her for teaching me—I left a message at West High, and they phoned back to tell me that sometime in the early 70s, Mrs. G had killed herself. I guess the only way to remember her and to thank her is by writing about her—and by trying to be a good teacher.

What is a good teacher? good teaching? what does it mean to be a good teacher? are teachers as good as they used to be? do we have reason to think teachers are not as good? what made them good? how do we define good? is there a model for good teaching? a system of meaning that we can attach to good teaching? are there different types of good teachers? what stories do we hear from teachers about good teaching? what stories from students? is good teaching intuitive? is it learned? how symbiotic should schooling and teaching be? what does learning have to do with teaching? can one really *teach* anything? what is the responsibility of the learner? what is the text of teaching? of good teaching? can we define good teaching?

In investigating a student's death, *Dragnet's* Joe Friday suggested "if you really want to know something about a kid, ask his coach". Embedded in Friday's observation is that the people who know children best are neither parents or academic teachers, but those that spend extra-curricular time, less structured time with children—fun time.

While describing a "good" teacher, a ninth grader told me that the teacher would have to be fun, even while teaching serious subjects; to allow humor in the class and to be able to make students feel loose, natural . . . comfortable . . . and above all, not to be on a "power trip."

Why isn't teaching fun time? Schools seem determined to impress upon children and parents that "being a good citizen" entails not having fun, and that good teaching consists of rule-making, structured lessons, stringent curriculum and right or wrong answers to formula questions. Our childrens' junior high handbook describes good teachers as those that are "competent" . . . "all teachers must meet minimum qualifications . . . students and parents will find the faculty willing to go beyond normal duty to assist them in any way." What qualifications are met? are these purely academic, or do these qualifications include certain attitudes towards children? what is a faculty member's "duty?" is teaching a duty? Many schools isolate learning time and fun time. The New Right's thrust to the "good ole days" of schooling have reinforced the lack of humor and diversity in teaching.

When asked what the purpose of schooling was, the student I spoke to divided schooling into three stages: the first stage of schooling is to keep one occupied until reaching the second stage, in which workbook-type teaching occurs; after students are taught, the final stage, from ninth grade to graduation is developed in order to keep students in, off the streets and out of society until they are old enough to know how to be responsible—to stay "out of trouble."

Teaching is considered a profession, yet when considering this young man's terrifying opinion of schooling, there is the undeniable evidence of the deskilling of a profession into a job . . . something to be filled competently and to be evaluated quantitatively: Lesson plans, time on task behavior—these reflect good teaching—high evaluations, high exam scores, good public relations images . . . all leading to a New Right definition of good teaching, which advocates a return to an unthoughtful respect for authority. "Back to basics" means far more than simple concern with the course of study. A meta-narrative works behind the concept, a story marked by a protection of patriarchy, Euro-centrism, and "family" values.

Teacher talk about surprise school visits, target evaluations, achievement test scores and complete lesson plans define a collective consciousness of what makes good teaching. Student talk about how easy he or she is, or how one can really "goof" off in class, or never has homework defines good teaching. Parent talk about Jennifer really "straightening up" or Nathan finally "settling down" or "Meghann actually doing homework," defines good teaching. Talk about teaching provides a tacit meaning about the importance of control, of conformist thinking, of good image, and of perpetuating my ninth grade friend's image of schooling: *Stage 1:* to be occupied, *Stage 2:* to be taught through prescribed workbook curriculum, *Stage 3:* to be held down.

Many who answer "no" to the question, "are teachers as good as they used to be?," blame the breakdown of family structure, drugs, lack of discipline and good parenting skills, and a failure of community will. In actuality, they are framing the teachers "good-ness" as dependent on their ability to cope with the problems of our age. The right-wing attributes bad teaching to "innovative" methods . . . schools that don't teach the basics produce teachers who don't know the basics. Innovative methods pose a threat to the Fundamentalist Right, many stories and myths are viewed as LIBERAL . . . exciting new facilitation of creativity is called NEW AGE and these labels translate to Satanic.

The success of the Ronald Reagans, George Bushes, Dan Quayles and Pat Robertsons rests on their ability to portray attempts to foster egalitarian educational policies and thoughtful graduates as misguided—indeed, as catalysts for a decline in teacher quality. If teachers are not as good as they used to be, then simple-minded tests of teacher aptitude, teacher-proof materials, deskilled job descriptions are justifiable. Such policies are necessary measures in the fight against the legacy of the "permissive, equality-obsessed" 1960s.

Do we find ourselves in the middle of the proverbial vicious circle? When the Right convinces the public that teachers are not as good as they used to be, and offers its shallow "quick-fixes" in the form of constraining teacher self-determination, then teachers really don't have the freedom, the professional perogative to be as good as they used to be. Frustration abounds. Students insist that schooling is designed to not let them learn to think, teachers complain that creativity and critical thinking is impossible to facilitate due to the structure imposed by administrative and governmental pronouncements. Civic courage, self-actualization are irrelevant, "learning" is public relations, a shallow attempt to present a positive image to the community—"putting our best foot forward."

No, teaching can't be as good as it used to be under the definitions set forth by education's right-wing critics, Bloom, Hirsch, Bennett, the Christian Right and the frightening Rush Limbaugh (who has taken it upon himself to define what education *should* be). Rather, teaching is relegated to a model of efficiency, quantitative evaluation, curriculum that defies social imagination and student handbooks that espouse rules that deskill teachers and oppress students. Images of the "good" student in the form of *Family Ties'* Alex Keaton haunt creative thinkers and students who insist on individuality through expression and/or appearance are quickly suppressed and taught to "love it or leave it."

But, possibility lives, images of alternatives flicker at the level of the popular. Fox television's Lisa Simpson was given a reprieve from her dreary teacher in the form of a substitute teacher who spent two weeks with her class. Lisa's world became a kalideoscope of investigation, open-ended questions and intrigue in the form of alternative methods of teaching the curriculum. Mr. Bergstrom was interested in who each child was and what they had to contribute to the class in the form of their own stories and knowledge. Dimensions of gender and class were acknowledged, not suppressed as Lisa was urged to see herself within the context of the forces which shaped her. The children were appreciated and in turn, appreciated the authenticity of the teacher and his desire to teach them. Teaching and learning became symbiotic and school was thought-provoking, fun. When Mr. Bergstrom left, a tearful Lisa was admonished to be herself and to follow her own vision, not the standardized, packaged vision promoted by "competent" teachers in National Schools of Excellence.

Martha Gatsinaris was a good teacher. How she taught, the effect she had on her students, the change she facilitated in me would never show up on a teacher evaluation form. Forms don't measure empathy, humor, driving three hours to visit a former student, or ability to connect students' lives with schooling and curriculum. The qualities that Mrs. G had as a good teacher could have easily been considered liabilities in many schools. As a result of being a student of Mrs. Gatsinaris, I was changed. I gained confidence, learned to channel my "enthusiasm," understood my place in the scheme of school and realized my potential as a student and finally as a teacher. No student should leave any classroom unchanged; without the empowerment to rewrite his or her own life in even a subtly different way.

If teaching is going to be good work, we have to be able to get beyond the simplistic, teacher-proof curriculums, standardization of evaluation, and an excellence read as conventionality. Making use of our critical system of meaning, our social imagination, while renewing our commitment to democracy, we can honor "good" teachers of the past by redefining the role of teacher of the future.

Post script for the second edition:

As I re-read this short chapter and review the past three years since its first publication, I think about those short steps forward and those pushing us backward as teachers and students of education. I want to dedicate this essay to the memory of Oswaldo (Ozzie) Toledo, a student of mine at Florida International University.

Ozzie read this essay in my class and was dismayed that the education that he was receiving reinforced the deskilled, mechanical, teacher-proof curriculum that has dominated education in North America. He felt frustrated and angry that even as a student, if he tried to be creative, inventive or student friendly, that he was criticized by his education professors. Ozzie had one professor in particular that reduced teaching to an assembly-line of behavioral objectives, attendance sheets and taxonomic check lists. In addition to questionable and abusive classroom techniques, the teacher treated students with disdain and ranted about the "puss-pocket" teachers in the victimized school system. The irony in this story is that this was the one educator singled out by his superiors—he won the teaching awards each year. This was the man that the college wished to set forth as a model teacher. Ozzie found this terribly painful; he chose Mrs. Gatsinaris' solution. We all miss him.

And power seeks always to reproduce itself.

Deborah P. Britzman

The slippery thing about history is that it must always be arranged. Some arrangements are more comforting than others and at times, the arrangement of the story hides its interestedness and thus the politics of selection. Milan Kundera's novel, *The Book of Laughter and Forgetting*, begins with the dangers of arranging history. He describes the evolution of one photograph: the original people who posed, and how years later, the empty spaces left because some individuals were suddenly erased, airbrushed from historical consciousness, because they fell from official grace. History is overpopulated with such stories and the familiar question, are teachers as good as they used to be, seems to provoke the impulse to airbrush and thus sanitize our memories of schools.

Thus some stories about the educational past are more comforting than others. And some questions invoke the stories we wish we could tell. Are teachers as good as they used to be is one of those oddly familiar questions that bestow cultural authority onto everyone. Teachers were an important presence in our past lives and, at times, they may even seem to haunt our present. We have all played a role opposite to teachers and because significant parts of our lives unfold in schools, we implicitly fashion some particular understandings of what a teacher is and does. Most of our childhoods were devoted to observing them, trying to anticipate their moods, and imagining their hidden lives. It seems almost secondhand nature to leave school believing we understand how teachers are made and what work they must do.

This cumulative knowledge of teachers is no such a part of us that it is taken for granted. Indeed, the mass experience of public education has made teaching one of the most familiar professions in this culture. Implicitly, schooling fashions the meanings, realities, and lived experience of our childhood: residing in our heads and hearts are contesting views of good and bad teachers. The question, are teachers as good as they used to be, may even seem pleasurable because it invites us to return to our won educational biographies. It is a question that is as much about who we are as it is about who they are. That is, one cannot tell stories about teachers without telling stories about students, schools, and the communities where we live. And yet this question is as slippery and as elusive as the histories it attempts to stabilize. The hidden dilemma is that the question of whether teacher are as good as they used to be traps us in an impossible chronology.

The particular phrasing of whether teachers are as good as they used to be couples our stories with the fictions of nostalgia. It would be nice to think there once was a time when schooling worked, teachers taught, and students learned. That once upon a time, schools were protected from contesting demands, incredibly complicated social strife, and were populated with smiling, satisfied subjectivities who did what they were supposed to do. In a story fused with nostalgia, things become simple: textbooks tell the truth, everyone listens quietly and waits their turn and when children are asked to line up, it really only expedites the smooth movements of large groups of children. The conjuring of this idyllic past depends upon an order of things somehow better than the disorder of the present It is a version of the past that implicitly says that somewhere along the road, the dream of education-for-all-involved became lived as a nightmare on Elm Street.

Embedded in this nostalgic narrative is a disturbing version of the present: the idyllic has its messy counterpart. This is the nightmare that rehearses what used to be good because of what we take to be bad. Its logic collapses multiple contexts and poses effects as causes because it offers reasons in the guise of motives. The question, whether teachers are as good as they used to be, requires no contextual distinctions and so the answers become so many ranting slogans. The next few paragraphs will suggest some of the anxieties conjured by this question.

The first anxiety concerns questions of preparation. This anxiety says that at some point, teachers stopped being as prepared as they used to be. Teacher education accepted anyone into their programs, and besides, only the worst students apply. Those who study teaching are required to take too many education courses and not enough courses in academic knowledge.

They then graduate from college without the proper skills. They even have trouble reading and speaking, and this makes necessary the mandatory literacy testing of teachers. Newly arrived teachers are too idealistic and lack the discipline techniques to control the students in the ways they used to control students.

A different anxiety addresses the conditions of teachers. Somewhere along the way, teachers became involved with things like teacher's unions and began to view their profession as labor. They became far too involved with negotiating the conditions of their work and thus are not negotiating the conditions of their work and thus are not concerned with their students. In this confused version, unions are viewed as constraining and manipulating teachers' actions. Teachers aren't as good as they used to be because nasty unions force them to limit their work. But with or without unions, this version also asserts that teachers became disenchanted with teaching because they are now required to do things that should have been done elsewhere: like teaching values, offering medical advice, counseling students, and even washing students clothes. In this conflated story, teachers could be as good as they used to be if families, communities, and cultures did what they were supposed to do and if unions would leave them alone. Students and their parents are also blamed in this version: teachers are not as good as they used to be because students no longer enter school with the proper respect for education and for teachers.

Yet another kind of anxious nostalgia, gathering different threads of history, becomes woven into this fictive sense of time and of identity. Teachers are not as good as they used to be because of the women's liberation movement. Today's women have more career choices than ever. Their choice of career is no longer determined by maintaining traditional gendered family roles and no longer tied to being the sole person to care for their children. In this story of gender tyranny, while their choice of career is no longer being determined by conventional imperatives, the actions of women are ruining both the sanctity of the family and the schools. So teachers are not as good as they used to be because women have abandoned the field and those male teachers left behind, as well as those male teachers just entering, are not as good as the female teacher.

The above versions of history are not comforting to those who work in schools. Not can they make sense of the fact that teaching and learning are overburdened with conflicting meanings. These meanings shift with our lived lives, with the common sense invoked to render our stories generalizable, with the deep convictions and desires brought to and created in education, with the practices we negotiate, and with the kinds of identities we try on as desirable, or shed as undesirable. The contradictory myths working through such nostalgia are that teachers should be both selfless and self-made, that everything depends upon them, and that teachers are always certain in their knowledge. The discomfort suggests that teachers are people who experience deep doubt about what schools actually do, that their understanding of competence and success are more vulnerable than imagined, and that the conditions of their work and daily lives are more complicated that our educational biographies are capable of imagining.

It is difficult to unravel all of the myths mobilized by the question of whether teachers are as good as they used to be because so many different voices speak and because this is a question that answers itself.

The past it conjures is too selective, and the present is too close to sort out. This is a question where the present can never be addressed on its own terms and where the future is overburdened with what is taken as the past. This implicit value on time hides the very process of selection and valuation. The question never requires us to define our criteria of the past or trace what it is that structures our sense of the good, the bad, and the ugly. When time supplants humanity, ethical responsibilities are abandoned. To ask the familiar question, are teachers as good as they used to be, is to reject the myriad relations that make education possible.

Are teachers as good as they used to be unleashes such dissonance because the question conjures an impossible time and this doubly shuts out thoughtful understandings of what good teaching means and critical considerations that are necessary for good teaching. As originally posed, this question can only invoke common sense. The problem is that what seems most obvious, most common is that which is never explained. Like the myths and the fictive chronologies that support them, common sense makes the world appear as natural, and as never in need of change. Common sense covers its own narrative tracks. And so, as posed, the question is overpopulated with assumptions that leave no trace.

But there is an additional explanation for why the question— are teachers as good as they used to be—seems to resonate with the familiar. And this has to do with the fact that this question has always echoed throughout the history of schooling. It hides the difficult reality that there has never been agreement as to what good teaching means and that what once seemed good twenty-five years ago may now be viewed as harmful. History does not stand still and neither do the meanings we make of it. One need only consider the history of corporal punishment in schools where beating the "good" into children, "for their own good" is now understood as child abuse. Caught within the question of whether teachers are as good as they used to be are contesting histories of what education might mean and of which version of the good holds currency. Caught as well in such a question are the insistencies of race, class, gender, ethnicity, and generation, and how these social differences contest or affirm dominant versions of "the good." The point is that this question about the past is only capable of invoking empty promises.

We are capable of raising intelligent questions about good teaching and still consider our deep investments in schools. Relevant questions can provoke us to refashion and articulate our educational, historical, political, and emotional imaginations. What kinds of teaching contribute to the building of democracy in the present as well as in the future? What might encourage students and teachers to imagine, in deep and compassionate terms, the possibilities offered by their own identities and the identities of others? How might teaching engage everyone involved in social justice and in the attainments of civil rights? What kinds of values allow students and teachers to work together in dignified ways? What conditions allow teaching and learning to be meaningful, creative, and pleasurable? If we can imagine schooling as a wonderful place, what kinds of identities would be available to teachers, students, and the larger communities? If education could lived as a utopia, what kinds of practices, values, beliefs, and relationships would sustain it? What if teachers and students could shed the stereotypes that trap them? How would their work and their lives be different?

These new questions suggest teaching as a social process of negotiation rather than an individual problem of behavior. This dynamic is essential to any humanizing explanation of the work of teachers. Teaching concerns coming to terms with one's intentions and values, as well as one's views of knowing, being, and acting in a setting characterized by contradictory realities, negotiation, and dependency and struggle. Engagement with these complications requires that we acknowledge that there is something quite vulnerable about teaching and learning. Teaching means coming to terms with the power to shape young identities and their views of the world. And given this encounter, the teacher is also in the process of becoming. This view of teaching admits an unknowable chronology because neither students nor teachers stand still. Teaching suggests an unsettling moment when new ideas disorganize what one thought was long settled. And so teaching means taking and inviting interpretive risks as part of the process of coming to know. Most unsettling, teaching means being intellectually and emotionally open to that which one cannot foresee, predict, or control. In other words, teaching means acknowledging and working with all of the uncertainties that are the sum of our lived lives.

Given such complexities, what kinds of conditions provoke good teaching? First, teachers need opportunities to move beyond their isolation from one another and their isolation from the community. As it is presently lived, teachers are expected to single-handedly work in crowded classrooms. Because teachers are expected to control the class alone, they implicitly understand this to mean that asking for help or support is viewed as a source of weakness. Moreover, rarely do students observe teachers interacting with other adults and thus cannot imagine teachers as people who also work with others, seek advice, and need support. To move beyond the terrible isolation teachers daily experience, teachers must have opportunities to shape their work collectively and to organize their time in ways that can allow thoughtful dialogue with their colleagues, creative interactions with students, and meaningful time in the communities in which they work.

A second condition is that teachers have the time and space to continue their education in ways they determine. Presently, in-service education is typically designed by administrators who rarely work in classrooms and whose imperatives are shaped by needs that are not pedagogical. Teachers are rarely given the time to determine programs that may be helpful, or even research what might be illuminating. Yet schools could be organized to facilitate the education of teachers and students. For example, part of the teacher's work should be devoted to teacher study groups that collaboratively research their teaching and learning needs. Such a direction necessitates a significant restructuring of schools where classrooms are not the only context for teaching and learning and where teachers have the opportunities to think through their practices.

A third direction for good teaching concerns carefully linking those just entering the profession to those already there in ways that value the contributions of the newly arrived and the experienced teachers. Everyone involved needs opportunities to experiment with new methodology, familiarize themselves with the most recent arguments in the research literature in order to construct their own views, and talk though their practices. As presently lived, however, those entering the profession are as isolated as those already there and far too often, learning to teach dissipates into the narrow terms of taking up existing practices without opportunities to practice in meaningful ways. Providing the time, space, and guidance for experienced teachers to work with the newly arrived would mean rethinking the work of teaching to include leadership in the revitalization of the profession.

A fourth direction involves extending the present boundaries of learning and teaching. The curriculum of school need not be confined to classroom settings and to the pages of textbooks. Communities have much to offer students and teachers when they become another context for education and the historic tension between the schools and the communities must be addressed in pedagogical terms. Like the isolation of teachers, the segregation of youth from their community context works to fragment education and the complexities of life. Community oriented schooling would mean involving new identities in the education of youth, extending the meaning of teaching and learning beyond the confines of classroom walls, and repairing the distance between school and life.

The question, what makes for good teaching, then, requires everyone to become more curious about the present structure of education and about the future possibilities opened when this structure is rearranged. Imaginative thinking can move us beyond the constraints of nostalgia and the anxious impulse to arrange history without an awareness of what it is that structures our destinations or how the inherited contexts and practices constrain our possibilities. Because we have all spent significant time in schools, we are obligated to shape its possibilities in ways that advance what we inherit. Imagining good teaching then, should invite us to move beyond the dreary cycle of self blame or blaming others and onto future visions of that which is not yet.

Chapter IV

Students Under Suspicion: Do students misbehave more than they used to?

Clinton B. Allison

Kathleen Berry

Clinton B. Allison

The Myth

Our mailbox in rural East Tennessee collects some of the darndest things. Among other unsolicited periodicals, we received the tabloid of a fundamentalist Bible college, located just a few miles down the road. Except for locality, we have little in common with the members of that community, nevertheless, I always dutifully read the Johnson Bible College *Blue and White*. In the April 1987 issue, there was an astonishing article, written by the president of the college, David L. Eubanks. "It sounds like to scenario of a horror story," he begins, and adds, "the problem is, it's true!" According to the article, "researchers" in 1948 surveyed teachers to find the "top" discipline problems in the public school. They found:

> Talking. Chewing gum. making noise. Running in the halls. Wearing improper clothing. Not putting waste paper in the waste paper basket.

Teachers in the 1980s were asked the "same question," with frightening results; "the degeneration in the span of only one generation is shocking." The current "top" discipline problems, according to the article, were:

> Rape ...! Robbery ...! Assault ...! Burglary ...! Arson ...! Bombing ...! Murder ...!

"The truth is that in one generation," the article continues, "our nation has been brought to the brink of moral and spiritual disaster." The surveys were found, according to Eubanks, in an article by Dr. James Dobson (the child-rearing expert of the religious right) in the March 1987 issue of his magazine, *Focus on the Family*, (Eubanks, 1987).

As an aging educational historian with a longtime interest in the history of childhood, I was bemused by the article. Surely, no rational person could believe that such a degeneration of discipline in the schools had taken place since 1948; researchers could not possibly have asked the same questions of a similar cross section of American public school teachers with that result. If the surveys existed at all, I suspected that the problem was in the ambiguous word, "top," which could mean either most common or most severe. Teachers across the generations have spent their lives warning children that they have about reached the end of their patience with whispering and admonishing students not to run in the hallways, and so it continues today. And serious crimes have always been committed by the schoolchildren; but rape, murder, assault (unless you count one ten-year-old bloodying the nose of another) and the other "top disciplinary problems" are not part of the daily life of most teachers, except in the most difficult of schools where they have always been problems. Surely, I comforted myself, only a minority that use such "evidence" of moral decay to spread their salvation message would accept such degeneration as fact.

However, the *Knoxville News-Sentinel* immediately reprinted the surveys on the editorial page of the Sunday newspaper, and on November 26, 1989, the newspaper, as part of article, concerning discipline problems in the Knox County Schools, included the following:

"Problems in School"
According to Knox County
Schools teacher surveys

1948
Loud talking
Throwing paper
Gum chewing
Disruptive Behavior

1988
Teacher assault
Student assault
Drugs
Weapons
Gang activity
Vandalism
Thefts

These surveys, of course, looked remarkably like the ones in the *Blue and White*. Were they really Knox County teacher surveys?" I called the feature writer of the story. He said that he had gotten the results of the surveys from security investigators with the Knox County School system. I telephoned them. One said, "I have no idea where it [the surveys] came from . . . The reporter must have found it in a newspaper somewhere." The other indicated that they were national surveys rather than Knox County surveys, but he could not remember their source. He graciously called back a few days later, telling me that he had gotten the results of the surveys from the Director of the National School Safety Center in a seminar at Pepperdine University.

On December 3, 1990, I saw the now famous survey without attribution, on the Donahue show. Deciding that I really needed to see the original article in *Focus on the Family*, I called the Johnson Bible College library; they did not keep issues of the magazine that far back. I called President Eubanks' office; he did not have that issue. I called *Focus on the Family*. The people in their correspondence department were helpful. They too, had read the surveys but they were not in the April 1987 issue (or any issue, they thought) of the magazine. One remembered a book in which the surveys had been reprinted and suggested that they might have come originally from Mel and Norma Gabler, the rightist watchdogs of school textbooks. Since thereafter, I received a notice that I would start receiving *Focus on the Family* in the mail.

The original source of the "research" is not particularly important; the surveys have become a part of our educational folklore. They only reinforce an already widespread, existing belief that children in the past were more innocent, better behaved, and less troubled than they are today. In the rest of this essay, I will first review some of the historical literature on student behavior and childhood delinquency, and then indicate some of the policy problems with believing in the myth of a lost world of good children.

The Myth Explored

Did children engage in violently disruptive behavior in public schools in previous generations? Of course. Unruly children is a problem as old as schooling. Horace Mann, often called the "father of the public schools," in his *Annual Reports* of the Massachusetts Board of Education during the 1830s and 1840s, kept a running account of schools closed because of student unruliness and rebellion. He publicized excerpts from the reports of local school committees which would be seized upon today as certain evidence that our nation has, in President Eubanks' phrase, "been brought to the brink of moral and spiritual disaster." "School broken up by the disorderly and insolent conduct of the scholars," read a typical excerpt (Mann, 1841, p. 87). He reported that, in the 1830s in Massachusetts, 300 to 400 public schools "were annually brought to a violent termination, either by the triumph of a rebellious spirit on the part of the scholars, or by . . . gross incompetency on the part of teachers" (Mann, 1843, p. 38).

In seeking a perspective on youth in contemporary society, historians of childhood and of education often look to the mid and late nineteenth century. Precursors of social changes which characterize our world were taking place: urbanization, industrialization, secularization, and immigration of diverse people. Ministers, educators, and other social commentators of the time were warning that families seemed to be losing their moral bearings, that there was a social and moral breakdown. There were already cries, as an example, that fathers were too often absent from the home, away on business, or too permissive. The failures of parents to discipline children properly were widely condemned. A mid-nineteenth century textbooks in teacher training warned teachers that "good government in the family is the exception and not the rule. Parents indulge their children at home nay, indirectly train them to utter lawlessness" (Kaestle, 1978, p. 9).

For those who perceive an epidemic of immorality in America today, perhaps even evidence of "end times," no better evidence exists than the sexual abuse of children. Mothers and fathers simply didn't do that sort of unconscionable thing in their fantasy America of the past. But, unfortunately, some children have always had to suffer the anguish and shame of sexual abuse. In her history of the first reform school for girls in America, Barbara M. Benzel, tells us that one type of inmate was there for protection against parental abuse, including forced incest:

> One 1863 entrant whose "mother says the girl is beyond control," was the victim of incest by her stepfather . . . Another entrant, a thirteen-year-old who arrived in 1875, was undoubtedly also a victim of sexual abuse . . . Susan K. [a twelve-year-old] another example from 1885, . . . had "been terribly abused by her mother and compelled to submit to lewd men on numerous occasions." (Benzel, 1983, p. 129)

Accompanying a perception of a moral breakdown in the nineteenth century was a widespread belief in an epidemic of youthful crime and violence that rivals the worst fears of doomsayers today. In 1849, New York Police Chief George W. Matsell warned of "the constantly increasing number of vagrant, idle and vicious children. Their numbers were almost incredible," he reported, and he feared that the situation was to worsen: "each year makes fearful additions to the ranks of these prospective recruits of infamy and sin, and from this corrupt and festering fountain flows a ceaseless stream to our lowest brothel—to the Penitentiary and to the State Prison!" (Hawes, 1971, p. 91).

Historian of childhood Joseph M. Hawes found an epidemic of juvenile crime in the nineteenth century *New York Times*: "Nearly every day small boys commit highway robbery—usually by snatching the purses of ladies—in the streets of New York and Brooklyn." In 1890, the *Times* reported a case in which two boys, one seven and one ten, were charged with stealing horses; for the ten-year-old, it was a second offense for the same crime. The *Times* also complained about juvenile gangs, "half-drunken, lazy, worthless vagabonds," shooting guns and sometimes terrorizing people in their homes (Hawes, 1971, pp. 130-31).

Children were, of course, not just committing crimes in sin-ridden New York. Hawes begins his book on juvenile delinquency in nineteenth century America with a chapter on Jesse Pomeroy, the notorious "Boy Fiend" of Boston, who tortured and murdered young children in the 1870s (Hawes, 1971). Down in mid-century Houston, a ten-year-old boy drew a pistol from his pocket and shot his younger protagonist, fortunately, in this case, without killing him (Mennel, 1973, p. 73). And at the turn of the century, the president of the University of Tennessee despaired that more than half of the persons indicted for crimes in Knox County, the home of the University, were children (Dabney, 1901, p. 46). If readers think that these examples of youthful crimes and violence are exceptions cited simply to support the thesis this essay, I challenge them to spend a few hours reading a daily newspaper of any previous period. Every generation has a youth crisis.

In the minds of many social reformers, the solution to the crisis of youth and the moral degeneration of society in the nineteenth century was public schools. They were established not just to foster literacy, but to teach proper values to the young; not only to save the individual from crime, poverty, sin, and aimlessness, but to save the society from social degeneration as well. Those who perceive a moral breakdown today because of court decisions on school prayer or "secular humanism" in textbooks would find comfort in the persistent evangelical Protestant messages in nineteenth-century school textbooks; moral relativity was not a theme. In the omnipresent moral lessons in textbooks, good boys and girls obeyed their parents and teachers or suffered dire consequences, and good deeds were rewarded, often immediately and materially. Ruth Miller Elson's *Guardians of Tradition* provides an analysis of the themes of nineteenth century schoolbooks (Elson, 1964). Those who hope for a moral regeneration by returning to the unambiguous teaching of virtue in school might also ponder Horace Mann's outrage about students' drawings in such books and their carvings on school desks: "with such ribald inscriptions, and with the carvings of such obscene emblems, as would make a heathen blush" (Mann, 1841, p. 59).

Faith in character education as the panacea for a perceived epidemic of societal "immorality" may have exacerbated the problems of school discipline. As state-wide systems of public schools were established and then made compulsory, schools enrolled a larger proportion of unruly children. In 1889, Illinois passed a new and tougher compulsory education law. The Chicago Public Schools attempted to enforce the law, and "a number of "incorrigible" children came into the schools," but they were soon dismissed because their behavior could not be controlled (Hawes, 1971, p. 164).

But the point should not be missed: incorrigible, even violent, behavior by some schoolchildren has been a continuing problem in American society. The growing size of the list of references collected for a projected study of discipline problems in the first half of the twentieth century is making me ponder early retirement. And severe discipline problems preceded compulsory education in urban schools. In my study of schools on the frontier, for example, I found numerous cases of flagrant misbehavior and sometimes outright rebellion. In a log school in Michigan, as a teacher (who from accounts of his cruelty got what he deserved) prepared to whip one of the students, the others "piled onto him like an enraged swarm of bees, with fistcuffs, kicks, pinching, biting, sticking pins and awls into him." Other students held the door closed, but some carpenters who had been working nearby forced themselves into the room and saved him from the enraged students (Williams, 1882, p. 547).

Ancedotal evidence may be interesting, but it can also bias our images of an era. The key question in this essay remains unanswered. Do a higher ratio of children and youth seriously misbehave than they used to? I don't know and, in a quantified sense, there is no accurate way to find out. As historians often point out, nineteenth and early twentieth century social statistics are notoriously unreliable. And misbehavior is contextual; perceptions of the seriousness of youthful behavior change over time. Masturbation and idleness (the latter especially by lower-class youth) were viewed as especially serious in mid and late nineteenth century. Gender, class, and racial bias were even more pronounced than they are today. Lower class girls were frequently punished or even committed to reform schools for alleged promiscuity or "sluttish" behavior. Behavior that might have caused working class or black youth to be expelled from school or sent to reform schools was often overlooked or tolerated when committed by middle-class children, especially by white children in the South (Schlossman and Wallach, 1978; Sutton, 1988). What is clear, however, is the constancy of a perception by each generation of American that it is in the midst of an epidemic of juvenile delinquency, resulting from a moral breakdown.

The Problem with the Myth

What is wrong with the myth of a more innocent time when children actually behaved as they do on reruns of "Little House on the Prairie" or "The Waltons"? When we live in a resented present, we like to "remember" a lovelier past, even if it is more fantasy than real. Such a past is akin to those idealized paintings of rural scenes that Southerners, and I suppose others, call barn art. They may not realistically depict the past, but so what? We can't hurt the past by distorting it. What harm does it do to idealize it?, lovers of such art might ask. Art critics may look down their noses at the picture of the Model T. Ford, rusting in front of the abandoned old home place. But their views can easily be dismissed by those who admire such pictures; are the critics not merely effete snobs anyway?

Isn't the same true with idealized history? The answer, of course, is no. History is a policy study—we justify particular policies rather than others on the basis of what we believe our experiences to have been. The way we remember our past will have much to do with our perceptions of our present and its problems. It is not enough to show that children were not the way they are depicted by the traditional minded, we must understand why they are depicted that way. And we must be aware of the dangers of believing the myth: it causes us to look in the wrong places for answers to real problems.

Historians understand that even personal memories do not represent objective reality; rather memories are constructed in particularly ways to meet present needs. Conservative-minded people in particular, are likely to recollect a past that is warmer, more harmonious, and more virtuous than a present in which their values may no longer dominate. In turn, their solutions to contemporary problems are likely to involve attempts to recreate conditions that resemble an idealized past. If they believe that the "surveys" cited in the *Blue and White* are just another piece of evidence for a loss of goodness in social changes such as insidious growth of "secular humanism". They may argue for solutions such as returning group prayer to classrooms, more corporal punishment, returning group prayer to classrooms, more corporal punishment, textbooks that reflect "traditional" values, and educational choice, including the right to attend private schools at public expense.

If, on the other hand, we understand that discipline problems are as old as schools and that some school children have always engaged in destructive, violent behavior, we may look to more realistic ways of reducing the need for children to behave in ways that are costly to them and to society. Nostrums based on distorted perceptions of the way it was only exacerbate the plight of troubled children.

References

Brenzel, B. (1983) *Daughters of the State: A Social Portrait of the First Reform School for Girls in North America, 1865-1905,* Cambridge, Massachusetts, The MIT Press.

Dabney, C. (1901) "The Public School Problem in the South". *Proceedings of the Fourth Conference for Education in the South.*

Elson, R. (1964) *Guardians of Tradition: American Schoolbooks of the Nineteenth Century,* Lincoln, University of Nebraska Press.

Eubanks, D. (1987) "Only God and His Word Can Save Our Nation", *The Blue and White,* 59.

Hawes, J. (1971) *Children in Urban Society: Juvenile Delinquency in Nineteenth-Century America,* New York, Oxford University Press.

Kaestle, C. (1978) "Social Change, Discipline, and the Common School in Early Nineteenth-Century America", *Journal of Interdisciplinary History,* 9, pp. 1-17.

Mann, H. (1841) *Fourth Annual Report of the Board of Education* Boston, Dutton and Wentworth, State Printers.

Mann, H. (1843) *Sixth Annual Report of the Board of Education,* Boston, Dutton and Wentworth, State Printers.

Mennel, R. (1973) *Thorns and Thistles: Juvenile Delinquents in the United States, 1825-1940*, Hanover, New Hampshire, The University Press of New England.

Schlossman, S. and Wallach, S. (1978) "The Crime of Precocious Sexuality: Female Juvenile Delinquency in the Progressive Era", *Harvard Educational Review*, 48 pp. 65-94.

Sutton, J. (1988) *Stubborn Children: Controlling Delinquency in the United State, 1640-1981*, Berkeley, University of California Press.

Williams, B. (1882) "My Recollections of the Early School of Detroit that I attended from the Years 1816 to 1819", *Michigan Pioneer and Historical Collection*, 5, pp. 547-550.

Kathleen Berry

What does it mean to misbehave?

In Anthony Burgess' book, *Clockwork Orange*, the youths of the community garnish their lives with incomprehensible language and acts of violence. Written in the 1960's, the images and actions of this fictional work have became a reality in the minds of the general public; an image that suggests the youths misbehave more than they used to. Before we survey the conditions that give predominance to the notion of students as misbehaving, the organic meanings of the word misbehave will be presented.

The Latin meaning of misbehavior return us to the original experience in which the word emerged. For misbehave, the Latin root is *male se gerere* which means: *male* - badly, wrongly, unfortunately, not; *se* - himself/herself; while *gerere* means to carry about, to wear, to display an appearance, to act a part, to conduct oneself or to entertain a feeling. Which now leaves us with the sense of a person who misbehaves as someone who badly or wrongly conducts himself/herself, does NOT act a part and so on. Now we cannot, as concerned readers, take the word misbehave for granted. Given different situational contexts in which the word misbehavior is used can actually create a fuller understanding to the question of whether students do in fact misbehave more than they used to.

Student behavior is situationally judged:

When others consider the way students behave, a judgment is being made; a judgment based on the assumption that there is a proper, correct, standard, or agreed manner of carrying oneself. In other words, to behave means to conduct oneself in accordance with recognized and approved criteria. Which criteria is used depends on many different situational contexts; historical, social, political, economic, religious and many more.

Popular books, such as those by Bloom (1987) and Hirsh (1987), are examples, which abuse the situational context in order to present the view that today's students are culturally illiterate and closed-minded. Authors, such as previously mentioned, use the propaganda techniques of degrading present day students by glorifying the past; a view which distorts the true conditions and attitudes of today's students. If students are being educated in an atmosphere of neo-conservatism and fundamentalism—the outcome of the dominant cry of "back to the basics"—authors like Bloom and Hirsch, politicians like those of the Bush administration, and religious leaders reduced to fundamentalism are only a few of the many who capitalize on the situational context to portray students as lacking many qualities of the students of the past. So what were the qualities of students in the past? Whose past?

For example, let me reminisce about student life in the fifties and early sixties. Students from that generation can share stories of conformity, complacency, and silenced voices. Stories about regulations that forced us to wear middle class clothes in spite of our parents blue collar incomes; incidents of writing lines and hours of detentions if we dared to question the information transmitted. And to be seen as different meant isolation. To be heard, for example, as a physical handicapped female with a voice and a curious mind was impossible. In fact, it seems students of the past, except for the select few, very few, were less interested, less exposed, and less able to participate in what Hirsh and Bloom romantize as cultural literacy and rigourous intellectual pursuits.

However, neither an attack on right wing education nor advocacy for left wing policies is what is ultimately in question here. The problem lies with understanding student misbehavior as a necessary means of questioning not only the allegedly required cultural content which "every American should know," but also seeing misbehavior as a means to challenge the status quo and cultural bias of the content. Another crucial aspect to consider about student misbehavior asks what it is about the students' life which evokes particular misbehavior; from that of "horsing around" in class to that of extreme physical and mental violence, to all the types of misbehavior in between. Deliberation on the contexts in which student misbehavior reveals itself leads us to ponder the value of their misbehavior as an indication about how we are as human beings and, more importantly, how we want the quality of our future life to be. The quality of life question requires critical thoughts and actions.

Misbehavior as critical thought and action:

When a student is labeled as misbehaving, two elements are in play. First, according to the previous definition, a student who misbehaves does not conduct himself/herself or play a part in the standard, expected behaviors. Secondly, to misbehave means to fracture the ordinary; to break from the conventional structures that are already in place. It is in the misbehavior of the latter type that we can find the seeds of critical thought and actions.

I intend, in the context of this discussion, for critical to be used in the metaphorically sense of a "critical care" unit of a hospital. A person in charge of a critical care patient is sensitive to every vital sign of existence, every minute detail, every fine discrimination. A time where every judgment and every action determines whether a person lives or dies. Thus critical, in the educational context, means to have teachers and students living together with a attitude of caring for every detail of life, to be aware of the dangerous and vital quality of our existence. Misbehavior is necessary to keep us alert and conditioned for critical thought and action. So what does this unconventional view of misbehavior evoke?

Misbehavior arises out of some sense of dissatisfaction with the structures of the human condition; out of boredom, meaninglessness, frustration, or curiousity about the way life is. In this manner of not behaving as expected there is an attentiveness to the details of life; an attentiveness that does not necessarily occur in the passive thoughts and conforming actions of standard behavior. As creatures of habit we can pass over or take for granted the critical details of life. Perhaps we have experienced separation, divorce, illness, death, or some other fracture in the structure of our daily lives. Whether by natural events or through misbehavior, it is in the collapse of ordinary, everyday structures where illumination and attentiveness to details receive critical thought and action. We no longer take life's moments for granted when structures which govern our lives are in jeopardy.

Once the structures that governed behavior are changed, eliminated, modified, clarified, or questioned by misbehavior, a student lives in that flux. On the one hand, the gaps left by a break down or elimination of familiar structures can be filled by exploiters ready to blame student behaviors or colonizers ready to fill the gaps with great promises of solutions and return to "the good old days". On the other hand, adults involved with students begin to accept the ideas of the exploiters and colonizers without noticing that students are usually caught in the middle, wanting only to make sense of their lives and trusting education to prepare them to create and live in future structures.

What emerges in all the chaos of break-down is what, as Foucault (1977) claims, are educational structures based on bourgeoise ideology which exercises functions that traditionally belonged to the police and also reinforces all the structures of confinement. Students who, living within these institutional organizations, attempt to find adequate forms of struggle against the confines of imposed powers, are labeled as misbehavior problems. In turn, to avoid confrontation, they fall prey to various forms of verbal battering and disenfrachished participation in their own education. A return to the old structures, such as the so-called basics (which really have come to mean the familiar structures of the past to those who use this term), only serve to confine students further and eliminate them from the initiatives needed for participation in the different struggles of their future.

No matter what the organizational structures, elements or idealogical bent is, a student in times of liberalism, learns in the liberal way and the liberal content. In the 1960's for example, when the left wing ideology was more influential in determining the view of what and how students should learn, the atmosphere of radicalism was the predominate view of students. If we remember correctly, passivity and conformity in students of the sixties would have been considered by some as misbehavior.

What is needed is an exposure to all the contents and forms of life but always with a critical understanding of what it means for the quality of life. A grandiose statement—the quality of life—but to keep the critical consciousness alive by asking what it means for our lives? So where does this leave the students at any time in their education?

With a critical consciousness the student learns the content and the form of all the games played in education. Whatever the political, economic, social, religious or other views of the world, it is the critical consciousness that must remain alive without succumbing to any of the pressures of one view. In this way the student recognizes the existence, not only of the world views available that construct the world but also how the student's knowledge and values are constructed. On the one hand the student recognizes the world as constructed of many views, knowledge, and values. On the other hand, and perhaps more significant, is that the student recognizes his or her place in the world. With these elements in place, the task is no longer just to be or know the world.. The task is to live critically in the world, with as vast and deep understanding as possible but with a constant questioning of the world and self. It is in this constant questioning that teacher and students become sensitive to gaps and shift in their knowledge, values, and actions.

To question is to open the mind:

Merleau-Ponty (1962) states: "We don't lose the life of curiosity as long as we keep the question before us, who are we? (p.81). When five year old Michael asked his mother; "Mom, how did you know I was going to be a Michael when I was born?" is an indication of the priority of the question as an attitude in life. However, research tends to show that by the age of seven or eight, the high-level curiosity questions, similiar to that asked by Michael, are very limited to non-existent in the repetoire of questions. But it is our critical questioning that excites and arouses us to be responsive to the matters being encountered. In the questioning of life's contents and forms of knowledge, beliefs, and actions is where the logical structure of openness is found. For a question to open the world for the student's exploration and interpretation, one is required to accept that to question means to "not conduct oneself as others." Similiar to the notion of critical thought and action as misbehavior to break, modify, change, or eliminate traditional structures that have no meaning, a question implies misbehavior also; that is, don't go along with the thoughts and actions of others just to "act the part."

A question refuses to take the world for granted; it becomes a way of being in the world as much as a knowing about the world. The intent of students' question should remain as a possible means for them, not just to grasp at facts, but to "apprehend a possibility for being" (Ricouer, 1981, p. 56). Openness to experience involves many moments of disappointment, risk-taking, and a terrifying energy of playing in the unknown. What may seem like misbehavior to the concerned adult, may be no more than the student's way of questioning the world. Yes, there are the little questions that create everyday misbehavior and there are the questions that emerge as violent. For our purposes, it is to keep in perspective the intensity of the questions, but also remind ourselves that misbehavior has the structure of a question; not to be spared the students but to emerge as possible insight into world and self.

Insight, a seeing into, a light into, is always an escape from that which was dark or unclear but is no longer just a question that holds the student captive in the behaviors of others or one's own. As students break through the knowledge of the before moments and into self-knowledge they are no longer deceived or captive. It is this break with the old that can be frightening and appear as mindlessness to the adult. The self-knowledge that comes from asking questions is not to be misinterpreted as selfishness (a misbehavior wrongly associated with the "do your own thing era"). Self-knowledge, which requires a question, propels the student from the external descriptions of the outside world to the inner discipline at the personal level of knowledge and being. The strength of self-knowledge empowers a student. The misbehavior of a questioning student is necessary and on-going.

The need for infinite misbehavior:

We can view life as the romantic, scientific, analytical, religious and in many other ways. But in all the history of thought, the cliche most appropriate is "the most constant thing about life is change" (taxes and death also but that changes too!). In so noting, we must accept life is in a constant flux of ways of being and knowing. Although some people might hold stedfast to life as a form of solidarity while around them, blindly so sometimes, lies, within that pseudo-solidarity, the notion of crisis.

To repeat the line of thought previously developed, crisis means a rupture of traditional thought and action. Within the gap left by the collapse of structure, lies a whole region of possibilities for revised or new thought and actions. It is this region of possibility, created by the critical and questioning "misbehavior" of students, where the original intention of education takes place; *educate* - the power to bring forth, lead forth the potential of students to reach their highest abilities. Until students enter into the region of infinite possibilities for thoughts and action does their real education begin. And that entry process depends on the student ability to question and break with the closed systems of thoughts and behaviors already in place; which leaves students and teachers with, instead of the comfort and enclosure of a finite system of knowledge and behavior, a compulsive power doe the development of an infinite consciousness.

Bloom, Hirsch and others may talk about the lack of tradition or structure in today's education. These authors and their proponents forget, conveniently, the flux in exposure to cultural knowledge and actions. In so doing, their ideas if put into action, retard if not eliminate the fundamental promise of education; which is the development of an infinite consciousness for creative thought and actions in our students. So what?

Why misbehave is like asking why bother with getting an education or, one step further, why bother with life like it is. Well, a question may evoke the infinite consciousness but it also has limitations. However, to impose limitations to the possibility for infinite thoughts and actions undermines the fundamental notion of democracy: the freedom of thought and action for every individual. Yes, individual thought and freedom has its limit also, given that we are social beings. So our possibility for the development of the infinite consciousness demands that students' "misbehaviors" begin to question and be critical of the way life is. Questioning is not necessarily a debate or argument to win or lose but a way to open the students and teachers up to a conversation; conversations about the world and self.

So in ending this conversation, I hope that students misbehave more than they used to. The complacency and passiveness of "behaving" students frightens me. Is the world really O.K.? Do we really live in Utopia? Why do students have to "know what every American should know"; to be contestants on game shows—or—to put into actions those ideas which will raise the quality of life for every "individual"?

References

Bloom, A. (1987) *The Closing of the American Mind*, New York, Simon and Schuster.

Foucault, M. (1977) *Language, Counter-Memory, Practice: Selected Essays and Interviews*, Oxford, Basil Blackwell.

Hirsh, E.D. (1987) *Cultural Literacy: What Every American Should Know*, New York, Random House.

Merleau-Ponty, M. (1962) *Phenomenology of Perception*, London, Routledge and Kegan.

Ricouer, P. (1981) *Hermeneutics and the Human Sciences*, Cambridge, Cambridge University Press.

Chapter V

Teacher Education: What is good teaching, and how do we teach people to be good teachers?

Eleanor Blair Hilty

Andrew Gitlin

Eleanor Blair Hilty

The past decade has produced numerous national reports that have called for the reform of American education. These reports have reflected the depth of public dissatisfaction with the schools. In a publication of the Office of Educational Research and Improvement (1990), Assistant Secretary, Christopher T. Cross added his voice to this call for reform:

> Schools have changed less than any other public institution in meeting the requirements of our changing society, even though education is the fundamental tool that enables all other public and private institutions to exist.

The schools are perceived as institutions that no longer "work;" a significant portion of young people fail or dropout of school each year and good teachers either leave the profession or "burnout." Critics of American education argue that the welfare of this nation is in jeopardy if the public schools do not commit to meaningful change in this decade.

The first wave of school reform efforts has focused on the need for good teachers. If we cannot train good teachers and place them in schools where they will be successful, then the future of American education is tenuous indeed. The focus of these reform efforts has been a reconsideration of teacher training and entry into the profession. This focus, while useful, may be premature. Attempts to restructure or "re-form" the schools in a new image lack an ideology that informs or shapes the direction of these efforts. While questions about good teaching and the training of good teachers are central to any serious effort to make the public schools more amenable to the needs of society, even these questions require a set of beliefs about the aims and purposes of the educational process. The calls for action, however, are general and provide little direction for the restructuring of teacher education. Recommendations for reform address selected problems, but a vision of the public schools that considers the social, political and institutional influences on the educational process is not evident in these reports.

A discussion of good teaching and the training of good teachers must consider the context of teacher's work, the schools. What good is served by restructuring teacher training in the absence of a consideration of how good teaching functions within the institutional constraints of most schools? Teachers operate in an environment that is structured in such a way that good teaching becomes the exception, rather than the norm. Jackson (1986) argues that a consideration of good teaching must include reference to the "cultural context" of teaching. Under this rubric he includes "the awarenesses, presuppositions, expectations, and everything else that impinges upon the action or that contributes to its interpretation by the actors themselves and by outsiders as well" (p. 96). The social milieu of schools perpetuate stereotypical gender roles. Bennett and LeCompte (1990) describe schools as "pedagogical harems" where the activities of female teachers are governed and directed by male administrators (p. 258). Most of the decisions that guide the daily lives of teachers are made by individuals removed from the daily tasks and responsibilities that characterize teaching. A lack of control over their work environment diminishes the attempts of teachers to practice as autonomous professionals. As a group, teachers are powerless to implement meaningful change in their own classrooms. The talents of individual teachers are "chained" to "teacher-proof" curriculums that limit independent and creative action (Giroux, 1988). This orientation has contributed to the deskilling of teachers; a process where there is a reduction in the level of skill required to teach (Pinar, 1989). Teacher education does little to prepare teachers to become leaders in institutions where they have little power, status or decision-making ability. A failure to recognize the lack of congruity between teacher training and practice means that potential teachers receive training that provides little preparation for placement in teaching assignments where the "realities" of teaching force new teachers to exchange their ideals for educational practices that do not meet the educational challenges of a new decade. Teachers are the key to good teaching, yet we won't see good teachers emerge in an environment that is authoritarian and does little to liberate the talents of individual teachers.

What is Good Teaching?

Good teachers *do* exist despite a preponderance of evidence to contrary. Efforts to define and identify good teaching have been plagued by attempts to standardize the form and function of good teaching. The language of "effective" teaching research denotes a focus on efficiency and outcome, rather than process. An Office of Educational Research and Improvement publication (1990), *Issues in Education,* included among its recommendations for middle school improvement the following proposal: "Education must be rigorous and interesting. The people who work in it must be accountable." The implication, of course, is that teachers are simply workers who must demonstrate their worth through productivity. Good teaching, thus defined, translates into good test scores. Recommendations like these reflect a view of teaching that is unacceptable.

Erickson (1984) recounts the story of a young Eskimo who learned to hunt seal from his father. The young man was advised that "if you want to hunt seal you have to learn to think like a seal" (p. 527). Likewise, if you want to understand, identify, or even teach good teachers you have to learn to think like a good teacher. This analogy is intended to convey two thoughts:

1) Good teaching is a cognitive process that cannot be understood in the absence of a consideration of "teacher thinking," and

2) Teaching is a personal experience. The voices of good teachers must be included in discussions of teaching. These propositions seem obvious, however this kind of thinking is not reflected in the literature on teaching.

Good teaching must be defined as an intellectual process. The process must be emphasized, not the outcomes. A focus on outcomes obstructs a consideration of the proper role of the classroom teacher as an intellectual (Giroux, 1988). Resnick (1987) recommends that "models of shared intellectual functioning" must shape our views of classroom practice (p. 19).

Contemporary research on teaching directs our attention to teacher thinking and the construction of meaning between students and teachers (Cochran-Smith & Lytle, 1990). There is an absence of research on the ways in which teachers understand and think about their teaching or even the manner in which students experience good teaching. Good teaching can never be a set of skills in isolation of a capacity to think about one's actions or reflect critically on the process or product of a teaching effort. Giroux (1989) admonishes recent efforts to define teachers "as clerks or technicians." Good teachers are intellectuals first and critical decision-makers second. It is the ability of teachers to be constantly reviewing their actions and evaluating outcomes that sets them apart from machines. At a minimum, teachers must constantly question the unstated or "taken-for-granted" assumptions and beliefs that guide classroom practice (Bennett & LeCompte, 1990, p. 257). Good teaching defies simple explanation and requires a vision of teaching that encompasses the creative and intellectual components of the process.

Seeing teachers in this manner requires that we have multiple models of "good" teaching. Teachers, good and bad, bring to teaching a culmination of experiences both personal and professional. It is imperative that the voices of teachers be integrated into any discussion of good teaching. McLaren (1989) discusses "voice" as a significant "pedagogical concept" because it acknowledges the interaction of cultural and historical variables in the dialogue that occurs between teachers and students (p. 229). Teachers come to teaching with a set of beliefs about the world generally, and about teaching and learning specifically. Good teaching is idiosyncratic and takes different forms. It is a process that is defined and mediated by the experiences of a particular teacher and a group of students. It is paradoxical that efforts to improve the schools have excluded teachers from the dialogue when ultimately they are the individuals who will fail or succeed at reforming American education. Discussions of good teaching that ignore the voices of teachers are incomplete and produce the lists of measurable skills and behaviors that characterize attempts to make teachers accountable.

Good teaching cannot be measured, but the process can be described. Good teachers view the teaching process as a creative endeavor. They establish learning communities that produce students who are independent, self-motivated learners. Good teaching is often exciting and seldom boring. The classrooms of these teachers are characterized by mutual respect, collaboration and connection. Good teachers recognize and support cultural diversity. A good teacher helps student to understand the democratic principles that shape our society while questioning practices that lead to the inequitable distribution of knowledge, power and resources (Greene, 1985; Giroux, 1989). Good teachers create a positive atmosphere for dialogue, reflection and debate. Good teachers encourage the development of intellectual skills that lead to critical, reflective thinking. An emphasis on basic skills, minimal literacy, and standardized tests are the antithesis of good teaching. Critics will, nevertheless, charge that classrooms should be well-managed and academically rigorous. Good teachers do share the responsibility for learning and behavior with students, however, I will argue that students taught in this manner are more successful on tests, in schools, in the workplace, and in social relationships. Good teaching produces good students.

Not surprisingly, good teachers are also good learners. They are exemplary models of a lifetime commitment to thinking, questioning, and learning. An appreciation of the many forms of good teaching would liberate teachers by giving them the freedom to develop a style of pedagogy that reflects their understanding of teaching and learning. No one would ever request, or even desire, that all doctors or lawyers practice according to *one* model. Does it not seem equally unreasonable to assume that all teachers must teach the same way?

Good teaching requires a restructuring of the school environment. Proposals for reform have emphasized "top-down" control of the profession (Hill, 1989; Bennett & LeCompte, 1990). This will *not* produce good teachers. Good teachers must have control over the instructional process in their classrooms (Giroux, 1988). Good teachers are pedagogical leaders who are attempting to transform and empower students through learning experiences that foster critical and reflective inquiry.

Teachers must work in environments that allow them to model these same skills. Administrators should work for teachers, or at the very least, they must be colleagues who share equally the responsibility for designing successful schools. Many people would find this latter proposition laughable, since it is a radical departure from the situation in most schools. However, it is the unequal distribution of power in most schools that has consistently led to the mediocre performance of both teachers and students. I argue that we will *not* see good teaching become the norm in our schools until new teachers enter the schools with the knowledge and skills to confidently demand the right to work in an environment that recognizes them as competent professionals and allows them to freely and optimally do what they have been trained to do, teach.

The Training of Good Teachers

The imperative for teacher education is to produce good teachers. Robert Maynard Hutchins stated that "the best education for the best, is the best education for all." Adler (1982) used this quote to support his proposals for educational reform in *The Paideia Proposal*. In discussing the education of teachers, the same principle holds true, "the best education for the best, is the best education for teachers."

Teacher education has historically been a second-class education; a ghetto for students (and teachers) who are perceived as intellectually shallow and lacking the ability to study a "real" discipline. These programs typically reflect a lack of commitment to scholarly ideals. This is not surprising when one considers that research findings consistently show a lack of scholarly activity on the part of teacher educators (Cruickshank, 1990). Correspondingly, the involvement of teacher educators in school reform has been minimal. In reality teacher educators suffer the same lack of status and power as the teachers that they train. It is not likely that teacher educators will ever be totally excluded from the preparation of teachers. However, even if their involvement is limited, the success of teacher preparation will hinge on the commitment of the education professoriate to a new model of teacher training; a model that is scholarly and intellectual. If that commitment is absent, a restructuring of teacher education will have little impact on the public schools.

There is a relationship between good teaching and the quality of the preparation of teachers. Teacher education is a bridge between content and practice through the study of pedagogy. Teacher education becomes the "scaffolding" that negotiates and supports the social and cognitive relationships between the "how" and "what" of good teaching (Wood, Bruner, & Ross, 1976: Erickson, 1984, p. 533). Shor (1987) argues that "all of school is actually 'teacher education,' a paideia socializing teachers in how to teach and what to learn" (p. 18). Thus, every aspect of the education of teachers must embrace the highest academic ideals and clearly reflect a renewed vision of good teaching. Good teachers will only become critical, reflective practitioners if their training encourages the development of those skills. In my syllabus for an undergraduate foundations class, I use the following quote from Paulo Freire (1987):

> This is a great discovery, education is politics: when a teacher discovers that he or she is a politician, too, the teacher has to ask, What kind of politics am I doing in the classroom? That is, in favor of whom am I being a teacher? The teacher works in favor of something and against something. Because of that, he or she will have another great question, How to be consistent in my teaching practice with my political choice? I cannot proclaim my liberating dream and in the next day be authoritarian in my relationship with the students.

Teacher education in a very broad sense is an education that recognizes the social, political and institutional influences that shape personal action. Good teachers understand the relationship of these influences to teaching and learning. Teaching, thus defined becomes an experience that liberates and empowers both practitioner and student.

The reform of American education demands that teacher education be fundamentally restructured and organized to be academically rigorous and interdisciplinary. Teacher education as it is presently conceived emphasizes vocational skills rather than intellectual skills (Pinar, 1989). Teachers spend a significant part of their training studying pedagogy to the exclusion of basic knowledge and concepts in the liberal arts and sciences.

Most recommendations for reform in teacher education focus on limiting the professional education requirements for teachers and increasing the teaching field component. These proposals translate into fewer teacher education courses and more content, less of the "how" and more the "what" of teaching. These changes, however, are quantitative rather than qualitative (Shor, 1987). The quality of the educational experience provided in all classes is a concern. Classes throughout the college curriculum are characterized by rote memorization of isolated fragments of knowledge. There are few attempts to situate knowledge within broader themes or concepts. Shor suggests a quality education that is shaped by Freirean principles and encourages active student participation that is "critical, values-oriented, multicultural, student-centered, experiential, research-minded, and interdisciplinary" (p. 22). These are the characteristics of a quality education. The education of teachers must reflect this orientation at every level of their training. Less or more of specific courses will not produce good teachers. Accompanying recommendations for a more rigorous education of teachers must be a commitment by all educators to *quality* educational experiences.

For many teachers, the most meaningful experience in teacher education is student teaching. The influence of this experience on teachers demands that teacher educators consider ways to connect this experience to a new understanding of the educational process. However, even this experience becomes problematic when preservice teachers are inadequately prepared and then placed with teachers who do not model good teaching as I have described it. Under the guise of "reality," these teachers demonstrate "tired" practices that get the job done, but do nothing to fundamentally change the way we "do" school. These experiences obviously leave an impression on new teachers who are frantically trying to cope with the demands of teaching, but these experiences frequently defeat the efforts of teacher educators to proclaim a new vision of teaching and learning. Student teaching, in this manner, indoctrinates and socializes preservice teachers to an unacceptable norm.

Obviously, there needs to be more collaboration between teacher educators and practitioners in the schools. A commitment to a new model of teaching requires that efforts be made to connect training to practice. This requires that *both* teachers and teacher educators combine their knowledge and experience to consider ways to bridge this gap (Cochran-Smith & Lytle, 1990). Good teachers should be deeply involved with teacher education programs in higher education and in the schools. A coherency between training and practice is the only way to make good teaching the norm rather than the exception.

The public fascination with school reform will not last. We must take this moment to seriously embrace meaningful change in the field of education. A reconceptualization of teacher training is the first step (Pinar, 1989). The problems that characterize teaching will remain unchanged until the *entire* process of teacher education is reconsidered and a new vision is articulated. The emphasis in the training of teachers must be on intellectual development. Within this realm, preservice teachers should have experiences that model and facilitate the development of the capacity to be a critical, reflective thinker. Remember, this is not just the best education for teachers, it is the best education for all students.

References

Adler, M. J. (1982). *The Paideia Proposal: An educational manifesto*. New York: MacMillan.

Bennett, K. P. & Lecompte, M. D. (1990). *How schools work: A sociological analysis of education*. White Plains, NY: Longman.

Cochran-Smith, M. & Lytle, S. L. (1990). "Research on teaching and teacher research: The issues that divide." *Educational Researcher, 19*, 3, 2-11.

Cruickshank, D. R. (1990). *Research that informs teachers and teacher educators.* Bloomington, IN: Phi Delta Kappa Educational Foundation.

Erickson, F. E. (1984). "School literacy, reasoning, and civility: An anthropologist's perspective." *Review of Educational Research, 54,* 4, 525-546.

Freire, P. (1987). *A pedagogy for liberation: Dialogues on transforming education.* South Hadley, MA: Bergin & Garvey.

Giroux, H. (1988). *Teachers as intellectuals: Toward a critical pedagogy of learning.* South Hadley, MA: Bergin & Garvey.

Giroux, H. (1989, May). "Rethinking education reform in the age of George Bush." *Phi Delta Kappan,* 728-730.

Greene, M. (1985). "The role of education in democracy." *Educational Horizons, 63,* 3-9.

Hill, D. (1989, September/October). "Fixing the system from the top down." *Teacher Magazine,* 50-55.

Jackson, P. W. (1986). *The Practice of Teaching.* New York: Teachers College Press.

McLaren, P. (1989). *Life in Schools.* New York: Longman.

Office of Educational Research. (1990, August). *Issues in Education.* Washington, DC: U. S. Department of Education.

Pinar, W. F. (1989, January-February). "A reconceptualization of teacher education." *Journal of Teacher Education,* 9-12.

Resnick, L. B. (1987). "Learning in school and out." *Educational Researcher, 16,* 10, 13-20.

Shor, I. (1987). "Educating the educators: A Freirean approach to the crisis in teacher education." In Shor, I. (ed.), *Freire for the classroom: A sourcebook for liberatory teaching.*

Wood, B., Bruner, J. S., & Ross, G. (1976). "The role of tutoring in problem solving." *Journal of Child Psychology and Psychiatry, 17,* 89-100.

Andrew Gitlin

Considering what is good teaching requires an analysis of the question itself and a response. To analyze the question, I will focus primarily on the issues of authorship—who is responding to the question—and purpose—what I hope this essay will accomplish. After doing so, I will then respond to the question as I conceive it. Included in this response will be a discussion of the tension between ambiguity and certainty, the politics of education and the school context.

The Question

Who is responding to a particular question or concern, the author, is not usually viewed as an important piece of information in examining the nature of the argument. As a consequence, the issue of who gets to speak and who is silenced is rarely considered. For example, without considering the question of authorship, the way this essay supports a historical trend where academics have been given the opportunity to speak about teaching while teachers have for the most part been denied such an opportunity, would not be apparent. By pointing to this trend, I don't want to suggest that only teachers should comment on teaching. Rather, my point is that one of the more hidden aspects of this essay is the way it strengthens a hierarchical relationship between teachers and outsiders that leaves those most intimately involved with students without much opportunity to speak out about teaching. While the intent of this essay is to raise some issues typically not discussed in debates about good teaching, when viewed from the point of view of who is speaking and who is silenced this essay is quite typical.

Besides clarifying the issue of authorship, it is also important to consider how my understanding of the question influences my response. Of particular note is the question of context. Is good teaching something that can only determined by knowing contextual factors such as the type of students found in the school, the mandated district policies, and the class size? Or, are schools so alike that one can make some generalizations about good teaching without explicitly considering context? Because good teaching takes place in a context that makes certain types of activities possible and likely, and others less likely, my position is that good teaching is enhanced by stripping away contextual constraints, thereby allowing the abilities and insights of teachers to emerge.

Another important issue that must be addressed before I launch into a response is what I hope this essay will accomplish. Is the purpose to lay out a singular notion of good teaching that others should adopt as their own? Is the purpose to provide several views of good teaching and let the reader choose? Or is the purpose to encourage debate, and through debate, assist others in clarifying their own positions about good teaching? Because I do not believe there is one model of good teaching, it would be inappropriate to outline a conception of good teaching to convince others to adopt some part of what is said. On the other hand, I do have opinions about what good teaching is and so to suggest that it really doesn't matter which version a reader chooses is not quite honest. In contrast to these two approaches, I have decided to outline my position about good teaching in the hope that the reader will use it as a text to consider the question for themselves.

The Response

Ambiguity: As one of my closest colleagues has often noted, teaching is a messy business. In fact, there are few questions about teaching that can be answered with a simple yes or a no. Instead, the response to any significant question concerning teaching is typically "maybe" or "under these circumstances" or "with these resources." Although outsiders, most notable the psychologically oriented researchers from the university, continue to assert that there are a set of laws or rules that characterize good teaching, at the level of practice the situation is always more complex, more conflictual, and less straightforward. While teachers clearly see this complexity, many strive to remove ambiguity and find certainty in what they do, no matter how fragile.

There are many good reasons for seeking out certainty in teaching, not the least of which is that teachers are rarely viewed as experts by other members of the educational community. Coupled with the never ending stream of criticisms directed at teachers and schools, this assault puts teachers in a defensive position, where acknowledging that ambiguity is a part of teaching only furthers the suspicions and doubts about their expertise and the educational experiences offered students. Striving for certainty has advantages, in that it promises a small amount of relief from the relentless criticisms voiced about teachers, teaching, and schooling. It also, however, can act to constrain a teacher's relationships with students and their development over time.

Teachers that have a strong sense of certainty about teaching often respond to teaching situations based on a set of informal rules that are the result of numerous experiences. Don't smile until Christmas, you're the teacher not the students' friend, high expectations achieve high results, are typical of the types of informal rules teachers develop over time. These rules may be valid in a number of ways, but they also make it less likely that teachers will see the need to find out who their students are, what their background is, and what they know. In essence, the informal rules become a substitute for the time consuming process of basing teaching practice on an in depth study of students. Teaching, as a consequence, becomes a one way process where the unique and complex characteristics of students are often obscured.

Teachers with a strong sense of certainty about teaching also don't have much of a need to involve themselves in a continuing educational process that investigates issues of schooling. Because they have worked hard to be seen as expert, to be certain about what they know and how they go about teaching, education is for those who are novice, who haven't taken teaching seriously, and who are not cut out to be teachers. Being certain is part of a rite of passage from those who need to those who know. One teacher I have worked with summarized this position by saying, "I don't have any problems, why should I raise concerns about my work?"

In contrast, other teachers try to deal with ambiguity, by accepting it, by seeing it as an integral part of teaching. The quest is not to remove ambiguity from the process of teaching but to find a balance between certainty and ambiguity. These teachers do not try to remove certainty completely from teaching, because to do so is to foster frustration and chaos. They do, however, allow ambiguity to play an important part in the teaching process by posing questions about their students, the curriculum, and the school context and base their practice on this understanding.

In my view, good teaching involves finding a point along the continuum between certainty and ambiguity that allows one to function while acknowledging the inherent messiness of the process. This point between certainty and ambiguity encourages teachers to view teaching as a process involving continuous inquiry as opposed to a product governed by rules, both formal and informal, that can "pre-scribe" how they are to act in the classroom. In this regard, thinking deeply about the culture, class and gender of the student before practices are outlined for what is to be done in the classroom, is part of accepting ambiguity as an inherent part of teaching. And finally, while good teachers are confident about their knowledge and abilities, they have enough uncertainty to want to rethink what they know and to know more. Within this view the expert is no longer someone who has arrived, who already knows, but one who is continuously engaged in educative experiences. Good teaching, in this sense, involves education for both student and teacher.

Potitics: Schools are political places and teaching a political act. One of the most obvious ways schools are political is that they serve a gate keeping function which helps determine job opportunities and career paths. Schools determine to a large degree who goes onto higher education, what types of institutions one can enter and the kinds of jobs that an individual is likely to get. Who goes through the gate, however, is not based on a set of objective criteria, but rather is closely tied to a number political decisions the school has to make about curricular form and content and the assessment of student performance.

Whether a social studies text includes information on Blacks and women and how they portray these groups, for example, is inherently a political question because it influences what knowledge is seen as legitimate and attitudes about the group.

Teaching is also political because it helps shape relationships between groups and individuals. While relationships may not seem political at first glance, almost all relationships reflect power and power is political. Because the teacher/student relationship, for example, often reflects a power struggle, political questions such as is the relationship just are part of understanding teaching. The teacher/student relationship, therefore, should be understood not only in terms of its effectiveness but also in terms of the relations of power that are constructed. Much the same argument can be made about teachers' relationships with other teachers, administrators, and parents.

Unfortunately, the structure of schooling is set up to hide the political nature of teaching. Given that many teachers' curriculum choices are constrained by mandated textbooks and that required assessment devices make seemingly objective judgments, issues of what is legitimate knowledge and questions about the gatekeeping function of schools seem to reside outside the teacher role. In much the same way, the popularity of standardized tests reinforces the notion that relationships of all kinds are to be assessed in terms of what they produce not the relationship itself.

In spite of these structural constraints, good teachers find ways to reflect on the political side of teaching. They find ways to examine the implications of selecting particular curricular content over other content, they think through what perspectives are included and left out and importantly they adjust their practice based on this understanding. In addition, they critically consider the implications of assessment approaches and use this understanding to develop or find new approaches that reflect the diversity of their students. Finally, good teachers pay close attention to their relationships with others. They don't simply accept the typical competitive and/or isolated teacher relationship or the dominant teacher/student relationship as the way it is, as natural. Instead, they work to develop relationships among teachers and students that are based on a set of articulated and examined political ideals. In summary, they under-stand that questions of learning cannot be separated from questions of equity, justice and even oppression, because what is learned by students is informed by the particular teacher/student relationship as much as the material covered. In this sense, the political is not something added on to concerns of effectiveness and efficiency but are integral to those concerns.

Context: As I have argued earlier, good teaching cannot be understood outside of the teaching context. Unfortunately, when one steps back and looks at the types of typical school structures found in schools, it is hard to deny that they are based on the assumption that teachers are the major source of educational failure, and in need of guidance and strict control. Put simply, given the view of good teaching espoused in this essay, structures for the most part act to limit good teaching. Good teachers must find ways around these structures to practice good teaching.

There is not room in this essay to illuminate all the common school structures, so I will choose a few that appear to significantly constrain good teaching. Over the last 20 years what is called a rationalized curriculum form has gained in popularity, especially at the elementary school level. This form divides curriculum into discrete units or objectives. For each objective there is a pre and post test that determines whether a student to ready to learn the objective and once finished with the material whether she/he has mastered the material. The intent of the curriculum is to help students move along as fast as possible given their abilities.

There are surely some benefits to the rationalized curricular form. However, this form creates a one-way approach to teaching where the teacher doesn't have to know if the student is Chicano, Black or from a working class neighborhood. The teacher also doesn't have to worry about the content of the curriculum, for it is predetermined and sequentially laid out. And finally the teacher doesn't have to be concerned with assessment because these instruments are part of the curriculum package. Put directly, the teacher doesn't have to be concerned about a range of political questions that are an inherent part of teaching.

Some teachers can and do find ways to get around the rationalized curriculum. However, given the small amount of time teachers have to develop curriculum, to consider alternative assessment devises, and, yes, even the small amount of time they have to get to know their students, the rationalized curriculum has the advantage of lessening the strain on their work. Many teachers, therefore, accept this curriculum as a trade-off, a compromise forced on them from the outside. To do otherwise is to further intensify their work.

Another structure that greatly influences teachers' work is teacher evaluation. Among other things, teacher evaluation has traditionally focused on teaching outcomes such as, a quiet classroom, a well organized classroom and the ability of students to proceed through their work in an orderly and efficient manner. There is nothing inherently wrong with classrooms that are quiet, organized and efficient, however, these outcomes ignore the political nature of teaching and importantly impose a product view of teaching that is less likely to acknowledge differences among students. Finally, teachers' ability to question what is legitimate knowledge and to consider issues of opportunity is not valued by traditional teacher assessment approaches. Rather, it is the ability to get students to digest information in an orderly fashion. As is true of the rationalized curriculum, teacher evaluation endorse a narrow view of teaching that challenges the need for continuous inquiry on a wide range of issues including the important political domain.

Finally, at a fundamental level nothing influences teachers more than class size. Although must has been written to show that class size really doesn't make much of a difference, the underlying assumption of this scholarship is that teaching is a one-way process of depositing information into the heads of students. And it could be that given this mode of teaching class size is not all that important. However, if good teaching involves taking account of who the students are, and a concern for the power relations between students and teachers, among others, then class size is an enormously important consideration. This is so for several reasons. First, the larger the class size the more difficult it is to get to know who the students are, what they know, and how they differ from each other. Second, even if a super teacher could gather this sort of information, trying to alter practice based on a study of students becomes nearly impossible with large classes. Finally, as the class size becomes larger so to does the need for the teacher to resort to techniques that will establish control *over* students as opposed to sharing power *with* them. Put simply, as class size increases so too does the need for types of teacher/student relations that are inherently unjust. For all these reasons class size works against the type of good teaching articulated in this essay.

If good teaching is something the public wants to see more of, then this analysis of school structure suggests that the nature of our schools needs to be radically altered. Teachers need to have more say on the form and content of the curriculum. They also need more time to not only get to know their students but time to reflect on a range of political issues that are part and parcel of curriculum making. However, the problem isn't one of simply giving them time, it is also one of changing the reward structure of schools so that reflection on what might broadly be called the politics of teaching is valued. This means that teacher evaluation schemes can on longer be limited to what teachers do but expanded to include consideration of what they think and what they see as problems. This does not mean that an evaluator accepts teachers' views but rather that these views as is true of their behavior is part of the assessment process. Finally, class size needs to come down to the point where teachers can act on their understanding of students, assessment approaches and curricula context and form among other things.

Conclusion

Good teaching is not simply a matter of teachers doing this or that. Instead, good teaching as outlined in this essay, is a complex process that results from what teachers do, as well as how they think about education, the relationships formed, and the context in which they work. Fostering good teaching, therefore, involves both changes in the structure of teaching and the teacher role. Structures need to be developed that encourage teachers to see ambiguity about teaching as a potential strength that enhances question posing. An once this process of question posing is firmly established as a part of the teacher role, further structures need to be put in place that enable teachers to examine and act on the vast array of political concerns that are often neglected. Finally, new structures need to be established that value and reward the types of thinking and activities I have outlined in this essay. Currently good teachers survive by getting around structures, and developing alternatives. While this is hopeful, it also makes more likely that our best teachers leave teaching after only a few years. What we need is not only an expanded teacher role but structures that complement such a role. Under these circumstances good teaching will be supported by our schools and importantly these teachers may just stay in the classroom to continue to provide quality educational experiences for our children.

Chapter VI

Education and Democracy: Should the fact that we live in a democratic society make a difference in what our schools are like?

Harvey J. Kaye

Dalton B. Curtis, Jr.

Harvey J. Kaye

Through schooling and education a people expresses and cultivates its public values, identities and aspirations, and prepares its newest generations to engage them. Thus, *a democratic society requires a democratic education.* Declaring ourselves a democracy, the proposition that America must provide a democratic education to its children and young people (at the least) is not really at issue. What has been and continues to be contested is the actual meaning of "democracy" and, in those terms, what a "democratic" education ought to entail. To appreciate the challenge we confront, we must see things historically . . .

Filled with paradox and contradiction, American experience, along with its record of economic growth and development and its chronicle of continental and imperial expansion, has been a long struggle to realize the democratic dream that *the people shall govern themselves.* The American Revolution and war for independence; the populism of Jacksonian politics, the Civil War between North and South and ensuing abolition of slavery; the campaigns for women's suffrage and equality; the many generations of farmer and labor movements and black struggles for survival, freedom and justice: the first 200 years and more of our history can be read as a narrative of continuous efforts *from the bottom up* to make real the aspirations that "We, the people" shall rule. Comprehending our past in this way, the struggles of the long decade of the sixties for the civil rights of racial and ethnic minorities, the social rights of the poor, and the equal rights of women, along with the movement against an imperial war in southeast Asia and the less-celebrated but, perhaps, equally significant insurgency of working people, white and black, male and female, in industry and the workplace, not to mention the environmental and consumer movements, are all recognizable as reassertions of the finest traditions of American life and history (Buhle and Dawley, 1985).

Yet, for almost a generation now we have been subject to a persistent and, arguably, concerted "class war from above" resisting, opposing and, even, seeking to reverse the "advances" which had been accomplished in the spirit of liberty, equality and democratic community. Against the achievements and reforms secured from the New Deal of the 1930s through the Great Society of the 1960s and, for most immediately, the threat they perceived of a coalescence of the several struggles of the day into a broader popular movement seeking ever more extensive radical-democratic changes in the American social order, the powers-that-be mobilized. And, in the course of the 1970s, with the encouragement and manifold support of significant sectors of American business and corporate capital, there was formed under the banner of the New Right Republicans a political coalition of conservatives and neo-conservatives which included cold-warriors, free-marketeers, moral-majoritarians, and a host of other right-wing single-interest groups and organizations variably committed to undermining the post-Second World War liberal consensus and to halting the democratic struggles from below of labor and the "new social movements". The ascendance to power of this diverse coalition was registered in the 1980 and '84 election victories of Ronald Reagan and, again, in that of George Bush in 1988 (Blumenthal, 1986; Himmelstein, 1990).

From the start there was inherent contradictions in this New Right alliance—for example those existing between the aspiration of the free-marketeers and those of the religious fundamentalists and, in another area, between the foreign-policy views of conservatives and those of neo-conservatives—and after a decade and more of Republican Administrations, it is not only clear that the New Right has failed to accomplish its many enunciated goals but that the coalition itself is breaking up. There is, however, little reason to be joyful or optimistic for there is no denying the consequences of a dozen years of New Right regimes. They have wrought confusion disarray and hardship. We have experienced a "decade of greed" and a "politics of inequality in which the rich truly have gotten richer and the poor have been made poorer—a process by no means limited to the margins, that is, to the Donald Trumps at one end and the poor and homeless at the other, but, rather, one conditioning the lives of the vast majority of America's working people (Philips, 1990). Moreover, the collapse of the New Right coalition has been due for less to organized and coherent opposition from the Left and resurgent movement from below than to the manifestation of its own contradictions and the difference between the various groups composing it.

In fact, in one major respect the Right has triumphed. That is, it has succeeded, to the decided benefit of the powers-that-be, in further fragmenting if not all but routing the struggles of working people and the oppressed. Evidently, the antagonisms of class, race and gender not only persist but are intensified, and studies reveal that there is continuing popular commitment to the programs and priorities of New Deal and post-war liberalism; never the less, the various movements for freedom and justice appear enervated and enfeebled, pursuing at best defensive actions. What we find is not merely increasing inequality, but political and cultural freedoms under attack and democratic activity becoming narrower and shallower, subordinated to the "freedom of the market," the imperatives of capital and the manners of the media. In short, public culture and discourse is more and more subject to commercial norms and values and devoid of critical thought and debate about the future of American society. The New Right's legacy, therefore, would seem to be the "depoliticization: of public life and, thereby, the enhancement of the status quo and the position of the powers-that-be, especially the political and economic elites of corporate capital. Philip Mattera has described the current scene:

> These days there is not much collective dreaming in America. The erosion of living standards and the increase in economic insecurity have brought about a climate of quiet frustration and cynicism. People have been caught between official pronouncements that these are the best of times and their personal realization that life is getting tougher every day. The contradictory evidence is having an immobilizing effect: most Americans do not see a way out of this Dilemma and consequently have grown wary of any change at all. While people in other parts of the world, notably Eastern Europe, are boldly confronting their oppression, the U.S. feels like a political backwater (Mattera, 1990: 187)

It is debatable whether or not the politics and ideas of the New Right have been actually *anti*-democratic. However, it is clearly the case both that their conception of democracy, of democratic life and practice, is a limited one and, stated in *historical* terms, that they conceive of it as already having been achieved. In other words, in their view *democracy in America* is accomplished. Indeed, they insist, not only does contemporary American liberal and capitalist democracy represent the high point of democratic development thus far, it represents *the* high point of democratic possibilities, the *culmination* of democracy's historical evolution. As one of their number, Francis Fukuyama, put it in a much-vaunted and widely-discussed article, we have at the "end of history" beyond which the choice is either more of the same or political, economic and cultural retrogression (Fukuyama, 1989; Kaye, 1991). The New Right's program of "democratic education" indicates just such an understanding of history.

Now, at first sight it would seem that there have been actually two different and conflicting campaigns pursued by conservatives and neo-conservatives (not necessarily respectively) for reforming and renewing American education in the 1980s and '90s. Both point to the apparently poor performance by American schoolchildren on standardized objective tests in comparison to their European and Asian counterparts and regularly blame liberal and Left educators for the problem; however; the respective campaigns proclaim different concerns and assert different priorities. On the one hand, there are those who warn of the dangers of American economic and industrial decline and propose that education be reformed to address it. Looking toward the creation (or *re*creation) and provision of a skilled, disciplined and productive workforce for American industries and enterprises in their competition with German and Japanese corporations (or, as is increasingly said, a workforce attractive to investments by the latter in the American economy!), they stress a "back-to-basics," teach the facts and nothing but the facts" approach to schooling generally emphasizing training in math and science. The priorities of this campaign are vocational, industrial and economic. On the other hand, there are those who speak less of economic decline and far more of political and moral crisis, that is, of the fragmentation and disintegration of America's "common culture" and "shared values." They, too, call for a "return to the basics," but, emphasizing schooling in the humanities, especially literature and history, they stress the restoration of a core curriculum of ideas and ideals entailing, at the least, a common body of knowledge and information and, preferably, a canon of Great Books and personages representing "Western Civilization." The priorities enunciated here are civic, political and cultural (Bennett, 1988; Bloom, 1987; Hirsch, 1987).

Yet, however much stressing seemingly different concerns and priorities—respectively, the making of workers and the making of citizens—the two New Right campaigns for American education arise from the same vision and register the same understanding of America's past, present and possible future, that we have arrived at the end of history, *and* express the same political project, that of assuring that we actually have! Both schemes for schooling delimit democratic education to a process of *transmission*, in the former that of skills and competencies and in the latter that of ideas and values. To be sure, schooling to develop skills and capacities for productive and valued employment and to communicate knowledge and ideals for informed and active citizenship are, in principle, essential to any vision of democratic education. However, bound up with a version of history which conceives of contemporary America as the terminus of democratic development, the New Right vision of democratic education aspires (at best) to no more than the *reproduction* of the American economy and polity and culture as they are presently constituted. Bluntly stated, the New Right notion of democratic education reduces schooling to being a support of the world *as it is*.

For those of us who do not believe that we have come to the end of history, who do not believe that the contemporary American social order—however "progressive," relatively speaking—represents the culmination of democratic development, such a state of affairs is obviously unacceptable. But our task is formidable. For a start, in the face of the triumphs of the New Right we need not only to make clear the inadequacies and limitations of their rendition of history and attendant conception of democracy but, also, to cultivate a popular awareness that the contemporary order of things, both the good and the bad, was not inevitable and that it need not remain this way. We must work towards the development of a popular comprehension that the present, too, is history and that nothing is gained without struggle. This entails both recovering and communicating the struggles for liberty, equality and democratic community which have contributed to the making of past and present (both the victories and the defeats) *and* revealing the possibilities which exist today for renewing that history.

Furthermore, along with our efforts to create a more critical and democratic historical memory, consciousness and imagination—indeed, as part of such efforts—it is imperative that we articulate and proffer a conception of democratic education which supports the project of extending further the development of democratic life and practice and, if enacted actually enhances the likelihood of its realization. The political scientist, Benjamin Barber, expressed it well when he wrote that "all education ought to be radical—a reminder of the past, a challenge to the present, and a prod to the future" (Barber, 1988: 173)

Unfortunately, all too often such aspirations have involved both a simplistic opposition to and a too hasty rejection of the educational initiatives enunciated by the New Right. I would argue that in certain crucial instances our response should not be that of opposing and disavowing their proposals but of critically appropriating, rearticulating and turning them in a more truly democratic direction. For example, at the cost of being portrayed as unconcerned about not only "academic standards" but, also, about the needs of working people and the oppressed to become literate and skilled and, moreover the economic future of our country, we have in the past too readily denounced the campaign to reform education in support of economic and technological development. Instead, we should have been taking the lead in this area, seeking to make all the more effective the acquisition of basic skills, literacies, and competencies by America's schoolchildren for the sake both of improving their chances to secure and pursue productive livelihood and of helping to assure continued American economic growth and development. *But that is not enough!* And this is where our conception of democratic life and practice differs from that of the Right. An Antonio Gramsci observed more than half of a century ago: "Democracy, by definition, cannot mean merely that an unskilled worker can become skilled. It must mean that every 'citizen' can 'govern' and that society places him, even if only abstractly, in a general condition to achieve this" (Gramsci, 1971: 40). In essence, we must develop a mode of education which not only does not predetermine or limit the "life chances" and livelihoods of young people but, beyond that, one which does not accept as natural or inevitable the socially-created division between economy and polity, between our lives as workers and consumers and our lives as citizens. A democratic education must, that is, not only prepare upcoming generations to be both capable and effective workers and capable and effective citizens, but, also, be capable of critically considering and, possibly, effectively challenging the separation between the two experiences, between the dictatorship characteristic of the former and the democracy of the latter, leading, hopefully, to the making of democratic changes and the developments in both.

To accomplish such changes will also necessarily entail a different kind of response to the New Right's educational initiative regarding the crisis of American polity and culture than those usually afforded by radical democrats. *There is a crisis!* And here, again, it is a mistake to simply reject the idea of a common culture, even when defined in terms of the "Western tradition." Rather, it is a question of critically appropriating—or, better, and more historically accurate, *re*appropriating Western *traditions* and American history and culture "from the bottom up," and of endeavoring to rearticulate them in a democratic and pluralistic fashion for ourselves and for future generations. Moreover, a democratic education must involve not just a process of transmission and inculcation of ideas and ideals but, also, an experience of engaging, working through, and possibly even transforming them (Kaye, 1991). That is, not only the ideas and ideals, but the activity itself must be recognized as contributing (or not) to the making of active and critical democratic citizens. As Gramsci insisted, a democratic education should be "forming" of a young person as one who is "capable of thinking, studying and ruling - or controlling those who rule" (Gramsci, 1971: 40).

Let us continue to insist that "We, the people" shall rule and, so inspired, create a democratic education whose purpose and promise is that of preparing ourselves and our children to do so.

References

Barber, B. (1989) "Cultural Conservatism and Democratic Education: Lessons form the Sixties." *Salmagundi*. 81, pp. 159-73.

Bennett, W.J. (1988) *Our Children and Our Country*. New York: Simon & Schuster.

Bloom, A. (1987) *The Closing of the American Mind*. New York: Simon & Schuster.

Blumenthal, S. (1986) *The Rise of the Counter-Establishment*. New York: Times Books.

Buhle, P. and A. Dawley (1985) *Working for Democracy*. Urbana, Ill.: University of Illinois Press.

Fukuyama, F. (1989) "The End of History?" *The National Interest*. 16, pp. 3-18.

Gramsci, A. (1971) *Selection from the Prison Notebooks*. New York: International Publishers.

Himmelstein, J. (1990) *To the Right: The Transformation of American Conservatism*. Berkeley, CA.: University of California Press.

Hirsch, E.D. (1987) *Cultural Literacy*. Boston: Houghton Mifflin.

Kaye, H.J. (1991) *The Powers of the Past*. London: Simon & Schuster International.

Mattera, P. (1990) *Prosperity Lost*. New York: Addison-Wesley.

Philips, K. (1990) *The Politics of Rich and Poor*. New York: Random House.

Dalton B. Curtis, Jr.

From the early years of the American republic, education has been seen as essential to the success of democracy. That idea certainly was uppermost in the minds of the nation's founders. Thomas Jefferson and Benjamin Rush, for example, believed that democracy needed an enlightened citizenry to ensure the protection of republican institutions and the effective functioning of government. To accomplish these goals, they proposed similar, albeit ill-fated, plans for tax-supported schools in their respective states. By the first half of the nineteenth century, industrialization, urbanization, and immigration as well as the continuing concern for republican institutions led Horace Mann, Henry Barnard, Calvin Wiley, John Pierce, and others into a campaign to establish common schools. The success of that effort in the Northeast and the Midwest, the advent of the corporate industrial state, and the desire to assimilate a second wave of immigrants helped to spread schooling throughout the rest of the country by the early decades of the twentieth century. By that time, schooling and democratic citizenship had become inextricably linked in the minds of Americans.

Today, most Americans say without hesitation that the school is responsible for teaching their children, and to the question, should the fact that we live in a democratic society make a difference in what school are like? They would probably answer, "Yes." Many Americans, however, are likely to be emphatic in answering "Yes!" to the question, Should the fact that we live in a capitalist society make a difference in what schools are like? They are far more concerned about the school preparing their children for the world of work than educating them for participation in public life. This attitude was clearly reflected by the National Commission on Excellence in Education in its 1983 report, *A Nation at Risk*. The commission expressed grave doubts about America's ability to compete with Japan, South Korea, and Germany in the world economy, but said little or nothing about the failure of Americans to be responsible citizens (National Commission on Excellence in Education, 1983).

This, the society expects the school to provide it with a trained workforce and only incidentally with enlightened citizens.

This essay is concerned with schooling for citizenship in a democratic social order and the concomitant responsibility of the society at large in the making of citizens. Without question, the fact that we live in a democratic society should make a difference in what our schools are like, but it should also make a difference in the behavior of adult citizens. If a democratic society depends on the rational decisions of its citizens in the practice of politics, then the school must teach the young both what it means to be a citizen and how to act responsibly in that capacity, and the adult citizenry must take seriously its commitment in democracy. This thesis raises several questions: What is meant by democracy, what are some of the ways of teaching the young how to be good citizens, and what must adult citizens do to make democracy work? These are the same questions the community and its educators ought to be trying to answer as they engage in the practice of democratic living.

Modern liberal democracy is a form of government in which power rests with the citizens who conduct the business of the state either directly or indirectly through elected representatives in what is called a republic. Democratic government is intended to serve public ends, to protect the rights of individuals, and to guarantee equality of all citizens before the law. To these responsibilities has been added ensuring material survival, which some see as the chief business of the state. Ultimately, the means of government are to be directed toward the purpose of liberal democracy; to free the individual to seek her own ends.

As Christopher Lasch has suggested, achieving the promise of democracy in twentieth century America has come to mean that government, whether in conservative or liberal guise, should foster material progress (Lasch, 1979, 1984, 1991). This attitude has contributed to the growth of unbridled individualism, the product of a consumer society. No longer is the principal purpose of work to produce high quality, durable goods that are the mark of excellent craftsmanship; rather, it is to enable the worker to consume the goods he or she makes or use the services he or she provides. Democracy in America has been further distorted by recent abuses of governmental power.

Thus, politics is seen as a dirty business, politicians are viewed as scoundrels, or at least of questionable character, and Americans are increasingly unwilling to engage in public affairs, all of which threaten democracy.

A way out of this quagmire is to conceive of a broader notion of democracy, one that encompasses government and society, and that enables the individual to achieve excellence in whatever she or he does, but particularly in the practice of politics. If democracy is seen as a form of associated living for the purpose of promoting individual achievement, then politics becomes the business of according equal rights to all citizens and creating the conditions under which human abilities can be cultivated to their highest level. This form of democracy combines the Aristotelian notion of virtue as individual excellence with the ethical concept of democracy as a way of life espoused by John Dewey. It tries to escape the emphasis on technique of the modern world by promoting the ancient ideal of *phronesis*, or practical reason directed toward moral perfection, it avoids the social restrictions of the ancient world by employing modern ideas of citizenship and equal rights; and it presupposes the interdependence of corporate society and its effect on modern life.

In order for democracy to become a way of life, certain conditions must be met. First, communities must be formed through effective communication, shared social ideals, and a commitment to solve common social problems. Second, local communities must communicate with and share in the common social ideals of the larger society. Third, although the particular structure of democratic government may vary, in all cases its ultimate purpose must be to create the good life by conferring equal rights and providing for human excellence. Fourth, the highest obligation of the citizen must be to engage in the practice of politics-that is, to participate in public life. Fifth, all citizens must be educated for participation in that way of living in order for the political conditions of democracy to be met.

The final condition of a democratic way of life brings us back to the problem of education in general and schooling in particular. If we are going to educate citizens for democratic living, what should our schools be like? Furthermore, should education be left solely to the schools? In answering these questions, I would like to examine two alternative schemes for citizenship education.

Recent proposals for the return of education have revived the tradition of civic education that centers on reading historic documents and the study of history, geography, and the civics as means of making good citizens. William J. Bennett, for example, published a series of monographs while he proposed top educate young citizens through a social studies curriculum that was to begin in the elementary school and continue through the junior year of high school. The elementary curriculum would start with myths, stories, fables, and biographies designed to lay a foundation for the formal study of history, geography, and civics. From the fourth grade through high school, students would take a series of courses in American and world history, geography, and American government (Bennett, 1986, 1987, 1988).

Unfortunately, this reform proposal suffers from the historic problem of civic education: It is too abstract. The social studies disciplines are studies apart from related disciplines, and there seems to be no connection between the formal study of history, geography, and civics and the actual problems of citizenship. Although Bennett emphasizes the important skills of reading and writing in social studies, he has no suggestions for enabling students to test their learning on public issues. His recommendations for the practice of citizenship are limited to a few civic tasks in the early years of elementary school. Yet he believes students should be "*learning* science by *doing* science" Bennett, 1986). His proposed science curriculum includes laboratory work for ". . . underlining and illustrating facts and principles of the scientific method, and demonstrating that order and sense may be made from the results of careful experimentation" (Bennett, 1987). If learning about society and the obligations of citizenship is to be as meaningful as learning about the physical environment, then students must have an opportunity to synthesize and apply their knowledge of the social studies.

An alternative to Bennett's civic education is called education for public responsibility. As the principal means of initiating the young into the democratic way of life, this scheme for citizenship education combines the Aristotelian concern for practical reasoning aimed at moral perfection, particularly in politics, with the Deweyan concern for problem solving at the heart of the democratic process. It offers the student opportunities to engage in the art of politics by posing social problems for them to solve. It emphasizes the importance of individual responsibility and social obligation through actual civic service.

Education for public responsibility begins in the first years of schooling and continues through high school. Its curriculum includes formal study of the social studies disciplines, regular engagement in solving social problems, and shared responsibility for the civic needs of the classroom, school, and society. Each year, students develop into the social studies as a part of their initiation into the culture and as a means of developing a sense of judgment to be used in solving the public problems put before them. They also are obligated to perform various civic tasks in their classrooms in the early years and in their school and community as they become older and more mature.

Their formal studies begin with American folklore and music, the patriotic symbols and events of American history, and the geography of their community. In the middle and late years of elementary school, students are introduced to American history, geography, literature, and fine arts in an integrated program that maintains the integrity of the disciplines while demonstrating the interrelationship of their content. The early years of the secondary school are devoted to an integrated study of the history, geography, literature, and fine arts of western civilization and of at least one non-western culture. In the last three years of the secondary school, students take work in American history, with a political and geographical emphasis, American government and international relations, and the problems of democracy. The study of the problems of democracy completes the social studies program and the problem-solving dimension of an education for public responsibility. Students from communities and political bodies to deal with actual public issues that draw on what students have learned throughout the school curriculum and that enable them to develop the broad outlines of solutions. Prior to this time, they have been challenged with increasingly complex social problems as an integral part of the social studies curriculum.

The final dimension of an education for public responsibility is the performance of civic tasks. As previously noted, young citizens do various civic tasks in their classrooms, school, and community from the earliest years of schooling. In their last year, individual students or student groups design and carry out a civic project under that guidance of members of the community.

Education for public responsibility avoids the pitfalls of Bennett's civic education. It considerably reduces the abstract nature of civic education by incorporating concrete social problems into the formal study of the social studies disciplines and by engaging students in civic tasks throughout their schooling years. It also helps students begin to synthesize their knowledge of America and the world by correlating the social studies disciplines with other related disciplines as they are being taught. At the same time, students gain skill in the exercise of judgment about public issues and practice at the tasks of public service in cooperation with the adult citizens of the community.

Cooperative public service is the final step in meeting the first condition of an education for public responsibility. The second condition is that adult citizens must see the example for the young by practicing the art of politics. They must engage in some form of public service if the school projects their children do are to have any real meaning. They must stop shirking their civic responsibility to vote. Voting is not a privilege in a democracy; it is a citizen's duty. Consequently, adult citizens must participate in the political process thoughtfully and demonstrate its importance to the young by including them in discussions of public issues. But this obligation cannot be met so long as citizens are willing to allow politicians to undermine the political process. In order to exercise their judgment effectively, citizens must demand rational arguments about public issues from their political representatives and they give those arguments serious consideration. They also must demand that politicians stop wasting time on image-making and devote their efforts to thoughtful debate about the business of the state.

Clearly, it is essential for the entire community to engage in education for public responsibility. The school must lay the intellectual foundations of citizenship and develop practical skill in the art of politics, and the citizenry must participate in public life. If excellence in politics were to become the highest practice for the citizen, then the moral stature of public responsibility would be demonstrated, the work of the school in educating citizens would be meaningful and effective, and the conditions most necessary for democracy to become a way of life would be achieved.

References

Bennett, W. (1986) *First Lessons: A report on Elementary Education in America*, Washington, D.C., U.S. Department.

Bennett, W. (1987) *James Madison High School: A Curriculum for American Students*, Washington, D.C., U.S. Department of Education.

Bennett, W. (1988) *James Madison Elementary School: A Curriculum for American Students*, Washington, D.C. U.S. Department of Education.

Lasch, C. (1979) *The Culture of Narcissism: American Life in an Age of Diminishing Expectations*, New York, Warner Books, Inc.

Lasch, C. (1984) *The Minimal Self: Psychic Survival in Troubled Times*, New York, Warner Books, Inc.

Lasch, C. (1991) *The True and Only Heaven: Progress and Its Critics*, New York, W.W. Norton & Company.

National Commission on Excellence in Education (1983) *A Nation at Risk: The Imperative of Educational Reform: A Report to the Nation and the Secretary of Education*, Washington, D.C., U.S. Department of Education.

Chapter VII

Women and Education: In what ways does gender affect the educational process?

Jo Anne Pagano

Janet L. Miller

Jo Anne Pagano

During the last decade, public discourse on education came to be increasingly dominated by the sentimental and nostalgic social and political agenda of the Reagan administration. Driven by certain economic imperatives, and enthralled by America's 1950's television image of itself, Reaganite intellectuals issued manifesto after manifesto reasserting faith in and commitment to an America in which all the moms wore shirtwaists and baked cookies, all the dads put their college educations to work earning good money, and all the kids did their homework and learned from their parents' fine examples to be good citizens. E.D. Hirsch rang praise for the successful and hardworking, thoroughly assimilated immigrant. Diane Ravitch persuaded many that the Civil Rights Movement unnecessarily disrupted the smooth and incremental progress toward racial equality taking place in legislature and courts. Allan Bloom mourned the idyll of upper class boys wandering among the groves of academe, now overrun with feminists and other Philistines. For all of these scholars, and others such as Lynne Cheney and Chester Finn and their military commander, William Bennett, the promise of America education had been betrayed by apostates of the canon. We are *no longer* culturally literate; we did not share vision or values and our cultural and educational disorder had brought us to the ruin of falling test scores and a falling dollar.

The tale they all tell is one of a past in which all Americans had access to the social and economic reward structure, in which all entered a cultural conversation organized by common history, knowledge, and understanding. It was a time in which all American could have identified, "Remember the Maine," The Monroe Doctrine, "Tippecanoe, and Tyler, Too," and had read Shakespeare and *Moby Dick*, some of the Bible and some of Plato, and knew the world's geography. Americans were literate, numerate, hard-working, and neighborly; schools were doing their job. But this, as we all know, is not an empirical description of the past. Yet even those who are most disadvantaged by it, are often mesmerized by this image of America; it retains a powerful hold on our imaginations. In our imaginations, we are all the same, therefore, all equally worthwhile. This is a version of the prelapsarian dream of original unity, before Adam and Eve knew that there was sex. As assertion of the importance of our differences, threatens America's dream of itself. To ask in what ways gender affects the educational process may provoke in some the struggle to sink deeper into sleep and cling to the dream.

Some will meet this question with surprise. Their unconsidered response will likely be a "No." Now these readers are not making an empirical claim, although their own educational experiences may have be beguiled them into thinking that they are. On the contrary, they are saying that gender *ought* not to affect the educational process. They have absorbed the values of their education, values which sustain a regime of enforced homogeneity. As we know now, the dark side of the expansion and democratization of education in this country was the impulse to appropriate and domesticate all who threatened to challenge America's nineteenth century pastoral vision of itself. Those contemporary educational criticisms which have captured the imagination of so many, and to whom, among others, the questions raised ion this book are directed, are efforts to recollect the nineteenth century's image of itself and are symptoms of a nostalgia for an edenic America that never was—an America in which race, class, ethnicity, and gender didn't matter.

Some will meet this question with a shrug and a knowing leer or sneer. I imagine Richard Bernstein, wise outsider and chronicler of the MLA and other academic meetings for readers of THE NEW YORK TIMES. He seems to think mention of certain topics of research and certain titles on programs sufficient to impugn the intelligence and integrity, not to mention the sanity, of the scholars associated with such topics and titles. Any paper with the word "difference" is a target for ridicule simply by virtue of the presence of the word "difference." "Sex" is another such word. The word "difference" employed in a title of any novel written in England during the eighteenth or nineteenth centuries is likely to be met with high hilarity. Its like saying the word "underwear" to an eight-year-old boy.

I meet this question with perplexity. This is one of those questions, the raising of which, is likely more interesting than any response I can imagine. Its having been raised may teach us about ourselves as other questions come crowding, pushing and shoving their ways into our minds. Why is the question formulated as it is? Certainly it teaches us that women and gender are perceived as situated precariously in educational debates. Why do we inquire instead into the ways in which the educational process affects gender? Whose conception of gender are we talking about? Whose gender is a stake in our investigation of the effects, if any there are, of gender on the educational process? And what do we mean by "educational process?"

It seems obvious to me that gender *ought* to have an effect on the educational process, just as it seems obvious to me that the educational process has an effect on gender. Regarding those two claims, I find nothing new for me to say. We've all said what there is to say many times before. That sex and other differences correlate in various ways with school performance has been well-documented, and the conclusion that our teaching ought to acknowledge the difference that difference makes seems unimpeachable to me. That academic achievement is more likely when the mode of teaching connects with the student's cognitive orientation is desirable if our goal is universal educational achievement. Equally obvious is the conclusion that it is desirable for human beings to orient themselves toward multiple axes of experience and cognition, that is desirable that we learn to think and feel the complexity of complex questions.

I suspect that, appearances to the contrary, I am not being asked to say really how gender affects the educational process. Were I to attempt to do so I should be met with yawns from those who agree with me and ridicule from those who do not. I suspect that I am being asked instead to argue that the question it itself a sensible one and that taking it seriously would yield educational benefits.

Still, I am perplexed by the question as it is articulated. For it seems that our interest isn't talking about gender and education at all, but about women and education. It seems curious that questions of gender should be so exclusively assimilated to my own sex, when masculinity is clearly equally implicated in the educational process. It seems that women are the problem, not gender. When this question is so formulated as it is,, certain expectations are sown. Foremost among these is the expectation that we will be talking about and perhaps sentimentalizing "women's ways of knowing." But we learn to be women, *and* we learn to be men. Women have certain cognitive and affective dispositions, *and* so have men. Why should gender effects be an issue in thinking about women's education only? An association among women and gender and education neglects the gendered nature of male knowledge. It can suggest to some that education as we know it is fine for men. Then women remain the problem, and the resistance to feminist and other theoretical analyses that employ the concept of difference is predictable. The question is, "Why can't a woman think more like a man?" The educational problem of those of us who teach women becomes then a problem of teaching them to be more like men in their cognitive approaches to the world. The problem of gender articulated as a question involving women and education only, can then be read as a problem of special pleading, rather than as a general problem of human knowledge and relationships. Moreover, it ignores the fact that many women can think more like a man than some men. That is many women are more oriented to abstraction and principled thinking, the sort of thinking usually associated with men, just as many men are more oriented to relational and contextual thinking. The point is that our approaches to education valorize the former and discount the latter. The first is called "thinking;" the second is called "feeling." The point is that we *ought* acquire both orientations, whether we are men or women, and that our educations ought to encourage our development in both domains.

I have a Ph.D., and I have a shameful memory of my behavior in a seminar I took as part of my program. The course was in the philosophy of science and one required of all Ph.D. students. That semester there were two women enrolled in the course. One day, the other woman presented to the seminar her research project. Her framework was ill constructed, and her methodology logically flawed, and I, along with the male students and the instructor in the seminar let her have it. Each time she tried to respond to a criticism, one or the other of us would point out the irrelevance of her considerations to the logic of our arguments. Before the afternoon was over, she left the room in tears. I was a good student, and it didn't occur to me to regret my part in pushing her to that point. I was scornful of her taking criticism so personally, of her thinking like a woman. I was disinterested, objective, and analytical—a scholar. I responded to the work and spoke in the normal style of academic exchange, and I humiliated another person.

I am culturally literate. I can identify most of the items on Hirsch et.al.'s list. I've studied classical as well as contemporary philosophy. The literary canon so jealously defended as source and sustenance of our highest and most noble aspirations is featured prominently in my educational history. I appreciate music and art, I can engage in intelligent discussions about science, and I can do some math. I have a good sense of history, and my S.A.T. and G.R.E. scores were very high. And yet these seem not to have made me a better person. This is not to deny that they can help.

At stake in all educational debates is the sort of person education should produce. They are moral issues, and not simply matters of skill and content. Our education ought to help us to be better persons. Decisions regarding the sort of education we want, are decisions regarding the sort of world we want to live in. The cultural literacy that is the outcome of a canonical education seems not to have accomplished much in the way of making this a better world. The social problems and global tensions which motivated the 1983 *Presidential Report on Excellence in Education* have escalated. The magnitude of unemployment, homelessness, world starvation, drug and alcohol abuse, child abuse and other violent crimes, declines in economic productivity has increased since then, as has the threat and actuality of war. This despite some reported rises in standardized test scores. The education that men and women receive is fine for neither men nor women.

What does all of this have to do with original question regarding gender and education? Simply that we associate certain traits and styles of thinking with women; that we relegate to women's work the labor of reproduction—the labor of sustaining and nurturing life, of caring for others. This is the labor Virginia Woolf called unpaid-for, and therefore despised labor. Feminist analyses and educational proposals in recent years have urged us to think of education not only in terms of production, whether economic or intellectual, but in terms of reproduction as well. Feminists argue that the world will be a better place and ourselves better people only if we can take multiple perspectives and orient ourselves simultaneously to the claims of caring and the claims of reason. Why should anyone find such a project threatening, and respond to research with a sneer?

Those who dominate educational discourse often respond violently to the suggestion that such should be our educational goals. I suspect that the strength of protest is related to the magnitude of the anxiety provoked by such suggestions. I suspect that for some it is an anxiety of control. For others it is an anxiety of responsibility. If we are forced to acknowledge that our education is rooted in a set of values and perspectives, *and* that those values and perspectives are neither universal nor obviously humane, then we shall have to take responsibility for the values and perspectives we choose to teach from.

My perplexity will now be seen to betray a certain disingenuousness. I teach at a university that has admitted women for twenty years only. We are not yet coeducational. Many of my colleagues do, however, have a will to coeducation as they do to enlarging in general education program. I am committed to this program and think that it makes us stand out from other colleges and universities of our sort. Now many may read the words "core program" and "general education" and immediately place us alongside Bennett and Bloom, Hirsch and Ravitch, et al. But what we have tried to do is enlarge the notion of the core such that the work of those outside the "canon" is not encountered as eccentric to the core, but as part of it, as part of the conversation that sustains the core. In the present political climate, our program disturbs some of our students and some of our colleagues. When some think of a core curriculum, they immediately think of dead white European males, to repeat a pretty worthless and finally unrevealing phrase. At Colgate, there are some who worry that general education is made to serve an ideological agenda, and when they say "ideological" they mean "left-wing." The inclusion of so-called "nontraditional" works seems to evoke that charge.

Our program is made up of four courses taken by all students. I chair one of them. It's called "The Modern Experience in the West" and is situated in the nineteenth century. Being sensitive to the politically charged climate, to the polarization among students especially, I invited a "conservative" outside speaker to make the point that the point is to learn to listen and speak across differences, to understand that whatever our affiliations, the continued existence of ourselves and even our planet demands that we recognize a common interest. As I look at the word "conservative," I see how very little that tells us. For he is a considerably more complex person and thinker, and no more "conservative" than I am "liberal". Certain designations no longer delineate the complexities of contemporary cultural politics, a scene redrawn partly as a result of research in questions of gender.

Our speaker was a very angry man. He is particularly angry with feminists and lesbians. It's interesting that I know that since women were not the topic of his lecture. Yet women were more present in his lecture than was the figure about whom he was lecturing. I was uncomfortable, but I learned something important. I learned, I think, why Bloom and Bennett, Hirsch and Ravitch and Cheney are so angry. They have not, as our visiting lecturer has not, as too many scholars on the political left as well have not, grasped the difference between scholarship and advocacy.

When we ask in what ways gender affects education, or in what ways education affect gender, we are suspected of violating standards of objectivity and disinterest. They assure immediately that we will cook the data—a fitting way to talk about research about women, I suppose. But it's a delicate line. As a student, I was exposed to all sorts of studies and "-ologies" that taught me, objectively and disinterestedly, against my own experience, that women are, in more ways than I can count, inferior. I call that advocacy or ideological research. We should pause a moment to notice that simply to announce our topic as "Women and" is to be met raised eyebrows.

Part of the problem is that women studies and the various racial and ethnic studies programs in this country are grounded in advocacy movements. But they have not remained there. We understood that advocacy required a basis. We needed to understand, intellectually, theoretically, empirically, questions of sexual difference in the contexts of our disciplines. This is knowledge with a passion, but no mere advocacy. There is a difference. Passion does not entail irresponsibility.

The educational challenge in the foreseeable future will be to teach people to acknowledge and understand their own passions, their own advocacy positions, without becoming reduced to them. It's that we have learned from women's studies. My guest, however, chose to understand his life, his work, endangered by our own. It seems clear to me, that gender is implicated in education, and that education has everything to do with gender. When I say, "Let's talk," he hears, "You're wrong." And as far as I can tell, that translation rests largely in his knowledge that I teach women's studies courses.

The real trick is to learn to do more than one thing. I find my teaching of canonical works immeasurably enhanced when I put them in conversation with noncanonical works, just as I find my students' understanding of print texts complimented by visual texts. Similarly, noncanonical works become richer when they are located with respect to canonical traditions. And now another distinction seems problematic, and that is the distinction between canonical and noncanonical. It does, after all, seem possible to do more than one thing at a time. It does, indeed, seem possible to acknowledge differences and to locate ourselves in communities and traditions larger than our differences. Virginia Woolf once said that poetry must have a mother and a father both. We should take our lesson from her.

Janet L. Miller

In the summer between fifth and sixth grade, I spent a lot of time hoping that I would get Mr. Brucker as my sixth-grade teacher. He was the best—everyone wanted to be in his class, because he was tough yet funny, serious yet caring. At least that's what all my friends said, and I couldn't doubt their wisdom, let alone my own fifth-grade observations of this teacher who always spoke gently to us amidst the shrieks and giggles that filled the hallways of our elementary school.

One hot July afternoon, as I was leaning out the front door, watching for my father to come home from work, I saw Mr. Brucker trudging up out front sidewalk, lugging what looked to me like a suitcase. My heart pounding, I ran into the kitchen and announced breathlessly to my mother that my wish had been granted. Mr. Brucker was here, and that must mean that I had been assigned to his sixth-grader class.

What I found out later, as he sat sipping ice water and talking with my parents in the living room, was that Mr. Brucker was selling encyclopedias during the summer in order to make enough money to support his family through the vacation months. His visit to our home had nothing to do with my assignment to his sixth-grade class. We were part of his neighborhood sales route, a route that meandered through the steel-girded south hills of Pittsburgh. And the encyclopedias, ordered by my parents only in response to my pleading eyes, I'm sure, arrived just coincidentally with the school notice that indeed placed me in Mr. Brucker's prized sixth-grade classroom. But my anticipation, my desire to be in his class, and my eager participation in all aspects of the classroom community that Mr. Brucker constructed with us that year have everything to do with my learning and subsequent re-learning and teaching as a woman.

What I already had learned, way before that summer between fifth and sixth grade, was that Mr. Brucker was prized among students and parents alike, not only because he indeed was a kind, caring, and enthusiastic teacher but also because he was the only male teacher in Sickman Elementary School. The other three sixth-grade teachers, all women, were supposedly equally as good as Mr. Brucker, or so the neighborhood lore implied. But to have a man as a teacher, in that last year of elementary schooling that still sanctioned childhood play even as it prepared us for the grown-up demands and rigors of junior high school, guaranteed for us the rites of passage into the rules and structures of the disciplines and forms of educating that would lead us into our appropriate roles and places as men and women. If we learned those rules and forms well, we perhaps could take our places in a society that could well extend beyond those burgeoning industrial hills that sometimes seemed to hem in, to constrain our parents' and thus our own visions of possibilities.

As I began that sixth-grade year, nervous and excited, I immediately could see why Mr. Brucker's reputation for posing such possibilities was so solidified within our community. We all, boys and girls, were charmed by his spontaneous grin and his willingness to join us in every aspect of our classroom life. In his spontaneity, he did not separate our learning from his teaching, and so, instead of sitting behind his desk, as so many of our earlier teachers had done, Mr. Brucker would straddle a chair as he coached us in our multiplication and division drills. He would leap from one side of the room to the other, foreshadowing the game show host as he attempted to keep our screams of excitement under a roar level during our spelling bees or math team contests. He was the sixth-grade pied piper, his glasses always slightly askew, and his tall lean body perpetually braced against the crush of students who constantly surrounded him as he tried to lead us through the tangled passageways of childhood and into that clearing known as "real school."

But, even as much as he talked to us about how junior and senior high school would be different from what we were sharing that year, and how we needed to prepare ourselves for those serious undertakings, I always had the feeling that Mr. Brucker never quite believed that was how it had to be. And so, I also experienced in that year some of the disruptive and contradictory positions that Mr. Brucker occupied within our particular elementary school culture. What I am still learning about are the ways in which those contradictory positions contributed to, affected, and ultimately disrupted many of my own contradictory understandings about myself as a female attempting to learn and later to teach.

I was aware, in that sixth-grade year, not only of some of the differences that Mr. Brucker as teacher represented for me, but also of some of the differences that characterized the kids in our class. Even though most of us lived within walking distance of our school, we girls who had known each other for a few years did not walk home with the new girls in our class who were part of the group known as "the hill" kids. Even though most of my friends' fathers worked in the steel mills ands most of their mothers worked at home, these new kids were part of a growing community of men and women from Appalachia who had recently moved to Pittsburgh to get jobs in the mills. There was a separation between the "old" and "hill" boys too, and I could see that Mr. Brucker tried to include these kids in every team event or partner activity that he proposed in class. And because this seemed important to him, I too tried to talk with my friends about including these kids in our daily school rituals.

In a way, I might have wanted to work toward such small attempts at inclusion because I felt different from my friends, in some ways. My mother, instead of staying home to care for my sister and me, needed to work a full-time job to help with family finances. She worked not in the mills, like some of the "hill" kids' mothers, but in a real estate office. And so I appreciated Mr. Brucker's discussion, in our unit on careers, of possible jobs that we girls might want to consider. He didn't just assume that we or our mothers would want or be able to stay at home in order to raise our children, and I remember that we girls talked, hanging from the monkey bars during recess that afternoon, about what we really might want to do in our lives besides be mothers. I, of course, had already determined that I wanted to be a teacher, just like Mr. Brucker.

But I was also learning that, even if I were to teach, and even if I were to explore with my students some of the alternative ways of living and thinking that Mr. Bruckers' gentle visions encouraged, I still would not be a teacher just like him. As we worked our ways through geography and grammar lessons, and built clay replicas of the Panama Canal, replete with water-tight locks, and recited declensions, I began to notice that the other sixth-grade teachers, the women, would often appear at our classroom door—to plead for our teacher's help in calming two students who were fighting in the lunch room, to ask him to open one of the old and constantly stuck windows in the room down the hall, to watch our class radio productions every few weeks, where we introduced and shared with classmates, through recordings and our own handwritten scripts, our latest research on Verdi's "Aida" or on the coal mining industry.

Mr. Brucker was the leader of Sickman School, whether he wanted to be or not. I think now that he tried in some ways to resist that role, and in our class, he constantly was encouraging us all, girls and boys, to consider possibilities for ourselves that did not automatically occur to many of us as we trudged home each afternoon through the ever-present yet gentle grayness of our steel town's southern hills. He challenged us girls to move beyond stereotypical images of ourselves that we reinforced every recess in our jump-rope and hopscotch play, for example, by insisting that we be part of the class kickball team. I still remember his gleeful yelp when I kicked the ball over the fence for my first-ever home run. He insisted that, on rainy days, the boys and girls play in the jacks tournaments that he set up for us during lunch and recess times. And he pushed us all in class, always asking us for another possible way to figure out the current math problem. But, even as he was attempting to disrupt our already deeply internalized conceptions of ourselves as gendered beings, as girls and boys who should fulfill certain socially constructed roles within our public and private worlds, I think that what I was learning in sixth grade had more to do with my desires to please this teacher rather than to emulate the disruptive and challenging perspectives that he perhaps was attempting to enact in his teaching. And in my desire to learn his acceptance and approval, I was learning the sanctioned forms of gendered relationships, discourses, and curriculums that structured and framed the lives of both Mr. Brucker and myself.

To please Mr. Brucker meant that I had to take some risks; I had to work to overcome my shyness about speaking up in class and I had to be willing to attempt to move beyond giving only the "right answers." He pushed us all not only to frantically wave our hands in our moments of certainty but also to offer explanations for those answers that we thought might be possible within each of our multiple points of inquiry. And, with that kind of encouragement, I was able, slowly, to participate in our class exchanges and debates and to articulate the connections that I could make among the various threads of our sixth-grade curriculum. I was enlarging my own capacities to enter into the official school languages of our textbooks as well as into the unofficial languages and relationships that signaled our connections to one another as we studies and learned together in the effusive sixth-grade community. And yet, as the year wore on, even as I was becoming aware of those connections among Mr. Brucker, the work our classroom, and ourselves as his students, I also was becoming increasingly aware, as the "hill" kids kept walking home in their own group, and as the boys more and more claimed their apparently rightful priorities in grabbing Mr. Brucker's attention on the softball field as well as in our classroom, of the differences between and among those relationships.

I was aware, certainly before sixth-grade, that the official languages of schooling were valued more than the discussions and bantering that characterized much of our interaction in Mr. Brucker's class. Even though I think that he clearly valued our dialogues above the facts that filled our textbooks and our "official" recitations of those disparate fragments of information, Mr. Brucker tried, for our own good, he said, to separate us as well as himself from the personal, intimate worlds that permeated our casual yet interrelated conversations about such topics as the geography of Western Pennsylvania, the economic interdependence of the industries that grew out of our "steel city," and the work in which many of our parents were engaged.

We knew that we had to "settle down" when his voice would modulate into the somber and serious lower register, and when he would unfold his long, lean frame into his chair that he positioned in the center of our double-layered concentric-circle desk arrangement. And then, even though our conversations had been filled with information we had gleaned from parents, siblings, friends, about what it was like to work in the mills, or to forge new communities in these still forested hills, or to worry about how to feed and care for children when lay-offs hit, we began to recite the facts of our textbooks, as Mr. Brucker questioned us in rapid-fire order.

I had become adept at such memorizations and recitations, having learned early in Mr. Brucker's class that such performances earned his praise. I think that we all worked at moving through such rote activities as quickly as possible so that we could get to the real parts of our learning, for I think now that we all recognized, even in sixth-grade, that the textbooks never captured the depths or complexities of our own stories. And I noticed that, even as I could recite lists of economic connection that tied our lives together, for example, there was no mention of the kind of bookkeeping and auditing work that my mother did in her job, or of the incessant housework that she, my sister, and I battled each night when we arrived home. The only women we had read about in our history books were Clara Barton, Florence Nightingale, and Jane Addams, and then we only knew of them through descriptions of their extensions of socially-sanctioned women's work.

And so, I learned that, even though the stories of our daily lives were the ones that Mr. Brucker asked about on the playground or during our lunch breaks or during the conversations of our class, he gave official recognition, official school praise, for those facts about Clara Barton as nurse during the Civil War, or about the geography of western Pennsylvania. Thus, as much as I learned from Mr. Brucker about the value of our connections and conversations, I also learned that, in order to receive the sanctioned merits of schooling, to receive his official acknowledgment and approval, I had to talk with others' words, to speak in the modulated serious tones of others' understandings, to memorize others' stories, to replicate others' knowledges. And in doing so, I neglected or repressed the unofficial, the desires inherent in our stories, our personal conversations and relationships that were at the heart of Mr. Brucker's teaching, and yet were separated as much from his conceptions of official knowledges as were my replications. And in my ironic desire to please, to receive authorization, I became Other.

I realize that this story too is only a partial telling, a story pieced together from myriad memories and recreated through the lenses of subsequent multiple experiences, conceptualizations, and enactments of teaching and learning. In this particular telling, however, are examples of the ways in which dominant educational constructions of gender, in which men teachers were more important, more valid in their associations with and transmission of official knowledge than women teachers, for example, undergirded my initial understandings of learning, curriculum, and pedagogy. In this telling, too, are vestiges of the ways in which those gendered conceptions of appropriate teaching and learning stances still manifest themselves in my educational work. I struggle still to hear my own voice, my own constructions and understandings of knowledge as emanating, in complex and changing ways, from both the personal conversations as well as the public representations of those knowledges. And as I grapple with those still institutionalized dichotomies, I still see Mr. Brucker also wrestling with what he seemed to perceive as artifical separations of our public and private knowledges about our worlds and our relationships to one another. He chose, for many reasons that I guess still substantiate many teachers' transmissions of others' knowledges, to officially support school knowledges, while, in his interactions with us, to offer us visions of other possibilities for ourselves. But I was so embedded in my own already internalized gender role as "good girl," seeking approval and thus replicating his official choices, that I missed, for years, the discrepancies between Mr. Brucker's pedagogical and personal representations of curriculum and learning.

While I do not claim my experiences or understandings as universal for all girls and boys who were educated in the United States during the 1950s, I do think that aspects of static role expectations for both teachers and students, of curriculum conceived as objective and measurable knowledge, and of teaching and learning as separated from the knowledges generated by individuals' relationships and interactions reflect those dominant constructions of gender that, for many, have separated and prioritized educational processes and experiences.

Thus, as we who educate now attempt to understand curriculum as representation of particular historical, social, economic, and political intersections in individuals' lives, we also view those intersections as mediated by multiple constructions of gender, race and class. As we engage in debate with those who argue for stable, unified canons that supposedly represent consensus on singular and universal traditions, we can point beyond inclusions of women's voices and works as a unitary representation, for example, and toward the multiple and shifting nature of those voices and their positions across various discourses which historically and currently constitute their lives in and out of school. Thus, it is important, but not sufficient to speak of elimination of sexism or sexual harassment in classrooms or of inclusion of minority voices into textbooks. It is important, but not sufficient to note how women are now integrated into educational institutions as students, teachers, administrators, as well as subject of scholarship. It is important, but not sufficient to point out the discrepancies, the separations between what counts as official school knowledges and what students and teachers construct daily as knowledges lodged in their interactions as well as their silences. We must scrutinize and work to change the very constructions of institutions, of disciplines and their representative curriculums, and of men's and women's internalizations of the gendered divisions and separations that historically have characterized educational processes, if we truly wish to work toward the creation of just and humane educational communities.

John Brucker's sixth-grade class provided me with a site for reflections and reconstructions of my own desires as a young girl, a student, and a teacher. As I work to understand the multiple ways in which the complex interactions of that year continue to both reflect and construct my conceptions of teaching, learning, and curriculum. I also am working to reconstruct my own versions, (now acceptable to me as possibly even subject to change), of myself as teacher, as learner, as knower. And while I still wonder what he might think of this particular version of our sixth-grade year together, and how he might construct his own stories of that year, I no longer need Mr. Brucker's permission to tell this particular tale.

Chapter VIII

Race and Education: In what ways does race affect the educational process?

Joyce E. King

Christine E. Sleeter, Walter Gutierrez, Clara Ann New, Susan R. Takata

Joyce E. King

"They can dress like us and act like us . . . but they still have the advantages of being white."
—Chuck Collins, Dane County
Youth Connection (Sanders, 1993)

Whites continue to wonder . . . whether 'blacks are capable of real intellectual achievement' . . . At the heart of the matter is a belief once voiced freely, but no longer openly aired, that African genes do not provide a capacity for complicated tasks.
Andrew Hacker, 1994, p. 459

For me the denial has ended. I can no longer tolerate the refusal of most European Americans to see that we African Americas are, independently of them, living, breathing, thinking human beings with a culture, a history, and an origin of our own.
Beverly McElroy-Johnson, 1993, p. 90

The problem here is that few Americans know who and what they really are . . . most American whites are culturally part Negro American without even realizing it.
—Ralph Ellison, 1986, p. 108

The historical practice of White people's emulation, envy, and impersonation of African Americans, often for financial gain— what I call the "prerogative of acting black"—has important implications for the status, curricular representation, school experience and response of African American students to their education or miseducation. An important distinction between education and schooling or mis/education that has been introduced into the literature along these lines follows a much earlier tradition of Black thought and writing about education. (See DuBois, 1935; Gordon, 1990; Shujaa, 1994; McElroy-Johnson, 1993; and Woodson, 1933). This chapter will suggest that understanding the dialectic of the burden of acting white requires a critical understanding of the prerogative of acting black in order to decipher the ways that culture, race, identity, and representation interact to influence the education of students in the U.S., especially African American students.

The "prerogative of acting Black" has received no such scholarly attention with respect to the African American education experience but remains unexamined in education research and scholarly writing. Another perspective in the literature, simply stated, is that African American culture exists as the above epigraph notes: it provides the material conditions and psychic context for *being* Black (Boykin and Toms, 1985). Moreover, such enculturation is universal. A body of literature also suggests that such enculturation has been an historically important survival strategy for African Americans, particularly with respect to their education under conditions of oppression. Finally, this does not preclude a variety of other strategies and cultural orientations that individuals may adopt, including bi-cultural accommodation (King & Mitchell, 1990). That is to say, "acting black" or choosing not to "act white" is not necessarily a defensive reaction to the dominant society, as Fordham and Ogbu's (1986) "burden of acting white" hypothesis suggests.

Ogbu and Fordham (1986) were the first to employ the "burden of acting white" hypothesis to explain the "school failure" of black youth. This hypothesis attributes the lower levels of academic achievement at least in part to students' lack of motivation and engagement due to peer pressure (Kunjufu, 1988) and to the "stigma" associated with blackness (Steele, 1992). Negative peer influences and other cultural deficiencies (Custred, 1990) are thought to limit students' identification with school. According to this "acting white" hypothesis, students limit their effort and engagement because they (mistakenly) believe that to do well in school, they have to "act white." This would constitute breaching racial boundary, maintaining peer group loyalties, which they are loathe to do. Spring, incorporates this argument:

> To avoid appearing "white" to other African American students, black children readily join in an anti-school culture. Of course, participation in this anti-school culture means that many black children will not attain the educational credentials that are required for participation in the mainstream economy (Spring, 1994, p. 101).

Interestingly, when researchers describe this phenomenon as a "culture of resistance" to schooling, what often gets ignored is that students are engaging in oppositional "collective autonomy" to protect themselves from assaultive schooling (Gilmore,

1985; Perry, 1993). The literature suggests that this includes "subtle and not-so-subtle patterns of exclusion" (Greeley and Mizell, 1993, p. 224) and teacher expectations and negative beliefs. These beliefs disparage African American culture undervalue or ignore "African American consciousness" (Gilyard, 1991 cited in Delpit, 1993, p. 291).

At least two other interpretations of what can also be referred to as the "burden of acting white" can be found in the literature and deserve to be mentioned. First, this literature suggests ways in which White teachers and students experience *being* and *acting* white as a "burden," particularly in situations where they may begin to feel guilty when learning about "white privilege" or begin to develop and/or resist "racial awareness" (Sleeter, 1993). On the other hand, African Americans who have successfully *mastered* the elements of "acting white" can also feel burdened by the demands, disappointments, and dread of being or becoming "mentally white" (Delpit, 1993, p. 290; King & Mitchell. 1990). Cose's (1993) recent study of "the rage of the privileged class"—middle-class African Americans—provides a compelling analysis of this reality. Perry (1993) critically re-examines the Fordham and Ogbu hypothesis and concludes that becoming "culturally white" is actually a prerequisite for schooling that these scholars fail to acknowledge. Further, if one considers not only the existing social science and education research literature but also works of fiction, both these dimensions of the acting white burden—for White and Black people—it becomes even more apparent that these are meaningful ideological and cultural correlatives for understanding the educational experiences of African American students from several vantage points.

These dimensions of the burden of acting white and the prerogative of acting black can serve as angles of vision to counterbalance the prism-like distortions that racial ideology and the process of racial formation (Omi & Winant, 1986) necessarily creates. When viewed from these different angles, the phenomenon initially described by Fordham and Ogbu, can be seen to occur within in a more holistic, *dialectical*, and historically specific, sociocultural context.

The Prerogative of Acting Black

A genealogy "traces the recorded history of a person or family from an ancestor or ancestors;" it is "the science or study of family descent" or "lineage" (Webster's New World Dictionary, 3rd College Edition, 1991, p. 561). The socially constructed roles of "conceptual blackness" as the alter ego to "conceptual whiteness" in this society (and globally, for that matter, are maintained according to rules and expectations that comprise the national culture, the racial identity of Americans and the ideology of white superiority that still exists in this society. Black people and White people have been united in an historically specific relationship that is constrained by the ideology of racism (Omi and Winant, 1986). This "racialization" of U.S. society has been and remains a determining feature of American cultural and social reality as well as the context of schooling. Therefore, an adequate social and cultural understanding of what acting white or black means with respect to the educational experiences of African Americans must be examined not in isolation but in terms of what these conceptualizations might mean *in relation to* each other. That is to say, we need an historical and relational understanding of how racial ideology works to define "acting" and "being" white or black (or Asian or Latino or Native American, etc.) under conditions of racial domination.

Not long after an article in a local newspaper in one Midwestern community asked, "But are whites genuinely interested in black culture, or is acting black just the in thing to do?" (Sanders, 1993, p. 20), *Jet Magazine* (January 10, 1994) reported that two White girls had to quit their junior-senior high school in Indiana because their peers harassed them for dressing black. Only in the popular press can such references to contemporary manifestations of acting black be found. Although, there is a dearth of scholarly writing on acting black, from institutionalized blackface minstrelsy to suburban "wiggers" (White (wannabe) niggers), no such scholarly attention is being focused on the possible educational implications of this national pastime of acting black.

Consider the way N'gai Croal (1994), a Black student at Stanford University, experiences and describes this paradox:

> As we watch basketball on television one of you wishes he were black. But do you mean black like Emmett Till or Usef Hawkins? Probably not. It's more likely that you mean black like Michael Jordan or Shaquille O'Neal. Yes. They're different, they're not really black, they're more than black—tortured logic plays in your mind like a drum.

Consider another, earlier example, this one is an excerpt from a book intended to prepare teachers for working in urban schools. Foster (1986) writes:

> When fear of physicalness is combined with a fear of blacks, the fear can become hate. Norman Podhoretz explained his special ''twisted' fear, envy, and hatred of Negroes as compared with other immigrant groups. While growing up in Brooklyn in the 1930s, he alternately envied, feared, and hated blacks because they 'were tougher than we were, more ruthless, and on the whole they were better athletes.' And they 'do not seem to be afraid of anything,' and 'act as they have nothing to lose' (H. Foster, 1986, p. 112).

Foster includes an extended quotation from Podhoretz's 1963 essay in *Commentary*, entitled: "My Negro Problem—And Ours". Podhoretz describes his envy of the "Negroes" who were "*really* bad, bad in a way that beckoned to one, and made one feel inadequate." Podhoretz asks:

> But envy? Why envy? And hatred? Why hatred? . . . just as in childhood I envied Negroes for what seemed to me their superior masculinity, I envy them today for what seems to me their superior physical grace and beauty . . . I am now capable of aching with all my being when I watch a Negro couple on the dance floor, or a Negro playing baseball or basketball (Foster, p. 113, cf., Podhoretz, 1963, pp, 93, 94, 97-98).

Indeed: "Envy, why envy? And hatred, why hatred?" Blackface minstrelsy is one starting point toward a genealogy for understanding the "twisted logic" of acting black and the racial prerogatives and perquisites that have been historically associated with it.

Although this form of minstrelsy has largely disappeared from American popular culture, its impact remains in the national consciousness. Vestiges of the "structure of racial feeling" (Lott, 1993) that are involved with it remain in the culture and psyche of African Americans and White Americans. Andrew Hacker and others cited here have observed the persistent suspicion that African Americans are intellectually inferior to Whites—a suspicion that is deeply embedded in the national consciousness. It was minstrelsy, as "popular" entertainment, that assisted a generation of Irish immigrants to develop a working class consciousness and permitted them to willfully assimilate from their similarly degraded status. As Lott (1993) notes, when Irish immigrants arrived in the U.S., native whites widely equated them with "blacks as an alien, subhuman, and brutal species" (p. 71). This working class consciousness that separated them from established white elites *and* blacks simultaneously enabled them to become "white."

The "tortured logic" of minstrelsy involved the performance and institutionalization of difference. This process of racial formation produced psychic and pecuniary rewards and privileges for the immigrant Irish. As a result of their participation in the disparagement of African Americans, antagonistic class relations were "soothed," or mediated at the expense of the further degradation of Black people. It is a *dialectic* of impersonal and envy that has continued from the 1920s when the Jewish jazz singer, Al Jolson, made his career in "blackface" (Rogin, 1992), to Elvis Presley's love/hate relationship with Black people and African American culture (Ventura, 1987) (i.e., love the music, but hate the people) to the "wiggers" in the suburbs "with black attitude" (Rogers, 1994; Wimsatt, 1994). These historically evolving manifestations of the racial ideology in this society have implications for the self-conceptions of students and teachers.

African American Culture Exists

African American culture is neither an epiphenomenon nor an instance of deficient socialization but consists of cultural practices, norms, values, behaviors, beliefs, attitudes and forms of cultural knowledge, consciousness and spirituality that constitute the group as a people. From this perspective Black culture is also regarded as a "culture of survival" and resistance (King &

Mitchell, 1990; Lemelle, 1991; Majors, 1986; Stuckey, 1987). As Lemelle observes, for example: Black culture is resistant to mainstream American social organization—our survival as a people has necessitated it (p. 11).

"Acting black" can be inferred, then, to refer in this instance to behaving, thinking and feeling in culturally appropriate ways that are consistent with membership and belonging in one's community and family and with collective survival (Richards, 1989). This perspective of the group status of African descent people in U.S. society is found in studies of the socialization or enculturation of African American students, primarily in their families (King & Mitchell, 1990; Peters, 1985; White, 1987) but also in their peer groups (MacLeod, 1987; Lemelle, 1991). Heath (1982) laments the gap between certain home and school communicative patterns that can also be said to involve "acting black" such as group loyalty and "keen interpretive talents." Still other research presents examples of the ways African American teachers have traditionally prepared Black students to "survive" the system (Delpit, 1993; M. Foster, 1994; King, 1991b; Ladson-Billings and Henry, 1990). The body of literature that delineates specific features of African American culture in comparison to the cultural practices and values of Euro-American schooling contrasts with Ogbu's (Ogbu, 1990) characterization of the problematic relationship between students' cultural frame of reference and school achievement (Boykin, 1994). Elsewhere I have discussed certain sociocultural deficit assumptions that the Ogbu-Fordham hypothesis shares with other scholarship (Steele, 1992) that is aimed at the re-socialization of African American youngsters to achieve "success" in school (King, 1994c).

The Racial Identity of Teachers and the White Man/Woman's Burden

Another body of literature addresses the consequences for African American students when their teachers have not developed an adequate understanding of their own ethnic/racial identity and the needs of African American students. For instance McElroy-Johnson (1933), an African American teacher, observes that "the failure of the educational system extends further ... into the political and psychological nature of the teaching body." She notes that teachers "who force a Eurocentric curriculum upon students from non-European backgrounds assume that these students ... want to be like European Americans" (p. 88). In other words, the "primarily European-American" female teachers at her urban school:

> ... for whatever reasons, are too often unaware of the non-European learners' needs ... ignore the need to translate curriculum and instruction into language readily accessible to these learners, and/or ... rigidly oppose acknowledging diversity and instead work for the "oneness of all" in "their image" of what that is" (p. 88).

Thus, the racial identity development and/or ethnic self-awareness of White teachers and students is a factor that is part of the sociocultural context that African American students experience in school. This factor is significant when students are learning together about racism and cultural differences (Tatum,1992); studying African American literature (Spears-Bunton, 1990); or when education students (and teachers) are learning to teach diverse populations (Hollins, 1990; King, 1992, forthcoming; King and Ladson-Billings, 1991; Sleeter, 1992). McElroy-Johnson is clear about the consequences for her mostly African American, Latino and Asian-Pacific Island students. She continues:

> This destroys the self-concept and individual power of non-European students, forcing them either into personal conduct that is destructive in nature or into a 'white-washed' imitation of the European-American ideal, an uneasy identity that is in opposition to their own natural cultural, ethnic, and racial identities (p. 88).

However, as the following example from my experience with student teachers shows, too many educators have not laid down the White Man/Woman's Burden. The following is an report from another classroom that supports this observation:

> To orient a new student teacher to her classroom a White teacher in an "exemplary" suburban school describes the Black children in her class this way: "Now, there are two groups of Black children here: The White-blacks, who will benefit from your teaching, because they have

white values and the Black-blacks, who will not. They are less capable intellectually and will be behavior problems, because they have black values" (King & Ladson-Billings, 1990, p. 17).

This is another dimension of what the notion acting white means, as well as what it does. That is, the "burden of acting white" account of Black students' lower levels of education attainment and academic achievement has become near orthodoxy in both the popular imagination and scholarly writing. Certain assumptions involved in this perspective are revealed in this earlier example of a cultural deficit beliefs regarding Black student's lower levels of academic achievement. Many of today's teachers were trained in graduate school education at a time when the viewpoint expressed in this incident was prevalent:

> In 1969, my educational psychology professor, an eminent scholar at Stanford University and author of one of the standard textbooks in the field explained to our graduate seminar that Black children were not successful in school because "they have no culture". "They don't appreciate Bach and Beethoven," and "research shows that their mothers don't communicate with them effectively."

The professor was probably referring to research like that of Hess and Shipman whose studies were emblematic of such cultural and cognitive deficit assumptions. Such research provided the rationale for compensatory education programs like Head Start. Eventually, this perspective and its conclusions were challenged by the assumptions of a "culture difference" perspective (King, 1994a, c). However, cognitive deficit assumptions have not been entirely displaced but are somewhat still at work in notions of *sociocultural* deficits. The following incident, again from my own experience, is presented to make this point:

> In 1987 the keynote speaker at a sociology of education conference, a prominent researcher, was asked if his findings regarding the success "minority" students achieve through cooperative learning strategies also applied to "model minority" Asians. He explained that his research focus was on Black students. But he added quickly with a laugh: "Maybe we should give all the Black kids Japanese mothers." The raucous laughter that erupted nearly drowned out another researcher who shouted this rejoinder: "No, no! Let's give 'em Jewish mothers!" (King & Wilson, 1990, p. 20).

A re-examination of the acting white hypothesis should also include consideration of how teachers, researchers, and students understand the racial signifiers that mark the difference between "blacks" and "non-blacks"—signifiers that have advantaged Euro-American ethnic immigrants and are at work in this quip about "Japanese mothers" and "Jewish mothers." This is an implicit critique of Black mothers—who presumably have "no culture."

The Burden of Coping with Black Representation and White Racism

Research in teacher education suggests that the expectations of experienced or beginning teachers regarding African Americans, their social status, cultural background, and needs as learners are not likely to be that different from prevailing views held in the general population. Here is one example of such a viewpoint. Joseph Sobran (1987) purports to explain why White Americans were so fond of the "Cosby Show"—a program that was considered to be a major breakthrough in the representation of African Americans on television:[1]

> Cosby appeals to white America's nostalgic affection for an endangered species—the Vanishing Negro. He's what we thought we were going to get by passing the civil-rights laws, and what we wish to hell we'd gotten (Sobran, 1987, p. 40).

The point is that the Cosby television show was valued, not for its representation of authentic African American distinctiveness, but for the extent to which these television Black folk fulfill White expectation of a wished-for "species" of "Negro." On the Cosby Show, despite its very positive contributions, Black cultural imagery and creativity were misappropriated to promote an idealized norm of success in "Blackface." The Cosby show was/is escapist fantasy.

In contrast, there is a body of literature that analyzes various media representations including "black/white binarisms" or dualistic constructions of African and European descent people in the U.S. and globally (Dyer, 1988) and representations in the other forms of "Western" (and European) popular culture

(Pieterse, 1992). Likewise, Toni Morrison's critical essays, including the book-length, *Playing in the Dark*, exemplify critical analyses of "the black" in the "white literary imagination" in U.S. fiction (Morrison, 1992). There is also a body of research and writing in postmodern "cultural studies" and "critical literary theory" that is beginning to link studies of the representations of race, culture, and identity with teacher education research (Britzman et al., 1993) and the education experiences of African American students (Ellsworth, 1993; McCarthy, 1993). There is also a growing body of literature that analyzes the representation of African Americans in textbooks (Crichlow et. al, 1990; King, 1992; McCarthy, 1990; Wynter, 1992a). However, research is needed that addresses the most effective ways to undo the ideological misrepresentations of African Americans in the school curriculum and textbooks, not only for students but for teacher preparation as well. The representation of slavery in the curriculum and textbooks is one source of the lingering doubts about Black people's intellectual capability. Such doubts plague students and cripple teachers (Greeley and Mizell, 1993; McElroy-Johnson, 1993).

Wynter (1992a) analyzes selected representations of "American history" in contrast to the lived experiences of African Americans and Native Americans that are marginalized but included in California's recently adopted textbooks. She demonstrates how these representations that perpetuate racism are inherently related to the views expressed by this letter-writer. Wynter analyzes the ideological premises, that is, of the cultural mode of rationality, that underlies the implied animalistic, "biologized" qualities the letter-writer attributes to African Americans. Wynter employs a Black Studies cultural model framework to decipher and challenge the notion of "genetic defectivity" that constitutes a founding "narrative" of our social order. This belief in genetic superiority/inferiority that made the enslavement of Africans seem rational and just is not the focus of analysis in the curriculum and textbook discussions of slavery. Moreover, according to Wynter, this structure of belief also legitimates the current global crisis of joblessness and the victimization of Black males in the U.S. (Wynter 1992a, b). It is epitomized in the acronym, N.H.I.; it refers to the phrase, "No

Humans Involved." Wynter (1992b) reports that this acronym was used routinely by judicial and police officials in Los Angeles to refer to young Black and Latino males in the wake of the insurrection there.

Interestingly, McElroy-Johnson (1993), as an urban teacher, perceives both the effects and the causes of this crisis in the failure of the education system to meet the needs of African American students. She states her commitment to a pedagogy that "gives voice" to her "voiceless" African American students, who are: "not graduating from high school," or "killed in the streets" or "ending up in prison" (p. 90). Asserting that, for her "the denial has ended". McElroy-Johnson writes:

> Our complaints are as real as those of our Japanese-American brothers and sisters who have received recognition and restitution for their grievances. The genocide, the destruction of our will, the enslavement of our ancestors has been, for us, and I dare say for the rest of human- ity, as vile as the Holocaust. I think we need to be heard and to be recognized, but not for revenge or restitution—there can be no restitu- tion or revenge to equal the death and destruction of millions of African souls traversing the middle passage to the Americas in slave ships . . . (p. 90).

With this observation McElroy-Johnson broaches a most crucial issue with respect to the education of African Ameri- cans: the mis/representation of slavery in the curriculum and textbooks—an issue that contributed to the controversy sur- rounding the history/social science textbook adoption in Cali- fornia several years ago. McElroy-Johnson's observations are worth quoting at length:

> It has never ceased to amaze me that, when the subject of African- American history is raised and the impact of slavery on this group is addressed, the response is often negative and resistant. If the subject were the dropping of the atomic bomb on innocent people at Hiroshima, one would select words carefully in raising any objection to the voicing of the terror of that deed and the effect it has had on the Japanese people and the world. If it were the Holocaust, one would be ill-advised to raise an objection to the constant reminders of these horrors in print, on television, and in film. We are encouraged to feel empathy and concern for the Southeast Asian people, who have fled oppression, or the Central American people, who are suffering from the ravages of war. Yet, when the subject of the psychological moral, emotional, spiritual, and physical effects of slavery upon African-Ameri-

can men, women, and children comes up, the responses are often very different, even hostile (p. 88).

This trenchant observation is consistent with my own teaching experience, research, and analysis: many teachers have a very damaging, distorted and incomplete understanding of the origins of slavery, its origins and implications for African Americans and the society (King, 1991a, 1992).[2] That is why educators like Asa Hilliard and Molefi K. Asante have emphasized the need to reconnect students to an accurate representation of the African American experience *before* the transatlantic slave trade.

It is important to note, however, that the prevailing account that teachers accept does not differ significantly from a standard historiography that essentially rationalizes the practice rather than provides a truthful, complete historical analysis (King, 1992, 1994b). My analysis of the misrepresentation in California's adopted textbooks of the origins of the transatlantic slave trade (King, 1992) builds on the critique that Wynter developed (Wynter, 1992a). For instance, by misequating the "Ellis Island" immigrant experience of some European Americans, the Middle Passage experience of the ancestors of many African Americans is represented as an anomaly—as an exception in the story of "the land of the free and the home of the brave." This is possible because the U.S. is characterized as a "a nation of immigrants." Moreover, instead of acknowledging, for example, as C.L.R. James (1970) does, that "every people, every race, has passed through a stage of slavery" (p. 119), the standard representation of the slave trade and slavery leaves students *and* teachers wondering, just as Hacker observes. They are wondering if there could have been "*something* . . . that rendered the black race [genetically] suitable for bondage" (p. 459, my emphasis).

By Way of Conclusion: A Coda

This chapter suggests that a more complete understanding of the school experience of African American students requires a genealogy of "acting black" in relation to what white means in this society. That is to say, a re-examination is required that includes *several* flip sides of the quadratic prism, of which the Ogbu-Fordham hypothesis angle of vision is only one. The question still needs to be asked: In societies characterized by centuries of the ideological racism, what does "white" and "black" mean to students, teachers and parents? What do these cultural conceptions *do* to students and to their education. What does acting white and acting black mean under such conditions? What are the implications for our system of education? for the curriculum, teacher preparation and parent involvement in education?

> And some black parents are just as reluctant to have their children associate with whites. 'My mom drills it into me all the time—it's a white world. Be proud of what you are but realize that people will treat you differently,' says Garietta, a black sophomore . . . 'My dad's afraid I'll be raped, or lose my heritage, or 'become' white' (Trebilcock, 1993, p. 100).

Notes

1 Sobran's comments appeared in the conservative *National Review* after a mob of White people attacked a group of Black males in Howard Beach, New York.

2 I served on the California Curriculum Commission, the State Board of Education advisory group responsible for developing and implementing curriculum frameworks and textbook evaluation criteria. In this capacity, I presented the training strand on the "inclusion of cultural diversity" to the panel of teachers and professors that was recruited to evaluate the history/social science textbooks in 1990. After this presentation, an elementary school teacher told me: "You have really educated me today. I never knew that anyone other than Blacks were slaves".

References

Baugh, J. (1994). New and prevailing misconceptions of African American English for logic and mathematics. In E. R.

Hollins, J. E. King & W. C. Hayman (Eds.), *Teaching diverse populations* (pp. 191-206). Albany, NY: SUNY.

Boykin, A. W. (1994). Afrocultural expression and its implications for schooling. In E. R. Hollins, J. E. King & W. C. Hayman (Eds.), *Teaching diverse populations* (pp. 243-274). Albany, NY: SUNY.

Boykin, A. W. and Toms, F. D. (1985). Black child socialization: A conceptual framework. In H.P. McAdoo and J.L. McAdoo (Eds.),*Black Children: Social, Educational and Parental Environments.* Beverley Hills, CA: Sage.

Britzman, D., Santiago-Valles, K., Jimenez-Munoz, G. and Lamash, L. (1993). Slips that show and tell: Fashioning multiculture as a problem of representation. In C. McCarthy and W. Crichlow (Eds.), *Race, identity, and representation in education* (pp. 188-200). New York: Routledge.

Cose, E. (1993). The rage of the privileged class. New York: HarperCollins.

Crichlow, W., Goodwin, S., Shakes, G., and Swartz, E. (1990). Multicultural ways of knowing: Implications for practice. *Journal of Education, 172*(2), 101-117.

Croal, N. (1994, March). Confessions of the N. H. I. *Stanford Magazine, 22*(1), 16-17.

Custred, G. (1990). Standard language in modern education. *American Behavioral Scientist, 34,* 232-239.

Delpit, L. (1993). The politics of teaching literate discourse. In T. Perry and J. W. Fraser (Ed.), *Freedom's plow* (pp. 285-295).New York: Routledge.

DuBois, W.E.B. (1935, July). Does the Negro need separate schools? *Journal of Negro Education, 4*:328-35.

Dyer, R. (1988, Autumn). White. *Screen, 24*(4), 44-64).

Ellison, R. (1986). What America would be like without Blacks. In R. Ellison, *Going to the territory* (pp. 104-112). New York: Random House.

Ellsworth, E. (1990). I pledge allegiance: The politics of reading and using educational films. In C. McCarthy and W. Crichlow (Eds.), *Race, identity, and representation in education* (pp. 201-219). New York: Routledge.

Foster, H. (1986). *Ribbin' jivin' & Playin' the dozens: The persistent dilemma in our schools.* Cambridge, MA: Ballinger.

Foster, M. (1994). Effective Black teachers: A review. In E. R. Hollins, J. E. King & W. C. Hayman (Eds.), *Teaching diverse populations* (pp. 225-242). Albany, NY: SUNY.

Gilyard, K. (1991). *Voices of the self.* Detroit: Wayne State University Press.

Gordon, G. (1990). The necessity of African-American epistemology for educational theory and practice. *Journal of Education, 172*(3), 88-106.

Greeley, K. and Mizell, L. (1993). One step among many: Affirming identity in anti-racist schools. In T. Perry and J. W. Fraser (Ed.), *Freedom's plow* (pp. 215-229).New York: Routledge.

Hacker, A. (1994, April 4). The delusion of equality. *The Nation, 258*(13), 457-459.

Heath, S. B. (1982). Oral and literate traditions among Black Americans living in poverty. *American Psychologist, 44*(2), 357-373.

Hollins, E. R. (1982). The Marva Collins Story revisited: Implications for regular classroom instruction. *Journal of Teacher Education, 33*(1), 37-40.

Hollins, E. R. (1990). Debunking the myth of a monolithic white American culture. *American Behavioral Scientist, 7*(2), 119-126.

Hollins, E. R. and Spencer, K. (1990). Restructuring schools for cultural inclusion: Changing the schooling process for African American youngsters. *Journal of Education, 172*(2), 89-100.

Irvine, J. (1990). *Black Students and School Failure: Policies, Practices, and Prescriptions.* Westport, CT: Greenwood Press.

James, C. L. R. (1970).The Atlantic slave trade and slavery: Some interpretations of their significance in the development of the United States and the Western world. In J. A. Williams and C. F. Harris (Eds.), *Amistad 1* (119-164). New York: Vintage Books.

King, J. E. (1991a). Dysconscious racism: Ideology, identity, and the miseducation of teachers. *Journal of Negro Education, 60*(2), 1-14.

King, J. E. (1991b). Unfinished business: Black student alienation and Black teachers' emancipatory pedagogy. In M. Foster (Ed.), *Readings on equal education, 11,* 245-271. New York: AMS Press.

King, J. E. (1992). Diaspora literacy and consciousness in the struggle against miseducation in the Black community. *Journal of Negro Education, 61*(3), 317-340.

King, J. E. (1994a, in press). Culture-centered knowledge: Black studies, curriculum transformation and social action. In J. A. Banks and C. A. McGee Banks (Eds.), *Handbook for Research on Multicultural Education.* New York: MacMillan.

King, J. E. (1994b). Perceiving reality in a new way: Rethinking the Black/White duality of our time. Presented at the annual meeting of the American Educational Research Association. April, 1994. New Orleans, LA.

King, J. E. (1994c). The purpose of schooling for African American children: Including cultural knowledge. In E. R. Hollins, J. E. King & W. C. Hayman (Eds.), *Teaching diverse populations* (pp. 25-44). Albany, NY: SUNY.

King, J. E., Hollins, E. R. and Hayman, W. C. (Eds.). (forthcoming). *Meeting the challenge of preparing teachers to teach diverse populations.*

King, J. E. and Ladson-Billings, G. (1990). The teacher education challenge in elite university settings: Developing critical perspectives for teaching in a democratic and multicultural society. *European Journal of Intercultural Studies, 1*(2), 15-30.

King, J. E. and Mitchell, C. A. (1990). *Black mothers to sons: Juxtaposing African American literature with social practice.* New York: Peter Lang Publishers.

Kunjufu, J. (1988). *To be popular or smart: The Black peer group.* Chicago: African American Images.

Ladson-Billings, G. (1994). *The Dreamkeepers: Successful teachers of African American Children.* San Francisco: Jossey-Bass.

Ladson-Billings, G. and Henry, A. (1990). Blurring the borders: Voices of African liberation pedagogy in the United States and Canada. *Journal of Education, 172*(2), 72-88.

Lee, C. D., Lomotey, K. and Shujaa, M. (1990). How shall we sing our sacred song in a strange land? The dilemma of double consciousness and the complexities of African-centered pedagogy. *Journal of Education, 172*(2), 45-61.

Lemelle, A. J. (1991). "Betcha cain't reason with 'em": Bad Black boys in America. In B. P. Bowser (Ed.), *Black male* adolescents: Parenting and education in community context* (pp. 91-114). Lanham, MD: University Press of America.

Lott, E. (1993). *Love and theft: Blackface minstrelsy and the American working class.* New York: Oxford University Press.

MacLeod, J. (1987). *Ain't no makin' it.* Boulder, CO: Westview Press.

Majors, R. (1986, Winter). Cool pose: The proud signature of survival. *Changing Men, 17,* 5-6.

McCarthy, C. (1990). Multicultural education, minority identities, textbooks, and the challenge of curriculum reform. *Journal of Education, 172*(2), 118-129.

McCarthy, C. (1993). After the canon: Knowledge and ideological representation in the multicultural discourse on curriculum reform. In C. McCarthy and W. Crichlow (Eds.), *Race, identity, and representation in education* (pp. 289-305). New York: Routledge.

Morrison, T. (1993). *Playing in the Dark: Whiteness in the literary imagination.* Cambridge: Harvard University Press.

Ogbu, J. (1990). Minority education in comparative perspective. *Journal of Negro Education, 59,* 45-57.

Ogbu, J. and Fordham, S. (1986). Black students' school success: Coping with the "burden of 'acting white'". *The Urban Review, 18,*(3), 313-334.

Omi, M. and Winant, H. (1986). *Racial formation in the United States: From the 1960s to the 1980s.* New York: Routledge & Kegan Paul.

Perry, T. (1993). Toward a theoroy of African American school achievement. Report No. 16. Wheelock College, Center on Families, Communities, Schools and Children's Learning. Boston, MA.

Peters, M. (1985). Racial socialization of young black children. In H. P. McAdoo and J. L. McAdoo (Eds.), *Black children: Social, educational, and parental environments* (pp. 159-173). Beverly Hills, CA: Sage Publications.

Pieterse, J. N. (1992). *White on black: Images of Africa and Blacks in Western popular culture.* New Haven: Yale University Press.

Podhoretz, N. (1963). My Negro problem—And ours. *Commentary, 35*, pp. 93, 94, 97-98.

Richards, D. M. (1989). *Let the circle be unbroken.* Trenton, NJ: The Red Sea Press.

Rogers, P. (1994). White B-Boys in the burbs, or; Up against the mall. *Newsweek*, January, 10:49.

Rogin, M. (1992). Blackface, white noise: The Jewish jazz singer finds his voice. *Critical inquiry, 18*, 417-453.

Sanders, D. (1993, October 29). Black is in. *Isthmus*, pp. 1, 20, ff.

Sobran, J. (1987). Howard Beach: The use and abuse of race. *The National Review, 39*(5), 28-38.

Shujaa, M. (Ed.). (1994). *Too much schooling, too little education: A paradox of Black life in White societies.* Trenton, NJ: Africa World Press.

Sleeter, C. E. (1992, Spring). Resisting racial awareness: How Teachers understand the social order from their racial, gender, and social class locations. *Educational Foundations, 6*(2), 7-32.

Spring, J. (1994). *Deculturalization and the struggle for equality.* New York: McGraw-Hill.

Steele, C. (1992). Race and the schooling of Black Americans. *The Atlantic, 269*(4), 68-78.

Trebilcock, B. (1993, October). Reading, 'riting, 'rithmetic . . . racism. *Redbook*, pp. 98-101, ff.

Ventura, M. (1987. Spring & Summer). Hear that long snake moan (Parts I and II). *Whole earth review*, pp. 29-43; 82-92.

Walker, E. V. S. (in press). Caswell County Training School, 1933-1969: Relationships between community and school. *Harvard Educational Review*.

White, M. M. (1987). We are family! Kinship and solidarity in the Black community. In G. Gay and W. L. Baber (Eds.), *Expressively Blacks: The cultural basis of ethnic identity.* (pp. 17-34). New York: Praeger.

Williams, S. (1991). Classroom use of African American language: Educational tool or social weapon. In Christine E. Sleeter (Ed.), *Empowerment through multicultural education* (pp. 199-216). Albany, NY: SUNY Press.

Wimsatt, W. U. (1994, September). In defense of wiggers. *In These Times, 18* (22):40, ff.

Wynter, S. (1992a). *Do not call us 'negros': How multicultural textbooks perpetuate racism.* San Francisco: Aspire Books.

Wynter, S. (1992b, Fall). No Humans Involved: An open letter to my colleagues. *Voices of the Diaspora. The CAAS Research Review, 8*(2), 13-16.

Christine E. Sleeter, Walter Gutierrez, Clara Ann New, Susan R. Takata

Muchos padres hispanos que inmigraron y continuan inmigrando a los Estados Unidos a través de muchos años, nunca pensaron; ni siquiera se dieron cuenta de las grandes dificultades que ellos encontrarían el tratar de educar a sus hijos en este país. El sueño dorado que les impulsó venir a este país fue la creencia que aquí todo es fácil, todo es bueno, todo es gratis, todo es posible y todo el mundo es rico y educado. ¡Qué triste que todo este sueño dorado se rompa en pedacitos al contacto con la realidad de la vida, la cultura, la educación, el idioma de este país! Pronto estos padres se despertaron y se dieron cuenta que nada entedieron y que todo fue una ilusión. ¡En verdad, un sueño y nada más!

Isn't this passage inaccessible for many readers? It is the same in reverse for many students who are not Anglo. American schools and the American population in general are rapidly becoming increasingly racially diverse. By the year 2000, 39% of the U. S. population will be minorities. Just the Hispanic population alone, from 1976 to 1987, increased more than 70%. Between 1980 and 2000, the Asian American population will have tripled. Often Whites believe that the best way to deal with this is to ignore race and try to be color-blind. That means in the process ignoring important factors such as how different people make and communicate meaning. Or, educators leap onto "quick fix" solutions that really do not change anything.

The investment of energy, money, and cultural resources in the education of citizens is necessary and recognized by any civilized country. But to deny a full and rich education to some based on their race and culture is chaotic and brutal, not to mention unproductive; it breaks the spirit of democracy and undermines civilization itself. It is important for Whites to realize that they (or we, depending on one's frame of reference) have tried to "hog" the resources of this country since its inception, and have built institutions and beliefs about people that perpetuate unfairness and discrimination. Dealing with this is very painful for Whites, but necessary if we are to build a just society in the future that provides access to a quality life and personal freedom for *all* its citizens. In this essay we will critique current approaches to addressing diversity in schools, then discuss some complexities of race and culture in the education process.

Diversity as a "PR Piece"

Discussions about diversity in schools and universities provide an example of "new" approaches to thinking about race that really are not new at all. In recent years, racist flyers and graffiti, name-calling, self-imposed segregated groupings (sticking with one's own kind) and fraternity pranks targeting particular racial and ethnic groups reflect the continued intensity and persistence of racism in schools and on university campuses. In an era of scarce resources, there is fierce competition for admissions, financial aid and other educational goods and services. Such scarcity has fostered this new racism. There is a threat of a power shift that was once dominated by Whites, as the minority is in the process of becoming the majority. The new racism is one response to this major social change soon to reshape American society.

In response, many schools and universities are designing for "diversity." Diversity is all about who should be "privileged" to the American Dream. Designing for diversity may be seen in the celebration of Black History Month or Native American Awareness Week, the development of ethnic studies courses, the hiring of more minority faculty and staff, and the admission of a more diverse student population. These things are done supposedly to clarify our understanding of racial and ethnic issues. But, is it realistic to expect new understanding to develop during a festival or a semester's course? Some students will change, while others will hold more tenaciously onto their prejudices and racist ideas. There is a backfiring effect of ramming diversity down the throats of students, who take such courses out of resentment and anger at another "required" course. The students ask, "who needs it?"

In the 1960's the focus of intense racial conflict was on access to quality education, university admissions policies, and ethnic studies; in 1990, the focus remains the same. Very little has changed for minorities. Is "Diversity" just a public relations scam of the 1990's? Although some see progress made, others see a frightening trend backwards. The ultimate bankruptcy came in 1974 with the Bakke decision, in which white males became victims of discrimination. More recently, Harvard University is accused of implementing an affirmative action policy for the rich (the practice of admitting the children of alumni). Then there is the false appeal to making it "on your own" or the "rugged frontier theory." The argument goes that to accept help is to lower one's self esteem. But help in any form, to undo the damage done, is essential to continued progress. In the '90's no one is making it "on their own." Are we really designing for diversity?

Education in the United States has undergone profound changes in the last several decades. Because education is the main vehicle out of poverty, open door admissions and affirmative action programs offered seductively quick solutions to the problem of equal access. Legal barriers to access based on race and gender were struck down, and society breathed a collective sigh of relief that discrimination has now ended. In other words, societal responsibility for oppression ended at the door to schooling with the charge that schools and the academy take up the challenge of educating those now within its ivy covered enclosure. But minority access to education has several built-in institutional biases reflective of a racist system.

Some believe that education is the cure-all solution to society's problems. But education did not create today's economic situation. The dilemma of education today merely mirrors the dilemma of our society. By 1990 it was clear that getting into schools and universities is only the first step. Because of institutional discrimination, women and minorities have been less successful getting out and on into other societal systems.

The Embeddedness of Prejudice

The immediate and long-term influences of oppression based on race were documented in excruciating candor in the book entitled *Something of Value* (Ruark, 1955). The premise (and conclusion) states that when you take everything from a people, you had better give them something of value; hence, the Mau Mau came into existence. South Africa has never been the same.

The notion of race is socially constructed, based on our ability to identify by sight people whose ancestral origins were on different parts of the globe. As a social construct, race has served to reinforce extreme opinions and biases held by some educators, and to condition significant segments of the population to accept passively inequality based on skin color as an incontrovertible way of living and learning in America. The fabric of prejudice is so delicately interwoven into attitudes, pedagogy and resulting behaviors that the mere suggestion that impaired academic achievement might stem from racist practices invokes responses akin to those attributed to the main character in a fairy tale called "The Emperor's New Clothes." Blinded by his prejudices, the Emperor paraded through the streets in the nude because he was so thoroughly conditioned by his tailor—who was too insignificant to lie to him—to believe that he wore invisible clothes that were magnificent to the human eye.

American society, too, has continued to ignore the problematic consequences of attempting to enforce color-blind notions upon those who benefit from oppression, and those who are perpetually victimized. Race, as well as color, has extensive ramifications which exist without meaning or reference to the intrinsic person, but which can exert painful day-to-day impact upon students of color as they struggle in the quest for identity, and frequently result in colossal self-denigration. Depending upon the length of life, for example, a person whose lineage can be traced to African origins has borne as many as five socially imposed designations: Colored, Negro, Black, Afro-American and African-American. Unlike white students, for whom the connotations of race appear to remain constant and positive, the capricious ambiguity inherent in this group-naming process Americans of color produces confusion and lack of self-worth.

Diminished estimation of self-worth has been found to correlate with lower academic achievement and other manifestations of undesirable behavior on an interpersonal level. When race is utilized as the dominant measure of worth for an American, that is, race determines what, when and how students experience education, it is small wonder that students of color and disadvantaged Whites exhibit severe feelings of worthlessness, helplessness, anger and isolation. In classrooms where varied ways of knowing, believing, assessing and behaving are considered to be innate deficiencies rather than cultural differences, the tendency for teachers to rely heavily on well inculcated systems of racism is great. One result is the statistically improbable numbers of school suspensions issued black males, and the disproportionate numbers of students of color placed in exceptional education programs, such as those for the mentally retarded, learning disabled, and emotionally disturbed.

A glaring example is that of a black male who was retained in the same kindergarten class for six semesters because the teacher was unable to elicit acceptable responses from him on a standardized IQ test. Instead of connecting related pictures by a single line, the student—who was an accomplished caricaturist —would add another related picture and circle the three (or more) concepts. This thought process was replicated in each battery of the test. The teacher attributed this behavior to his being black, as the other members of the primarily white class followed the manual instructions explicitly. Since this youngster was generally reticent and did not participate in class discussions, the teacher assumed that his quiet demeanor signified lack of comprehension, and his "bizarre" responses on the same test for six semesters justified her beliefs.

Similar encounters may be observed consistently, due to the ignorance and racism that permeates the educational arena, where the popular remedy seems to be a steady proliferation of stigmatized programs that exclude students based on race. It appears that placing the blame on race is far more palatable than examining the players who are participating in the arena, in that benign attention can be given to the students and school can continue as usual.

Institutional Racism

Most people equate racism with individual prejudice, but it goes far beyond that. Institutional racism comes about when a group of people have the power to enforce their prejudices by creating social institutions to buttress their privileges. Over the course of America's history, until recently we have had a dual system of institutions: those for people of European ancestry, and those for everyone else. The segregated school system was an example. Further, this dual system maintained white control over wealth and power, and at various points in history, helped Whites extend their control through conquest. For example, the Southwest was part of Mexico until the U. S. took it over through war, following which Anglos took land from Mexicans living on conquered territory by manipulating property laws and taxes.

It has been only since 1954 that this dual system of institutions was declared illegal by the Supreme Court. However, 1954 was preceded by over 400 years of constructing a dual system. Therefore, legal declaration that race is no longer to be a legitimate factor for allocating access to jobs, housing, education, and so forth, only began to dismantle institutional racism. Legalized racism was replaced by more subtle forms of racism.

For example, the school curriculum has been constructed around the European and Euro-American experience: history moves from Europe to the East Coast of the U. S. and west from there; most literary, musical, and art figures taught about are white; and European notions of linear progress and conceptions of circular time and mastery of the natural world are taught (as opposed to, say Native American conceptions of circular time and living in harmony with the natural world). While a few heroes and contributions from other groups have been added, the curriculum remains essentially Euro-centric. Students are regularly tested for their mastery of it, then rank-ordered, and sorted into ability groups and tracks for different instruction. Those who enter school most familiar and comfortable with a Euro-American perspective about the world tend to leave school well prepared for the best college and life opportunities. This is institutional racism; children are not overtly denied access to instruction based on their race, but instruction is still organized in such a way that white students, on the average, profit most from it.

White Americans often confuse race with white ethnicity, and wonder why Americans of color are experiencing difficulties that go beyond those of their white ethnic ancestors. The main difference between race and white ethnicity is skin color and other visible differences, and their use both historically and currently. During the period of colonization, Europeans destroyed as best they could the cultures and peoples of Africa and the Americas, enslaving Africans because their skin color allowed easy identification of slaves. Strong as conflicts were within Europe, with the exception of the Holocaust during the 1940's, Europeans generally did not attempt to destroy and subjugate each other as brutally. When Eastern and Southern Europeans immigrated to the United States, they were not immediately accorded the privileges of White Americans, and did face considerable persecution and discrimination. But they succeeded, as Omi and Winant (1986) put it, in drawing "the color line *around*, rather than *within*, Europe" (p. 65). Further, they were able to bring with them families and communities that could remain intact and provide economic and cultural resources for survival and growth.

In contrast, African, Native American, and Mexican families and communities were attacked with intent to destroy over a long period of time, and to some extent, such policies are still intact. For example, the Chinese Exclusion Act of 1882 specifically prohibited immigration based on race, and in the process splintered many families by preventing them from joining their men who had already immigrated to the U. S. A bachelor society developed, and Chinatowns today are still impoverished partly as a result. As another example, Whites today are agitating for the termination of Native Americans' treaty rights, while on many reservations natives experience a high rate of disease and unemployment, leading to self-inflicted death and alcoholism. Adequate health care and health insurance are unavailable for low-income Native Americans, African Americans and Latinos, resulting in high infant mortality rates and shorter life spans than Anglos experience. African American males can look forward with greater likelihood to spending their young adult years in prison than in college.

Race, Culture and Language

Racism is made to appear legitimate by trying to convince Americans that the most worthwhile culture and knowledge comes from Europe and Euro-Americans. The teacher who believes that regards children who are not white as culturally impoverished.

One need only immerse oneself in the language, philosophy, art, and accomplishments of a non-white group to realize that such a teacher is the one who is culturally impoverished. There are fundamental *cultural* and *language differences* in what students bring with them to school, that are based in their racial or ethnic roots. For example, the Hispanic style of learning is to be dependent on the caring teacher. In Hispanic cultures people work together rather than independently, so Hispanic children often wait to secure a personal relationship with the teacher and other students before attempting to complete a task. The teacher needs to be aware of the sensitivity defining how the Hispanic learns best. As another example, the syntax of the Spanish language is broad, open and free in its structure. The English language is restrictive, it is economic in word usage because Anglo thought is different from Hispanic thought. To an Anglo who does not understand this, a Hispanic student might appear to talk around a point imprecisely; conversely, to a Hispanic student, an Anglo may appear to speak too bluntly and even rudely, and to move through with ideas with excessive speed.

Our nation's educational system has been the subject of much negative attention over the past few years, and nowhere is this more deeply felt than in minority communities, who view education as the main road out of poverty. For example, about 45 percent of Hispanics are expected to drop out of high school, according to former Secretary of Education Lauro Cavazos. Alarming statistics link low levels of education with high incidence of teen pregnancy, unemployment, and even suicide among minority youth. A lack of roots or identity can impede the academic development of a child, and the risk is even greater when coupled with low economic status. Many minority parents, faced with racism and low paying jobs, compromised their ethnic identity for a chance at the American dream. As a result, a significant number of language minority babyboomers never learned their parents' language nor gained an understanding and appreciation of their heritage. They are often more familiar with negative and limiting stereotypes projected through the media than they are with poets, thinkers, and leaders who shared their ancestry.

Bilingual and multicultural education should provide the deep understanding of the minority student's roots, culture, heritage, people, and the people's ambitions. Of course language minority groups have to learn English, and as quickly as possible, in order to survive. But these are necessities, not blanket exclusions. Most language minority people cannot forget their language, nor do they want to. Language itself encodes values, literary works, and world view. To learn a second language is to open new horizons; to lose one's first language is to sacrifice one's identity and roots.

Connection with one's ethnic and racial ancestry will give a student roots. A good education will given him or her wings to soar as high as his or her potential will allow. Roots and education can be combined in an effort to give minority children motivation for the future by teaching them about their language, their heritage. One must know where one came from before one can know where one is going.

A well designed bilingual and multicultural approach to education can help minority children to stay in school and grow. It can also help white students understand their diverse and inequitable environment better. The country's changing racial and ethnic composition will demand sweeping changes in the delivery of education. Obviously minorities are disenfranchised, and this is the nation's very survival that we are talking about. Demographics will dictate that most people, especially those in positions of power, understand, accept and even encourage cultural diversity. Schools should concentrate on changing themselves, developing the capacity to serve all students, instead of consistently trying to change the nature of the students.

Conclusion

Teacher education programs are critical points of departure for aspiring educators whose socialization tends to be disparate from the populations that they will be entrusted to teach. As such, it is imperative and incumbent on teacher education personnel that curricula prepare teachers to interact successfully with and diligently teach students, regardless of their race, to become aware of different styles of intellectual acumen, and to be adept at helping students recognize and reject attempts to exploit them because of their race. This is hardly a simple endeavor, as it entails self-exploration and objectivity which bring curriculum content and pre-teachers together without violating either for *all* its citizens.

References

Omi, M. & Winant, H. (1986). *Racial formation in the United States*. New York: Routledge.

Ruark, R. C. (1955). *Something of value*. Garden City, NY: Doubleday.

Chapter IX

Socioeconomic Class and Education: In what ways does class affect the educational process?

Joseph W. Newman
William Stanley

Joseph W. Newman

Most Americans take pride in our nation's efforts to educate children from all socioeconomic backgrounds, and there is much to admire in our commitment to sending all children to school. We should be concerned, however, that once the students get to school, social class plays such a strong role in their success—or lack of it. As pleasant as it would be to pretend schools take in students from diverse backgrounds and give then all the same opportunities to succeed, that simply does not happen. It is easy to underestimate the effects of social class on education because social class is such an underdeveloped term in our national vocabulary. Social class is a concept Americans talk around rather than talk about.

In fact, we often talk more openly and pointedly about race, religion, and (to a lesser degree) gender—the subjects of other chapters in this book—even though we claim the discussion makes us uncomfortable. When we discuss race, religion, or gender with a group of friends, educational issues often come to the fore. We may talk about school desegregation, for example, or prayer in public schools, or female cadets at West Point. The news media give us at least a surface awareness of these issues, for they are part of our nation's political conversation. The courts constantly call our attention to race, religion, and gender, for there is a well-documented record of discrimination based on these factors in the schools and throughout society.

Americans regard social class as a different kind of factor. Do poor children *as a group* receive unfair treatment in school? We may be hesitant to answer yes. The courts, too, have hedged their answer, for judges usually do not consider social class a factor comparable to race, religion, or gender in discrimination suits. Try discussing social class with a group of friends, and notice how the conversation wanders, most often into race or ethnicity. Educator and civil rights activist Mary Frances Berry contends the media show little interest in poor people without an added minority "teaser." Stories about poor black people, poor brown people, or poor red people get attention, she says but "nobody cares about poor Whites—not even poor Whites."

Who are the poor? Answering that question helps explain our reluctance to confront social class head on. A poor person is somebody else, many white Americans want to believe. Yes, African Americans, Hispanic Americans, and Native Americans are disproportionately poor. That is, compared with the total population, a much higher percentage of the people in these groups are poor. When we try to understand their plight, we cannot ignore the continuing racial and ethnic discrimination they face. But U. S. Labor Department figures show almost 70 percent of all poor people are white. The reason is almost 80 percent of the population is white, and even though Whites have a lower incidence of poverty than the total population, Whites still constitute the largest group of poor Americans. Statistically, the typical poor family in the United States consists of a white woman—a female head of a household—and her children. Trying to understand this family's plight. We cannot ignore continuing discrimination based on gender.

Although social class is tightly interwoven with other social forces discussed throughout this book, class has a powerful impact in its own right. As Americans we cannot afford to pretend our nation has avoided the social stratification we like to criticize in other nations, for the United States too has social classes, a class structure that exerts a strong influence on the process of education. Socioeconomically, some Americans are more equal than others, and this chapter explains how inequalities in education mirror inequalities in social class.

Unequal Children, Unequal Schools

Consider how the circumstances of a child's birth influence the kind of school the child attends. This example makes use of a model sociologists have developed and refined since the 1920s, a five-tiered class structure based on such factors as income, occupation, education, and housing. A child born into the *upper class* (the top 2 percent of the population) or *upper-middle class* (the next 15 percent of the population) usually experiences American education at its best. This child's family literally goes shopping for a school. The child will probably attend a public school patronized by other families of high socioeconomic status, a Roman Catholic school with a similar clientele, or a selective Independent school.

A child born into the *lower-middle class* (about one-third of the population) or *upper-working class* (another one-third) is likely to attend a neighborhood public school that gets fair-to-good reviews from parents. Lower-middle class and upper-working class families are still the backbone of American public education, but those who are dissatisfied often opt for a religious school-Roman Catholic or fundamentalist Protestant.

A child of the *lower-working* class (the bottom 15 percent of the population) encounters American education at its worst. Born into a family with a few educational options, this child will almost certainly attend a neighborhood public school dominated by other poor children, a school many students, parents, and teachers regard as inferior. From the 1960s through the 1990s, the educational label placed on the lower-working class student has changed from "culturally deprived to "culturally different" to "disadvantaged" to "at risk." Although educators have tried to make each label less condescending than the one before, whether the treatment the student receives in school has changed along with the label is a subject of intense debate.

Language and Dialect

To understand why, consider the issue of language and dialect. Linguists help explain what the casual observer in a school notices: the lower a student's social class, the greater the differences between the dialect used in the student's home and the dialect used at school. To linguists, dialect is not at all a pejorative word. Everyone speaks a dialect—a cultural variation of a language. Dialects vary in pronunciation, vocabulary, and syntax. Standard English is simply the dialect of English that appears in grammar books. No one speaks or writes standard English perfectly.

Students from middle and upper-class backgrounds, though, usually acquire a fairly close approximation of standard English just by growing up with their families and peers. These students come to school with a tremendous advantage, for they already know the "official" dialect of the school. They can use the dialect to make sense of what goes on at school, from the teacher's morning greeting to the afternoon math lesson.

Students from working-class (especially lower-working class) backgrounds enter school with a double burden, for they must try to learn a new dialect at the same time they are trying to understand the formal and informal operation of the school. Their task is much more difficult than the one middle and upper-class students face. Evaluated against *norms*, standards that by definition reflect average performance, working-class students have to try harder just to keep up they have to run faster just to stay even. Here is one of the most pressing problems of American education.

William Bennett and Chester Finn, secretary and assistant secretary of education, respectively, during the Reagan administration, have definite opinions on how to deal with the problem. The causes of this and other educational problems seem obvious to them: during the 1960s and 1970s, Americans "simply stopped doing the right things." Bennett and Finn are especially critical of educators who, led astray by liberals and radicals, lowered their expectations of students. Academic and moral standards plummeted down a slippery slope. To start doing the right things once again, the schools must saturate students with standard English. Teachers must once again stress corrections in language, for teachers are role models and more: authority figures who must insist on learning. All students will profit from this reversion to tried-and-true methods, Bennett and Finn conclude, and working-class students have the most to gain.

Such proposals, couched as they are in tough but egalitarian rhetoric, have strong political appeal. Bennett and Finn along with *Cultural Literacy* (1987) author E.D. Hirsch, Jr. and education professor Diane Ravitch, are staking out the high ground in America's ongoing educational debates. These conservative critics are billing themselves as traditionalists with a social conscience. They want the best for all students, they say, placing special emphasis on the *all*. Critics on the opposite end of the political spectrum, temporarily outflanked by this maneuver, sometimes find it difficult to counter the democratic posture.

In their efforts to be more egalitarian than the traditionalists, critics on the left must be careful not to apply a double standard. When scholars with graduate degrees and great facility in standard English use their impressive skills to brand standard English elitist, the arguments sound unconvincing at best and hypocritical at worst. Those who owe their own success to the use of the "prestige dialect" should be the last ones to encourage others to reject the dialect as an instrument of "cultural imperialism". Critics can be more constructive by agreeing standard English is indeed valuable, both intellectually—it can help unlock a storehouse of knowledge—and economically—it can help students move up in the social structure.

Bennett, Finn, and other traditionalists quite properly defend the value of standard English, but they offer no new suggestions fore helping working-class students grasp the value. The notion that students will learn if authority figures insist they learn is certainly not new. The noses-to-the-grindstone approach has been around for years. But has it ever worked with large number of students? Traditionalists believe it has, and they seem nostalgic for a Golden Age of American education, a time when teachers were able to push all students to high levels of achievements by demanding hard work and promising rich awards.

Such an age never existed. There *was* a time when only a few students entered high school and fewer still graduated. According to statistics from the U.S. Department of education, In 1900 only 10 percent of the eligible age group went to high school and only 6 percent graduated. In 1920, 31 percent started and 17 percent finished, and in 1940 the percentages were 732 and 51. These figures are for all 14-to-17 year olds. The attendance and graduation rates for working-class students were much lower. Throughout these years, moreover, teachers complained many students fortunate enough to graduate from high school left with inadequate skills in standard English. Does this sound like the Golden Age of education traditionalists pine for, a time when, according to E.D. Hirsch, schools "effectively taught . . . disadvantaged children under a largely traditional curriculum"? Surely this is not an age we would want to recreate in the 1990s.

Nor would we want to return to the days when it was standard practice in schools to make working-class students feel ashamed of their home dialect. Traditionalists down play the harsh treatment students suffered in an educational system committed to safeguarding correctness at all costs. Today, linguists know attacking a student's home dialect is the same thing as attacking the student. The suggestion here is not that teachers abandon standard English for "anything goes" approach to language. Instead, teachers can help students learn to use different dialects in different settings. Most people, in fact, shift back and forth between formal and informal language, between standard and non-standard English, depending on the situation. We speak differently in a job interview than at a baseball game. We write differently in a letter to the Internal Revenue Service than in a note to an old friend.

Here is a more realistic gauge of correctness; the concept of *appropriateness.* According to linguist, working-class students need practice in making deliberate choices about which dialect to use in which situation. Some school are having success with an approach that calls on students and teachers to envision specific situations requiring standard English. Students can role-play job interviews, for example, or talk with people from the immediate neighborhood who use standard English in their work and a less formal dialect in most other situations.

More fundamental reforms will be necessary in society, however, in order for these techniques to be more than empty exercises for working-class students. Many students do not view themselves as upwardly mobile. They have difficulty imagining themselves in jobs that demand standard English, for they have already encountered social and personal barriers that, from their point of view, look insurmountable. They see no connection between what the school has to offer and what they will need as adults. Seeing the world through these students' eyes can help us understand why they find the advice to work hard and reap rewards at once laughable and infuriating.

Traditionalists offer little more than a pep talk, an upbeat message that doors of opportunity will open to students who master standard English. Don't give up, traditionalists urge. Don't make excuses for yourself. You can be successful. Much of this advice is not bad *in* itself, but *by* itself—in the absence of political action—the pep talk rings hollow. The traditionalists' political commitment to reducing discrimination and increasing opportunity rarely matches their rhetorical commitment. William Bennett is a perfect example of this phenomenon. He urges poor people to word hard while he opposes legislation designed to reduce discrimination at school and on the job. He challenges working-class students to speak well, fit in, and move up while he supports cuts in higher education grant and loan programs. Bennett practices double-standard politics of the worst sort.

Ability Grouping and Tracking

Social class is at the heart of the ongoing debate over ability grouping and tracking, practices so deeply entrenched in American education many people cannot imagine schools without them. Ability grouping and tracking became popular at the turn of the twentieth century, when schools faced an influx of working-class children. Since then educators have continued to diversify the curriculum in an effort to accommodate students from different socioeconomic backgrounds. Some educators, speaking bluntly, have argued working-class students lack both the interest and ability necessary to succeed in school. They need a special curriculum just to get by. Other educators, trying to sound less judgmental, have taken the position that all students differ in their interests and abilities. Only a diversified curriculum can "meet the needs" of all students. Whatever the justification, the results are clear: the schools are divided by social class. Ability groups and tracks in schools reflect socioeconomic divisions in society.

Ability grouping involves placing together students of similar ability for instruction in particular subjects. Elementary school teachers usually form separate groups for fast, average, and slow readers, for example, The conventional wisdom among teachers is today's students are too sophisticated for the names teachers once assigned to reading groups: bluebirds, robins, and redbirds. Invariably, teachers say, students redesignate one of the bird groups buzzards. In an effort to stay a step ahead, many teacher now allow students to select the group names, and in 1991 the students favored New Kids, Ghostbusters, and Ninja Turtles. Now students have to be more creative to come up with an insulting nickname foe one ability group. Popular choices in 1991 were Iraqis and Scuds.

The names in this account are already dated, but the point is not. The lowest group is the one that gets the bad name, for ability grouping puts the label of "losers" on low-group students. Students from working-class backgrounds are more likely that other students to be placed in the lowest ability groups in the first grade, for their home dialect differs more from the school's official dialect. Thus working-class students can acquire a stigma almost at the start of school.

Evidence on the academic effectiveness of ability grouping is mixed, with about as many studies unfavorable to the practice as favorable. The most favorable studies show it offers a slight advantage to students in the top group. The least favorable studies show it does significant harm to students in the bottom group. Instead of reducing the academic and social differences children bring with them to school, ability grouping seems to increase the differences. As students move through the grades, the gap between top and bottom widens.

After examining the evidence, some educators are looking for alternatives to ability grouping. One promising strategy is *cooperative learning*, in which teachers form learning teams composed of students with different socioeconomic backgrounds and different academic abilities. Students cooperate rather than compete. Faster students help slower students. Teachers assign grades based on a combination of individual progress and group performance. Whether assign grades based on a combination of individual progress and group performance. Whether cooperative learning can dislodge ability grouping from its entrenched position in the schools, however, remains to be seen.

When students move from elementary school to middle or high school, tracking helps ability grouping accentuate their differences. Tracking involves placing students in different academic programs, often called college preparatory, general, and alternative/basic/vocational. Sociologists have documented how the tracks reflect the social structure. The more affluent a school's student body, the more emphasis the school is likely to place on college prep programs. Schools with poorer students, by contrast, tend to have smaller college prep tracks and larger general and alternative tracks. In the nation as a whole, college prep programs enroll about 80 percent of upper and upper-middle class students are eight times as likely as lower working-class students to be in their schools' most prestigious track. Enrollment in alternative programs is weighted in just the opposite way, heavier on working-class students and lighter on others.

Tracking promotes even deeper academic differentiation than ability grouping. In ability grouping, all students take a particular subject—reading or mathematics, for example—albeit on different levels. In tracking, students follow different programs that may involve completely different subjects. Students in a high school's college prep track may take four years of math, for example: algebra I, algebra II, geometry, and trigonometry. Students in the general track may take three year: general math, consumer math, and algebra I. Alternative track students rarely take more than two years, typically general math and consumer math. Tracking parcels out science in the same way, with more years and more demanding courses going to college prep students. Tracking usually reserves foreign languages for the same favored students. Even English and social studies, subjects all students take for three or four years, are differentiated because of tracking. While college prep students are learning to write essays and analyze issues, other students are filling out worksheets and looking up answers in the back of the book.

Since the release of *A Nation at Risk* (1983) and a flood of other reports decrying the poor quality of American education, tracking has come under attack by critics from throughout the political spectrum. Today tracking has fewer defenders than at any other time since the 1940s. Tracking does more harm than good, most critics agree, and it does the most harm to working-class students. A consensus is forming that now is the time to reduce tracking.

Debating why tracking is so resistant to change, though, points up differences of opinion among the critics. William Bennett, Chester Finn, and other traditionalists place much of the blame on the education system. The adults in charge of the public schools are allowing students to take the easy way out, traditionalists contend. Even when state legislatures and state boards of education raise high school graduation requirements, teachers find a way to let the weakest students water down their education. To fulfill the two-course math requirement most states have imposed for graduation, alternative-track students usually select the easiest courses available. The same thing happens in every other subject, and teachers who know better stand by and let it all happen. Parents and other citizens must share the blame for this tragedy, traditionalists argue, for we have not held the schools accountable. Now is the time to demand, in Diane Ravitch's words, "the schools we deserve."

All students deserve excellent schools, to be sure, but the traditionalists' arguments are out of touch with the world of the schools, the world students and teachers know from the inside out. Teachers' working conditions are their students' learning conditions, and they are blocking attempts to reduce tracking. Bennett and Finn shy away from discussing such matters, but people who spend more time in schools remind us of the heavy workload teachers carry. It is not unusual for high school teachers to be responsible for teaching five classes of thirty to forty students each—a total of 150 to 200 students every day. Just interacting with so many human beings is a wearying task. After school, there are not enough hours in the afternoons, evenings, and weekends for teachers to do justice to their many other responsibilities, one of which is grading papers. Do the arithmetic and see how much time it would take a high school teacher with the above workload to spend just ten minutes per week on each student's written work. Now put yourself in the teacher's shoes and ask whether it would be possible to double or triple that time in order to give working-class students some of the help they would need to succeed in an academically rigorous program.

Class, Dollars and Programs

Reducing tracking and pushing all students to their limits are admirable goals, but given current conditions in the schools, the goals are out of reach. Even if teachers were superhuman, they could not compensate for the lack of resource in many schools. The public schools in the nation's poorest school districts, supported by weak local tax bases, cannot afford many of the programs other districts can. An affluent suburban high school often spends $7,500 per student and offers four foreign languages, six math courses, and eight science courses. Most students in this school take the challenging program Bennett recommends for every American student. Only a few miles away, a rural or central-city high school is able to spend only half as much money per student and offer only half as many courses in each academic area. If schools cannot provide programs, students cannot take them.

Throwing money at problems will not always solve them, traditionalists like to remind us, but without more money our poorest students will never have access to the academic programs that help privileged students become privileged adults. An encouraging sign on the horizon is the success of lawsuits seeking additional state funding for school districts unable to raise enough local revenue to offer quality programs. As these cases work their way through the courts, judges are finally saying what they have been reluctant to say in the past: poor students *as a group* do indeed receive unfair treatment in America's schools.

William Stanley

Introduction

Our society appears to have great difficulty coming to terms with the question of social class (McDermot, 1990). For example, most Americans describe themselves as middle class despite large differences among them in terms of wealth and income. Educator/philosopher Mortimer Adler (1983), has even referred to the United States as a "classless" society. There is a lack of consensus regarding the meaning of social class and the criteria we should use to determine an individual's (or group's) class identity. Class has been determined in many ways throughout history, (e.g., family heritage of an aristocracy), but in modern industrial societies, some combination of the following criteria are likely to be employed: wealth, income, occupational status, educational attainment, housing, lifestyle, cultural orientation, and one's relationship to the means of production. There is also disagreement over the actual nature of social class structure in our society and the extent to which genuine social mobility exists among classes. Finally, how class and education are related in the United States remains a controversial question.

Despite the lack of consensus and occasional assertions of classlessness, most people do understand that classes are a major feature of our society and that there are wide differences of wealth, income, status, culture, and power. Furthermore, most Americans seem to believe that class background has a significant effect on a student's educational attainment and socioeconomic success.

Research on the relationship between class and one's life chances has been underway throughout this century. Some of the results have been unclear or even contradictory. Still, there have been some indisputable findings. For example, the rates for infant mortality and serious childhood illness are significantly higher among the poor than they are for the more affluent. Children of the poor also have significantly less access to schooling, both in terms of quality and total number of years completed. And since the level of schooling is highly correlated with occupational status and income, one's class also has a significant affect on attaining each of these goals.

Some of the Specific Effects of Class on Education

Most educators in the United States, despite their differences, have understood class to have a significant affect on education. Early in this century, Dewey (1916) discussed the negative influence of class on education, as did leading social reconstructionists like George Counts and Theodore Brameld during the 1920's and 30's. Another important contribution to this literature was August Hollingshead's (1949) *Elmstown's Youth* which described the differential treatment received by the poor, middle-class, and upper-middle-class students. James Conant (1961) also noted the negative impact of poverty on education in the postwar period. *The Coleman Report* (1966) is among the most influential studies involving the effect of class on education. Class was found to affect student attitude toward school, classroom participation, level of prior knowledge, and time denoted to homework. Many of Coleman's findings were confirmed by Jencks (1972) and more recently by Wilson (1987). And Ted Sizer (1984), in his book *Horace's Compromise*, made the following observation:

> Among schools there was one important difference, which followed from a single variable only; the social class of the student body. If the school principally served poor [students], its character, if not its structure, varied from sister schools for the more affluent. It got so I could say with some justification to school principles, "Tell me about the income of your students' families and I'll describe to you your school. (p. 6)

Since local control and financing of schooling is still the major form of school organization in this society, social class has a significant impact on the level of expenditure per pupil. One recent estimate contends that, on average, affluent suburban school districts spend approximately $9,000 per pupil compared to $4,500 per pupil in inner city and rural schools. This amounts to a $58,500 per pupil gap in spending over the thirteen years from kindergarten through senior year (Nelson, Palo, and Carlson, 1990). Of course, these are averages and actual amounts will vary from district to district. Nevertheless, it is the case that most districts with a predominantly lower class student body receive significantly less funds per pupil than the districts serving middle or upper class students. The impact of this differential funding can be observed in several ways. Lower class school districts are more likely to have deteriorated school buildings and drab classrooms in need of repair. Generally, such schools are less well supplied, have inadequate science laboratory facilities, and out of date or inadequate numbers of textbooks. Teachers in these schools often have less training and receive lower salaries. The work environment is frequently quite unpleasant, even violent. Crime, drug abuse, and teenage pregnancy rates are higher than in most affluent suburban schools. It is difficult to retain teachers, and many classes are taught by substitutes. Lower class inner-city schools have much higher student dropout rates (50% or higher) compared with the national average of about 25% (McLaren, 1989, pp. 8-10).

There is also evidence that lower class children are more likely to be diagnosed as having learning disabilities and placed in special education programs. The pervasive use of tracking and grouping is also influenced by class with the bulk of lower tracks and groups being populated by lower class students. And once a child is placed in a lower track or group, he or she is unlikely to move to a higher one. Finally, there is evidence that lower class children generally have a harder time learning than do middle class students. I will say more about this as we go on. For now, it should be clear that a lower class background can have a significant negative impact on educational opportunity and future life chances (Darling-Hammond, 1990).

Given the negative effects of class on education, it is alarming to note the evidence for the persistence of hard-core poverty in our nation. During what has been called "the longest period of economic expansion in the post-war period"—1982-1990, the economic gap between the bottom fifth and the top five percent of our population has actually increased, and twenty percent of all children under age six live in poverty (McLaren, 1989, 7-8).

The Origins of Class in our Society

Sociologists have posed two main explanations for the existence of class and social stratification in our society: a functionalist (or consensus) theory and a radical (or conflict) theory. There are many variations of view within each of these theoretical orientations. However, each general theoretical position reflects a major way scholars have tried to explain social class and its function. Most important for our purposes, each theory has very different implications for educational practice.

The Functionalist Account of the Relationship Between Social Class and Education

For functionalists, the existence of social classes or social stratification is an inevitable outcome of the process necessary to stabilize our social system. Social organization and stability require people to perform many different roles, some far more difficult or complex than others. In the main, people are induced to perform social roles by extrinsic rewards, especially income and prestige. The functionalists also believe that human intelligence and skills vary widely and that there are relatively fewer people available for the more difficult social roles (e.g., surgeons, physicists). The combination of high social need and scarce human resources results in higher income and prestige for certain occupations that satisfy important social roles. Over time, this process results in a society wherein different groups performing different social roles form classes or social strata defined by income level, education, occupational prestige, housing, lifestyle, and culture.

In other words, the existence and evolution of classes is explained as a natural feature of social organization. Therefore, it would be both unrealistic and dysfunctional to try to eliminate social classes. Rather, we need to ensure that our society has genuine social mobility so that people have an equal opportunity to achieve the class position equal to their abilities. No one should be kept from entering the middle or upper class strata because of his or her race, ethnicity, gender, religion, class origin, or other similar variables. Functionalist theorists acknowledge that our class system is far from perfect and that racism, sexism, and other forms of discrimination continue to limit social mobility. In addition, economic decline often reverses the course of social mobility, with the negative consequences of recessions tending to fall more heavily on those in the lower classes. Nevertheless, functionalists believe that ours is a relatively open society, and we are working to remove the remaining barriers to social mobility.

Public education plays a crucial role in this regard. Our public schools are open to all children regardless of their class background, and educational attainment is highly correlated with future income and occupational prestige. While discrimination limiting social mobility still exists, differential social rewards are generally linked to real human differences in terms of one's ability to make a social contribution. If we accept these functionalist assumptions, then our social stratification can be understood as both natural and fair. As long as our society provides genuine equality of opportunity to all citizens, our present social class system is more properly described as meritocracy and not a society based on a rigid class structure of owners against workers or elites against common people.

The Radical Account of Class and Schooling

Radical or conflict theorists are far more skeptical than functionalists regarding the inevitability of social classes, at least in their present form. Most radical theorists have been influenced to some degree by Marxism. Early forms of Marxist thought understood modern industrial societies as divided into two major classes, i.e., the dominant bourgeoisie who owned and controlled the economic means of production and the proletariat or industrial working class. Over time, the Marxist interpretation of class (e.g., rejection of the inevitability of a classless society following a successful worker revolution) has undergone major revisions to reflect the significant socioeconomic changes that have occurred since the death of Marx. In fairness to Marx, he never held a rigid or fixed definition of class, understood that modern industrial society was far more complex than a single two-class model, and would have supported the reinterpretation of social class in terms of specific historical conditions.

The important point for radical theorists is that, in general, social classes do not reflect genuine human differences but are the result of unequal power arrangements. Radicals argue that most of the measures (e.g., I.Q. tests, SATs) we use to determine human differences are not objective scientific measures but pseudo-scientific constructs employed to help maintain control over the lower classes. Obviously, it is in the interest of the dominant social classes to have most people, particularly those in the lower classes, accept the functionalist account of social classes as necessary and inevitable.

For radicals, the dominant social classes use education to help reproduce their power and existing social arrangements. While this process is never entirely successful, it is effective. The dominant classes exercise control over education in several ways. First, education is generally organized in such a way as to reflect present social arrangements. Schools are hierarchical organizations with white males holding most leadership positions and teachers having relatively little power. Second, the curriculum is largely designed to support the views of the dominant classes. For instance, there is little criticism of the current social order, and course content mainly reinforces traditional values, economic theory, and functionalist views of human behavior and institutions. Third, the very practice of education is conducted in ways that function to undermine the competence of the lower classes. Almost two decades of research (e.g., Labov, 1973: Bernstein, 1971: Bourdieu, 1973, 1977; Bourdieu and Passeron, 1977) have documented the very different forms of language used by students with different class backgrounds. These different forms, language codes, or discourses can have a powerful effect, because they either enhance or diminish a student's potential for gaining from his or her educational experience. *Different* discourses do not mean either inferior or superior as Labov (1973), Bernstein (1971) and others have demonstrated. For example, the dialect of urban black children is no less a complex, meaningful language code than the traditional middle class dialect of white children (Labov, 1973; Gee 1988, 1990).

The consequences of using one dialect as opposed to the other can be devastating. As sociolinguist James Gee (1988, 1990) explains, the discourse style one brings to school might be the single most important variable that explains student failure or success. Most schools (and school materials like texts, workbooks, films, etc.) feature the mainstream discourse spoken by the white middle class. Thus, white middle class students are inducted into a familiar process of schooling that gives them the opportunity to practice and improve their linguistic competence. In sharp contrast, most poor children, particularly black and Hispanic students, enter school using a very different discourse inconsistent with the mainstream discourse of the middle class. Students from lower class families must simultaneously attempt to learn a new (middle class) linguistic discourse along with the content of school subjects. It is no wonder that such children tend to fall behind and have higher failure and dropout rates. Moreover, schooling teaches such students, at least indirectly if not overtly, that their mode of discourse is inferior and that they need to learn to speak and write *the* correct way.

I am not suggesting that schools should not attempt to teach lower class (as well as other culturally different) children to become competent users of the standard English of the middle class. Rather, this necessary competence (given our present society) must be accomplished in a very different way which respects the culturally different student's discourse and does not seek to replace it with another. While bi-dialectical competence should be a goal for children of the poor and culturally different, it should also be part of the linguistic competence required of middle class children. This implies a comprehensive approach to language acquisition that includes the study of the literature of culturally different groups, as well as an analysis of language that illustrates how middle class English is merely one possible dialect among others and without any intrinsic structural superiority. On the other hand, culturally different children need to have a realist understanding of the dominant role played by middle class English in our society and how a lack of competence with this discourse can influence their life chances.

The evidence that education helps to reproduce the present class structure does not mean that there is no significant social mobility in our society. Rather it suggests the social mobility that does exist is largely shaped and controlled by the classes with the most power. According to radical theorists, a certain amount of mobility is necessary to keep the lower classes contented, avoid social revolution, and provide evidence for the functionalist position that our society is a democratic meritocracy. In this way, a limited amount of social mobility can function mainly to preserve the present class structure. Indeed, the evidence available indicates that our class structure has not changed significantly throughout most of this century. And as noted earlier, the income gap between the top and bottom classes has actually widened over the past decade of economic prosperity. We must also recall that those who are able to improve their class position (generally) must acquire the values of the higher classes. Thus, the more successful one becomes, the more likely he or she will come to identify with the dominant class view.

Conclusions

While the debate continues over the relationship between class and schooling, we can draw certain conclusions. The existence of social classes representing great differences in wealth, income, occupational prestige, and cultural orientation is a dominant feature of our social order. It is also clear that one's class position has a powerful effect on the quality and level of education attained. Lower class children also tend to have more learning difficulties even when placed in high quality schools. In other words, lower class children generally require more educational assistance, yet they typically receive less than their more affluent counterparts.

What remains in dispute is the extent to which the existing class structure is more a natural reflection of human abilities or the artifact of unequal economic, cultural, and political power. Even most conservatives agree that significant barriers exist to social mobility and that these (e.g., racism, and sexism) should be identified and removed. Unlike radicals, however, the conservatives remain convinced that removing artificial barriers to mobility will not eliminate significant social stratification. Conversely, radical educators would like to put such assertions to the test. They wonder what our society and schooling would be like if we eliminated most forms of discrimination and created genuine educational opportunities that did not penalize culturally different students.[1] Until this occurs we should remain skeptical regarding the conservative (functionalist) assertions regarding the inevitability of our present class structure.

Note

1 The reader should consider Chapters 7 and 8 for some other perspectives on the links among class, gender, and race.

References

Adler, M. (1982). *The paideia proposal*. New York: Macmillan.

Bernstein, B. (1971). *Class, codes and control: Theoretical studies toward a sociology of language, 1*. New York: Schocken Books.

Bourdieu, P. (1973). "Cultural reproduction and social reproduction." In R. Brown (Ed.). *Knowledge, education, and cultural change*. London: Tavistock, 71-112.

Bourdieu, P. (1977). *Outline toward a theory of practice*. Cambridge: Cambridge University Press.

Bourdieu, P. & Passeron, J. C. (1977). *Reproduction in education, society and culture*. London: Sage Publishers.

Coleman, J. S. et. al. (1966). *Equality of educational opportunity*. Washington, DC: Government Printing Office.

Conant, J. B. (1961). *Slums and suburbs*. New York: McGraw-Hill.

Darling-Hammond, L. (1990). "Achieving our goals: Superficial or structural reforms?" *Phi Delta Kappan*, 286-295.

Dewey, J. (1916). *Democracy and education*. New York: Free Press Edition, 1967.

Gee, J. P. (1988). "Discourse systems and aspirin bottles: On literacy." *Journal of Education, 170* (1), 27-40.

Gee, J. P. (1989). *Social linguistics and literacies: Ideology in discourse*. Falmer Press.

Labov, W. (1973). "The logic of nonstandard English." In N. Keddie (Ed.)., Tinker, Taylor: *The myth of cultural deprivation*. Harmondsworth, UK: Penguin Publisher.

McDermont, B. (1990). *The imperial middle: Why Americans can't think straight about class*. New York: Morrow Publishers.

McLaren, P. (1989). *Life in schools: An introduction to critical pedagogy in the foundations of education*. New York: Longman.

Nelson, J. L., Palonsky, S., & Carlson, K. (1990). *Critical issues in education*. New York: McGraw-Hill.

Sizer, T. R. (1984). *Horace's compromise: The dilemmas of the American high school*. Boston: Houghton Mifflin.

Wilson, W. J. (1987). *The truly disadvantaged: The inner city, the underclass, and public policy*. Chicago: University of Chicago Press.

Chapter X

Media and the Schools: What is the effect of media on the educational experience of children?

Eugene F. Provenzo, Jr.

Joe L. Kincheloe

Eugene F. Provenzo, Jr.

Media in the form of television, film, recorded music, comics and video games play a major role in the experience of contemporary childhood. In doing so, they shape the values and beliefs of children, as well as providing them with critically important cognitive and interpretive models for understanding the world.

One need only visit an elementary school to see the extent to which this is the case. A third grade teacher gives an open-ended writing assignment to her children and they return with essays on television and video game characters such as the Care Bears, the Teenage Mutant Turtles and the Mighty Morphin Power Rangers. On the playground, the same children participate in rough and tumble play based on their favorite television and video game characters. Conversation in the lunch room focuses on video game scenarios and the television programs which the children watched the previous afternoon and evening. Sandwiches are taken and eaten from lunch boxes emblazoned with media figures from the cartoon characters the X-Men to the fashion doll Barbie. Action figure trading cards and comic books are swapped and exchanged while waiting for the school bus. In the classroom, children constantly refer to concepts and ideas by explaining them in reference to television: "It's like something I saw on television . . .," or "I remember a story on TV where . . .," are common starting points for discussions with classmates and teachers.

Children come to school with a vast knowledge of the world based on television and other media. One hundred years ago most children would be hard-pressed to tell you how a kangaroo jumps or how a tiger stalks its prey. Children familiar with nature specials have no problem describing these movements. Likewise, they can tell you which deodorant will make you feel fresh, which toothpaste will give you sex-appeal and which hamburger you need to eat if you're having a hard day.

In the following essay, I focus on television and how it affects the educational experience of children. While other forms of media could be analyzed at length (film, recorded music, comics and video games), I emphasize television because of its pervasiveness and singular importance in the lives of children.

Electronic Versus Typographic Cultures

In 1964 Marshall McLuhan published *Understanding Media: The Extensions of Man.* In it he wrote prophetically that:

> The young student today grows up in an electronically configured world. It is a world not of wheels but of circuits, not of fragments, but of integral patterns. The student encounters a situation organized by means of classified information. The subjects are unrelated. They are visually conceived in terms of a blueprint. The student can find no possible means of involvement for himself, nor can he discover how the educational scene relates to the "mythic" world of electronically processed data and material. (pp. viii-ix)

McLuhan's dictum that "the medium is message," is particularly relevant in the context of this essay. Television and the other electronic media have created a new environment for childhood—one which includes a new environment for schools as well.

The issue is not whether children will learn though television in the schools, but the extent to which traditional learning will be superseded by what children learn from television. In this context, the situation is similar to the experience of medieval culture confronting the new print culture of the book during the Renaissance. The oral schoolmen of the Medieval tradition, rather than creating a new synthesis of written and oral education, allowed themselves to be swept over by the technology of the printed page. (*McLuhan*, pp. 75-76).

Today television is in fact the dominant mode of education in our culture. It has clearly superseded book culture as the primary source of our society's information. One can see this in the vast amount of time and resources we invest in television. Nielson estimates as of January 1, 1994 put the total number of televisions owned in the United States at 93,100,000, or approximately one for every three people in the country. Of these, 98% are color televisions. (*Information Please Almanac Atlas and Yearbook: 1994*, p. 748)

For the average child, television plays a major part in their lives. The typical child, between the ages of 2 and 11, views approximately 28 hours of television per week. (Barry, p. 48) When combined with other electronic media sources such as films, videos, video games and recorded music, the total media exposure for the average American child approaches nearly forty hours per week. Unlike school, this is twelve months a year, day-in and day-out. In fact, it can easily be argued that other than sleeping, electronic media represents the single most important activity of children in American society today.

Like the media theorist Neil Postman, we assume that "the media of communication available to a culture are a dominant influence on the formation of the culture's intellectual and social preoccupations," and that media forms such as film, television, recorded music, or video games, represent social constructions of reality. (*Amusing Ourselves to Death*, p. 9.)

Television integrates the culture for children in ways that have never been possible before. The rich watch the poor and the poor watch the rich. As Richard Rodriguez has pointed out:

> In the suburbs we use TV to watch the mayhem of the inner city. But on the TV in the inner city, they watch us. The bejeweled pimp in his gold BMW parodies the Beverly Hills matron on Rodeo Drive. The baby with the gun in his chubby fist is spiritual heir to John Wayne and his feminist cowgirl wife Annie Oakley, and to the country that was settled with guns in the cowboy movies, and in truth. (pp. 53-54)

In this context, Neil Postman argues that television has recreated the language and meaning of our culture:

> ... although culture is a creation of speech, it is recreated anew by every medium of communication—from painting to hieroglyphs to the alphabet to television. Each medium, like language itself, makes a unique mode of discourse by providing a new orientation for thought, for expression, for sensibility. (*Amusing Ourselves to Death*, p. 10)

For Postman:

> ... television is the command center of the new epistemology. There is no audience so young that it is barred from television. There is no poverty so abject that it must forgo television. There is no education so exalted that it is not modified by television. And most important of all, there is no subject of public interest—politics, news, education, religion,

science, sports—that does not find its way to television. (*Amusing Our-*
selves to Death, p. 78)

If, as Postman argues "television has gradually *become* our
culture," then this raises a number of important issues for the
schools and the future of education and learning in our culture.
"What is television? What kinds of conversations does it permit?
What are the intellectual tendencies it encourages? What sort of
culture does it produce?" (*Amusing Ourselves to Death*, p. 84)

In addition to these questions, other questions can be asked
as well. What is television evolving into? And, how will the
emerging technologies of hypermedia, virtual reality and interactive television further transform the experience of how we
and our children know and learn in American society?

Television's Lessons

The first and foremost lesson that needs to be realized about
television is that it is a teaching machine. The basic premise
underlying commercial television, for example, is that people
learn from the programs they view. When they watch a thirty-
second commercial selling soap or an automobile, they are
being taught to desire and imitate what they see on the screen.

Television, however, teaches us much more than simply what
goods to buy and consume. Television also teaches us how to
conduct conversations and interact with other people, as well as
how to interpret visual information and deal with issues critically. As a university professor I have become increasingly
aware of the fact that my students are often better at seeing
things than listening to them, of skimming information than
reflecting on ideas. The image of a close friend's thirteen year
old daughter comes to my mind: She was talking to me one
Sunday morning while her father was making coffee in the
kitchen. She told me about her schoolwork as she watched the
television out of the corner of her eye, "channel surfing" even
after her father came back into the room to continue his conversation she flipped from one station to another with the
remote control, never staying for more than ten or fifteen sec-
onds on a single program.

In talking to teachers, they frequently talk about having to compete with television in their classrooms. A high school chemistry teacher, for example, has described to me how her students want things to go wrong in experiments—how they want the excitement of television and its special effects in her classroom.

One also is led to speculate whether or not children want to "channel surf" information. Why should children be patient in a traditional classroom setting when with cable television and a remote control device they can flip from one program or piece of information to another. In this context, viewing TV makes information process and learning a kinesthetic process, a melange of sounds, and more importantly, visual images streaming in front of one's field of view. How does this affect children and their readiness to learn in more traditional settings such as the classroom?

Of course none of this addresses the even larger issue of what is actually taught by television. When a program is finally settled on, the images tend to be graphic and often sexually explicit—very often they are also violent.

Television keeps few secrets from children. As Neil Postman and Marie Winn have pointed out, it has eroded the dividing line between the world of the adult and the world of the child. Television does not systematically segregate its viewers. In reality children have access to virtually anything that adults have access to. Unlike reading a book, television does not take special training or experience to understand. Children are cable and television ready as soon as they learn to speak and can set still in front of the tube (Postman, 1982, p. 80).

Children, according to Postman and Winn, are no longer sheltered from adult life the way they used to be. As a child growing up in the 1950s and 1960s, I knew almost nothing about incest or homosexuality. Violence—even television mediated violence was extremely rare in my life. My most memorable experience in junior high school, for example, was sitting in front of the television in November of 1963—the Sunday following John F. Kennedy's assassination—and seeing Lee Harvey Oswald being shot by Jack Ruby. That image, and my memory of sitting there with a glass of milk and a baloney sandwich in my hand,watching a man being murdered,remains clear and fixed in my mind—my first "eyewitness" murder. Perhaps that weekend marking the beginning of my becoming an adult.

For the average child today, however, television mediated violence, whether real or imagined, is commonplace. A child who views two to four hours of television daily will have witnessed 89,000 murders and 100,000 other acts of televised violence by the time he or she leaves elementary school. This represents roughly five violent acts per hour in prime time and more than twenty-five per hour in the context of children's programming (*Schumer*).

To what extent do children come to believe through viewing such programs that violence is normal and commonplace—that might rules over right? What models about society are provided to children through television?

TV has a tendency to glamorize violence for both children and adults. It does this not only with fictional characters but with actual murderers. Thus Ted Bundy, Richard Speck, Wayne Gacy and the Hillside Strangler have all had television programs done about them. In testimony before Congress on television violence Marvin Kitman, television critic for *Newsday*, explained how:

> . . . TV movies are rarely about good people. They glorify bad guys. When a cop gets blown away, his killer gets more coverage on the TV news than the cop and his funeral. . . . The fate of Amy Fisher is not lost on young people. What a message TV gives to kids. You can be a spoiled brat who didn't become a killer only because of bad aim and have three TV movies made about you in 1 month, January. (p. 15)

The connection between media violence and violence in our culture, especially among our youth population is consistently denied as being a problem by members of the film and television industry. There is, however, a significant research literature that connects violence to media exposure. Joy *et al* investigated the impact of introducing television for the first time to an isolated Canadian community. The community, which was called "Notel" by the researchers, had never had television because of signal problems. Using a double-blind research design, forty-five first and second graders were observed over a two year period to see if aggressive behavior such as hitting, biting and shoving increased. In the two control groups aggressive behavior did not increase significantly. In Notel, during the same two year period, however, such behavior increased by 160%.

Huesmann, in a twenty-two year study of 875 men in a semi-rural setting, examined whether or not the viewing of violent television predicted the seriousness of criminal acts committed by the time the subjects were thirty years old. After controlling for the subjects' baseline aggressiveness, socio-economic status and intelligence, it was found that violent television viewing was a significant predictor for criminal behavior.

In a June 1992 article in the *Journal of the American Medical Association*, Dr. Brandon Centrewall of the University of Washington Department of Epidemiology and Psychiatry, looked at violence in the United States from an epidemiologically point of view. Centrewall compared homicide rates in the United States and Canada, where television was introduced in the mid-1940s, with the Republic of South Africa where television was introduced thirty years later. Canada, which had not gone through the political and social unrest of the 1960s, provided a control model for the United States. In order to rule out the effect of racial conflict in South Africa, only the white homicide rate was considered by Centrewall.

Centrewall found that the homicide rate in both Canada and the United States increased by almost 100 percent between 1945 and 1970. Television ownership increased at almost the same percentage as the homicide rate for the same period. In South Africa, the white homicide rate gradually declined between 1945 and 1970. When television was introduced in 1975, however, the white homicide rate exploded, increasing 130 percent by 1983. Centrewell concludes from his research that in the United States and Canada:

> . . . the introduction of television in the 1950s caused a subsequent doubling of the homicide rate, ie, long-term childhood exposure to television is a casual factor behind approximately one half of the homicides committed in the United States, or approximately 10,000 homicides annually. (p. 3061)

Centrewell goes on to argue that while other factors such as poverty, crime, alcohol, drug abuse and stress contribute to violence, the epidemiologic evidence suggests that

> . . . if hypothetically television technology had never been developed, there would be 10,000 fewer homicides each year in the United States, 70,000 fewer rapes and 700,000 fewer injurious assaults. (*Ibid*)

Conclusion

Television, and media in general, are profound shaping forces in American culture, and more specifically the experience of school age children. Children are taught to consume, as well as how to view the world and what the world is about through television. Cognitive and interpretive models clearly derive from television and other media as well.

How much the media ultimately shapes the world view of children and conditions them to accept or reject the lessons of traditional schooling is almost impossible to determine. To ignore the significance of television and other powerful forms of media on shaping childhood, however, is clearly foolish.

This issue is even more important as new forms of television and technology emerge that have an even greater capacity to attract the attention of our children and educate them in new ways. Recent developments in video game technology using digitized pictures and CD-ROM when combined with virtual reality technologies that allow you to interact with computers and television, suggest that we are in the first stages in the creation of a new type of television—an interactive medium as different from traditional television, as television is from radio. This new media is very much like the interactive movies or "feelies" described by Aldous Huxley in his anti-utopian novel *Brave New World.*

I believe that the remaining years of this decade will see the emergence and definition of this new media form in much the same way that the late 1940s and early 1950s saw television emerge as a powerful social and cultural force. What the effect of this new medium will be on the experience and attitude of children is yet to be seen.

References

Barry, D. (November-December 1993). "Screen Violence: It's Killing Us," *Harvard Magazine*, pp. 38-43.

Centrewall, B. (1989). "Exposure to Television as a Cause of Violence. G. Comstock (ed.), *Public Communication and Behavior*, Vol. 2, pp. 1-58. New York: Academic Press.

Centrewall, B. (1989). "Exposure to Television as a Risk Factor for Violence," *American Journal of Epidemiology*, 129(4), pp. 643-652.

Centrewall, B. (June 10, 1992). "Television and Violence: The Scale and Problem and Where to Go From Here," *Journal of the American Medical Association*, Vol, 267, #22, pp. 3059-3063.

Huesmann, L. R. (1986). "Psychological Processes Promoting the Relation Between Exposure to Media Violence and Aggressive Behavior by the Viewer," *Journal of Social Issues*, Vol. 42, #3, pp. 125-129.

Huxley, A. (1969). *Brave New World*. New York: Harper and Row.

Information Please Almanac Atlas and Yearbook: 1994. Boston: Houghton Mifflin Company.

Joy, L. A., M. M. Kimball and M. L. Zabrack (1986). "Television and Children's Aggressive Behavior," in T. M. Williams, editor, *The Impact of Television: A Natural Experiment in Three Communities*, pp. 303-360. Orlando, Florida: Academic Press.

Kitman, M. (December 15, 1992). "Violence on Television," Statement prepared for the Subcommittee on Crime and Criminal Justice of the Committee on the Judiciary House of representatives. 102nd Cong., 2d sess.

McLuhan, M. (1964). *Understanding Media: The Extensions of Man*. New York: New American Library.

Postman, N. (1985). *Amusing Ourselves to Death: Public Discourse in the Age of Show Business*. New York: Viking Books.

Postman, N. (1982). *The Disappearance of Childhood*. New York: Delacorte.

Provenzo, E. F., Jr. (December 6, 1993). "Video Games and the Emergence of Interactive Television for Children," Statement prepared for the United States Senate, Joint Hearing of the Judiciary Subcommittee on Juvenile Justice and the Government Affairs Subcommittee on Regulation and Government Information on the Issue of Violence in Video Games.

Rodriguez, R. (January/February 1994). "Gangstas: Hard Truths from the Streets of East L.A.," *Mother Jones*, pp. 46-54.

Schumer, C. E. (December 15, 1992). Opening statement of Chairman. U.S. Congress. *Violence on Television*. Hearing before the Subcommittee on Crime and Criminal Justice of the Committe on the Judiciary House of representatives. 102nd Cong., 2d sess., 1992. Serial No. 115.

Winn, Marie (1983). *Children without Childhood*. New York: Pantheon Books.

Joe L. Kincheloe

Any question that focuses on the relationship between the media and education by necessity opens a cultural can of worms. In this chapter I will address only a few of these cultural issues (the worms)—in particular, the meaning of the term "education," the power of media in the shaping of identity, and the need for media literacy in teacher education and ultimately in the schools themselves. Many of us already realize that all those years of watching re-runs of Arnold Ziffle on *Green Acres* or acne commercials on MTV affect us in some way. No one has to tell us that we typically know more about the history of *Star Trek* than the history of democracy in America. And what about those Happy Meals at McDonald's with the Flintstones "action" figures and, of course, Barbie? Where do they fit?

Many traditional educators may consider the question—*what is the effect of media on education?*—beneath their dignity, not worthy of investigating and answering. Meantime, while these guardians of tradition turn their backs on TV, popular music, video games, and movies, their students gain much of their education, their understanding of the world from these sources. Education takes place most often *outside* the walls of school and, as a result, those of us who are seriously concerned with its nature and effects have developed new ways to analyze and make sense of these media-grounded educational dynamics. Indeed, who can deny the power of Disney's history of *man*, the Marlboro Man's curriculum of masculinity and the role of women—*look at those babes on the beach*—in Budweiser commercials? Everyday in America, civics students are captive audiences bombarded by Channel One's version of world news blended with Pepsi, M and M's and Clearasil commercials.

A media curriculum would address such issues as it explored larger questions of how power produces knowledge. The legitimated knowledge purveyed by the media, in turn, helps shape our identities and values, revealing in the process the way our culture, our everyday lives are increasingly constructed by activities of gigantic corporations. A culturally grounded media education would explore the complex ways culture is shaped by corporate power holders, while at the same time exploring how such a reconstructed culture is inscribed on individual lives. Such a cultural inscription can be sensed in the echo of a harried mother imploring her child "to hurry up and get your *Reeboks* on." The emerging field of cultural studies has produced important analyses of these education-related issues, focusing often times on media as a signifying practice. A signifying practice makes meaning by attaching symbolic significance to a contested item or practice. Advertising, for example, attaches love to diamonds, authenticity to Levis, good times to Old Milwaukee, and family values to McDonald's. Whoever commands the ability to signify cultural artifacts holds the power to construct consciousness. The fact that the analysis of such phenomena are excluded from curricula this late in the twentieth century is hard to fathom.

Thus, contemporary culture becomes what Henry Giroux calls a terrain of struggle for cultural authority. Various companies compete to produce their own, self-interested version of the American story past and present (Giroux, 1993, 1994). For example, McDonald's advertisements depict the history of the American family and, in the process, create an artificial tradition of historical meaning. Using a film antiquing process to produce simulated historical family photomontages along with sentimental music and mawkish lyrics, the McMarketers portray America as one big happy family, a combination of mini-families who work the land, own small grocery stores, wave Old Glory on holiday celebrations, and today eat at McDonald's. The journey from "then" to "now" conceals all evidence of the violent struggle to move from an economic system grounded on harming and small, locally-owned businesses to multinational conglomerates.

In the process of presenting this seamless celebration of Americas' history of family values, the advertisers deftly sidestep the burden that corporate capitalism has placed on family life with its industrialization policies of the 1980s and 1990s. As corporations shut down their U.S. plants in Shreveport, Louisiana and Flint, Michigan and reopened them in Mexico and Malaysia, the resulting stress placed on the families of unemployed fathers and mothers was of little concern. The well-being of American communities that had supported firms for decades was not as significant a factor as quarterly corporate earnings charts. Corporations use the power of the media to teach a "curriculum of legitimation" that depicts them (despite all evidence to the contrary) as family-oriented good citizens who value the beliefs and principles that made America great. The expectation that families can live in stable communities with long-standing friends and social networks is rendered increasingly unrealistic in an era where one out of every four workers is fired, laid off, or transferred every year.

As most consumers of media have by now learned, those who shape programming often have limited concern with accurate representations—ratings, profit, and power are their obsessions. For those dominant groups who seek legitimation in the larger attempt to secure political and economic power, access to TV and other media becomes a necessity. When we come to understand, for example, the political ramifications of "innocent" media messages, we begin to appreciate the subtle relationship between media access and power. Images of children excited as they open gifts on Christmas morning have no *overt* political message. At a deeper level, however, such images may be politically influential, as they tell us that such happiness in our children can be evoked only by the consumption of goods and services. If we truly love our children and want to see them happy, then we must support the interests of the corporations who produce these valuable products. Thus, when Mattel Inc. calls for lower corporate taxes and a better business climate in which to produce its toys, we accede to its wishes. After all, this is the company that allows us to make our children happy—indeed, this is a company with political and economic power.

The development of new media technologies over the last couple of decades has not served (as proponents of techtopia once predicted) to create a new era of empowered citizens. The corporate control of the media and the control of knowledge production that accompanies it dramatically affect individuals' perception of the world. The corporate ability, for instance, to represent American blue collar workers as lazy and unproductive shapes the politics of labor-management relations. Corporate managers using the media to disseminate their portrayal of workers can rally the public to support their denial of higher wages to workers while raising their own pay. The last two years, for example, Lee Iacocca was chair of Chrysler, he made over nineteen million dollars per year. At the same time, Chrysler management was exhorting labor to cut waste because of falling profit margins in the company (DeYoung, 1989). Few labor complaints are heard on the American mass media.

A progressive media education would cultivate the notion that media literacy involves seeing through the myth that technological innovations in TV and computers have simply served to produce a better informed community. A better explanation of the impact of such technological innovations, students of the media learn, revolves around the creation of a new form of technologically-facilitated power—let's call it techno-power. With the aid of hypermedia private interests are building undreamed of information monopolies; the public nature of information is quickly mutating into information as a private commodity (Smart, 1992; Harvey, 1989). As fewer and fewer large corporations control the flow of information (two percent of publishers, for example, now control 75 percent of the books published in the U.S.), public assessibility to information contracts. In this circular process techno-power expands.

It is important for educators to understand that this shaping of public opinion by way of media control is never simplistic. Many times efforts to manipulate opinion backfire, as men and women perceive what is happening to them and rebel. Also, technologies such as computerlinks and information highways can be used to convey alternative messages that challenge corporate control. Still, however, most Americans are unable to comprehend the degree of influence power wielders attain as they control TV and other media that by-pass reason and focus directly on the management of human feelings and emotions. Techno-power becomes a medieval alchemist that instead of turning base metals into gold transforms "truth" via its power to speak directly to our feelings and desires into "what sells" (McLaren, Hammer, Reilly, and Sholle, 1995; Brosio, 1994; Kellner, 1989). Valuable information in this context becomes not

that which explains or empowers but that which creates a cooperative community, a culture of consumption. Techno-power's
communication media do not exist to help ordinary citizens
take control of their lives or understand the demands of democratic citizenship. The need to capture the attention and the
emotions of consumers transcends all other media uses. In the
process of improving ratings, the techno-power of TV reduces
everything to the same level—everything that happens must be
reconstituted to capture viewer interest. In terms of traditional
notions of importance all events and messages are equally triv-
ial—death, destruction, war, famine, unemployment, beer femi-
nine hygiene, weight loss programs, acne medications, etc. . . .
CNN presents *War in the Gulf*, brought to you by Depends
Undergarments.

Such understandings of techno-power and media influence, I
would argue, should instigate massive changes in formal education. The curriculum should be expanded to included previously excluded cultural processes, popular and youth culture in
particular. Such a reconceptualized curriculum would be centered around the development of a critical media literacy. Such
a literacy (McLaren, Hammer, Reilly, and Sholle (1995) label it a
critical pedagogy of representation) encourages teachers and
students to *read* TV commercials, for example, as more than
mere attempts to sell products (Seiter, 1993). Commercials in
such a curriculum are read as multidimensional visual, aural,
and narrative texts that provide entertainment, stimulate our
desires , speak to our social and interpersonal investments (for
example, our relationships with peers or authority figures), and
inscribe our consciousness with the imprint of power.

Sit with a child watching Saturday morning cartoons and the
children's commercials that accompany them. Notice how
adeptly commercial producers situate the child in relation to
the world of adults, as toys, games, and food are presented as
tickets to a utopian kiddie cosmos free from the restraints of
parental or other authority figures. There is little authentic
effort to educate children—indeed, the power of the ads
involves the fact that they appeal to kids as kids. Educational TV
always assumes that children are deficient, somehow less than
adults in some ways. The understanding is not lost on kids—

their different responses to the different types of programming is dramatic. Few know children as well as the media surrogates of techno-power. My argument here is that teachers should understand children and their media world at least as well (Steinberg and Kincheloe, 1995).

A critical media literacy understands that TV advertisements don't simply sell products, they sell lifestyles and identity (see Alan Block, 1995 for an insightful discussion of literacy). As teachers and students apply their critical analysis, they uncover scores of social assumptions that are made and discarded in the instant it takes to make sense of an advertisement. As these social assumptions are studied, hidden political codes emerge. The analytical process turns into a political act. Now we understand, students exclaim, what McDonald's is trying to do with its family-oriented hamburger commercial. Such a theme, they realize, cannot be separated from the larger debate in American politics surrounding the deployment of the issue of family values. The McDonald's marketers, students assert, want us to think of McDonald's every time Bill Clinton, Dan Quayle, Lamar Alexander, or Jack Kemp allude to their concern with the preservation of family values. As teachers and students move beyond that which is immediately visible in video of any type, thinking moves to a new level of sophistication. Media literacy becomes a higher order cognitive act.

Without the grounding that media literacy provides teachers become the unwitting accomplices of power interests. A dynamic understanding of media and techno-power not only helps teachers avoid complicity, but it provides the grounding for a politics of resistance to such authority (McLaren, 1994). Such a resistance often emerges as an act of cultural recovery that takes, for example, McDonald's pseudo-history of the American family and rewrites it in light of the struggles for social justice that have been waged in defense from the ravages of power elites. Such cultural recovery would bring to light the stories of immigrants and their fight against discrimination, the labor wars of the late nineteenth and early twentieth centuries waged by industrial leaders against workers and their families, and the ways African American families fought to support one another in light of Jim Crow laws and lynch mobs.

A critical media literacy as it provides answers to our question—what is the effect of media on education—operates within a larger democratic system of meaning that promotes education for critical citizenship. Recognizing the power of media to shape identity, a critical media literacy empowers men and women to assume conscious authority over their own identity formation. So empowered, these critical citizens ask whether media presentations promote democratic values or serve to further oppression. In this context critical media literacy becomes an invaluable skill for those engaged in broader political projects such as the women's movement, the fight for economic and workplace democracy, and the struggle for racial justice. Teachers and students who have acquired such literacy can use it to link the crusade for democratic school reform to these movements.

James Jennings (1992), for example, writing as an African American engaged in the movement for racial justice calls for a media literacy that will unite individuals concerned with the media portryal of black and other non-white men and women. Black identity, self-concept, is shaped in part by these media images, making it more difficult, as a result, for black parents and teachers to impart racial pride to their children. This African American issue is only one of countless social and political dynamics revaluing around the educational effect of media. What I am asking teacher education students to do is not easy. Indeed, the development of a critical media literacy will bring few rewards and may even impede success in the school hierarchy. Nevertheless, I implore teachers to put issues of justice and democracy first and join the resistance to the anti-democratic machinations of techno-power.

References

Block, A. (1995). *Occupied Reading:* . New York: Garland.

Brosio, R. (1994). *The Radical Democratic Critique of Capitalist Education.* New York: Peter Lang.

DeYoung, A. (1989). *Economics and American Education*. New York: Longman.

Giroux, H. (1994). *Disturbing Pleasures: Learning Popular Culture*. New York: Routledge.

Giroux, H. (1993). *Living Dangerously: Multiculturalism and the Politics of Difference*. New York: Peter Lang.

Goldman, R. (1992). *Reading Ads Socially*. New York: Routledge.

Harvey, D. (1989). *The Conditions of Postmodernity*. Cambridge, Massachusetts: Basil Blackwell.

Kellner, D. (1989). *Critical Theory, Marxism, and modernity*. Baltimore: Johns Hopkins University Press.

Kellner, D. (1992) "Popular culture and the construction of postmodern identities." In S. Lash and J. Friedman (eds.) *Modernity and Identity*. Cambridge, Massachusetts: Basil Blackwell.

McLaren, P. (1994) "Multiculturalism and the postmodern critique: Toward a pedagogy of resistance and transformation." In H. Giroux and P. McLaren, *Between Borders: Pedagogy and the politics of Cultural Studies*. New York: Routledge.

McLaren, P., R. Hammer, S. Reilly, and D. Sholle. (1995) *A Critical Pedagogy of Representation: Rethinking Media Literacy*. New York: Peter Lang.

Seiter, E. (1993) *Sold Separately: Parents and Children in Consumer Culture*. New Brunswick, New Jersey: Rutgers University Press.

Smart, B. (1992) *Modern Conditions, Postmodern Controversies*. New York: Routledge.

Stam, R., R. Burgoyne, and S. Flitterman-Lewis. (1992). *New Vocabularies in Film Semiotics: Structuralism, Post-Structuralism and Beyond.* New York: Routledge.

Steinberg, S. and J. Kincheloe. (1995). *Kinderculture: Exploring the Cults of Childhood.* Boulder, Colorado: Westview Press.

Tomlinson, J. (1991) *Cultural Imperialism.* Baltimore: Johns Hopkins University Press.

Chapter XI

Educational Reform: What have been the effects of the attempts to improve education over the last decade?

Stephen Nathan Haymes

Douglas J. Simpson

Stephen Nathan Haymes

What have been the effects of the attempts of educational reform to improve **urban** education over the last decade? With regards to the educational reform agendas of the Reagan and Bush administrations one of the main focuses of *A Nation at Risk* and *American 2000* is on "functional illiteracy" and "basic skills." The National Commission on Excellence in Education, the author of *A Nation at Risk*, argued that illiteracy is one of the major "indicators of risk." The Commission reported that "[s]ome 23 million American adults are functionally illiterate;" and "[a]bout 13 percent of all 17-year-olds in the United States can be considered functionally illiterate." The report concludes by saying that "functional illiteracy among minority youth may run as high as 40 percent" (1983:8). Eight years later, *American 2000* reported that the number of functionally illiterate Americans increased to 25 million (1991:16). What I will point out in this chapter is that functional illiteracy has been used by New Right conservatives to insist that educational reform be supportive of the back-to-basics movement. Second, I will discuss how the back-to-basics movement has been a way for conservative educational reformers to prescribe traditional values and norms, and ideologically constructs certain populations, in particular blacks and Latinos as the Other. And third, the attempt to improve urban education by the New Right has been mostly about securing white supremacist cultural domination.

However, the cultural domination of mainstream white society has been mostly expressed through a racialized form of corporate ideology, which I call "white enterpreneuralism." That is to say, the purpose of education for conservative mainstream reformers is to improve America's global economic competiveness and dominance, or more pointedly to better the authoritarian power and privilege of the wealthy in the United States and throughout the world. For the New Right, education is simply an appendage of its free-market ideology. The significance of this for race is that the subtext of mainstream conservative free-market ideology assumes that wealth is the result of hardwork, and poverty laziness. Put another way, in a white supremacist post-industrial corporate culture such as the United States, hardwork and therefore self-discipline is equated with whiteness, and blackness with laziness and the lack of self-regulation.

The assumptions and beliefs that informed mainstream conservative educational reform during the 1980s and early 1990s have been implicitly or explicitly about urban poor African American and Latinos(as), and therefore about race. More generally, what this essay will discuss is that the education reform ideology of the New Right movement, in particular its definition of functional illiteracy and basic skills, has operated to delegitimate the claims of oppressed racialized urban communities that the existing logic of the post-industrial corporate social order in the United States is premised on a system of racial discrimination and racial inequality. The attempts of educational reform to "improve" urban education over the last decade was not the intention of the New Right. Instead, its political aspirations was to regulate and control the cultural, political and social life of blacks and Latinos(as) within American education and the wider society.

In the context of a broader right-wing politics, this New Right aspiration is of significance given that radical antiracist and cultural nationalist movements of the late 1960s and 1970s, in conjunction with demanding community-control of schools, were responsible for a "resurgence, reevaluation, and transformation of notions of the *differentness* of peoples of color from the white dominant culture" (Frankenburg, 14:1994). For the New Right, the radical social movements of racialized communities were seen as disruptive to the traditional American values of individualism and hardwork; to "bootstrap" ideology. One important reason is because their (racial minority movements) redefinitions of difference as the "autonomy of culture, values and aesthetic standards and so on" were also linked "with an analysis and critque of racial inequality as a fundamentally structuring feature of U.S. society" (Frankenburg, 14:1994).

In light of the New Right's political project with respect racialized urban communities, what struck me the most about *A Nation at Risk* and *American 2000* was how the language of both reports appeared to be "deracialized;" both reports seemingly silent on racial matters avoided making explicit references about the racial politics of New Right conservative educational reform. The assumption of *American 2000* is that it is not the racial politics of America's white supremacist patriarchal corporate order that is socially and morally responsible for the horrible social conditions experienced by racialized urban communities, but those particular communities inadequate education.

> . . . if we want to combat crime and drug abuse, if we want to create hope and opportunity in the bleak corners of this country where there is now nothing but defeat and despair, we must dispel the darkness with the enlightment that a sound and well-rounded education provides (1991:2).

Again, notice the way in which *American 2000* addresses race without mentioning it directly accept through the use of "coded words" such as "crime" and "drug abuse" which the reports identifies with specific places which are described as "bleak corners of this country," meaning the inner-cities.

This covert way of discussing race reminds me of Michael Omi and Howard Winant's comments in *Racial Formation in the United States* that to dismantle or limit the political gains fought for by racial minorities in the 1960s the New Right used coded words. Strategically, the New Right understood politically that it could no longer as previously "defend patterns of racial inequality by demanding a return to segregation or by reviving simplistic notions of biological superiority/inferiority" (1994:123). Omi and Winant noted that as a key device to limit the political gains of racial minorities "coded words" operated as "phrases and symbols which refer indirectly to racial themes, but do not directly challenge popular democratic or egalitarian ideals" (1994:123). Troyna and Williams refer to this process as "discursive deracialization", that is, "a situation in which persons speak purposely to their audience about racial matters, while avoiding the overt deployment of racial descriptions, evaluations and prescriptions" (1983:4). They point out further that "[t]his covert use of racial evaluation is often capable of justifying racial discrimination by providing other non-racist criteria for the differential treatment of a groups distinguished by its racial characteristics" (1983:4).

In the context of educational reform over the past decade "basic skills" and "functional illiteracy" are the non-racist criteria used to justify the racially undemocratic character of American education. More specifically, the discussions found in *A Nation at Risk* and *American 2000* pertaining to basic skills and functional illiteracy have an implicit racial subtext that legitimates the exclusion of a form of education that takes seriously the diverse and specific cultures, histories, narratives, experiences and ways of learning of racialized minorities in United States. In fact, it delegitimates the claims of racial minorities that American institutions, particularly its schools, are premised on a racist logic that supports white supremacy, whether in its gendered and/or class manifestations. Both *A Nation at Risk* and *American 2000* point to high rates of functional illiteracy as evidence that racialized poor urban communities lack basic skills. I should add that for New Right conservatives, it was the supposed permissive nature of progressive and egalitarian educational reforms of the 1960s, the outcome of political struggles of the racial minority movements of that period, that is viewed as responsible for the serious problems of functional illiteracy experienced by racially defined minority communities during the decades that followed.

The New Right argued that the egalitarianism of the educational reforms of the 1960s—ideological and cultural diversity in the curriculum, student knowledge as an object of inquiry in the classroom, non-standardized forms of evaluation and testing, and nonauthoritarian forms of teacher authority—was responsible for the breakdown of traditional authority in American education. For conservatives, egalitarian educational reforms contributed to societal disorder, that is, to social pathologies that were believed to be responsible for joblessness, crime, single-parent households, teenage pregnancy, drug abuse and gang violence. Functional illiteracy was also believed to be a product of the perceived social pathologies supposedly generated by the egalitarianism of past educational reforms. J. Elspeth Stuckey points out that "deeply believed about illiteracy is its strong relationship with antisocial behavior. She shows study after study in which illiteracy is associated with either prison populations, high school dropouts, welfare mothers, unwed teenage mothers, and the chronically unemployed. Stuckey concludes by saying that "certainly, illiteracy is a fact of disfranchised life. It is not on par with pregancy, however, or abuse, or criteria for imprisonment. That is, illiteracy is neither a trespass nor, actually, a redress" (1991:101).

What New Right conservative educational reform has done over the past decade is to use non-racist criteria to ideologically construct racialized urban populations as Other, as pathological communities. This ideological construction is implicit in the racial subtext of *America 2000* and *A Nation at Risk*. Just before describing the inner-city as "bleak corners of this country," *America 2000* emphasizes the lack of basic skills and functional literacy pointing to the "25 million adults [who] are functional illiterate and the 25 million more adult workers [who] need to update their skills and knowledge." Presumed in *America 2000* is that adults and parents of color devalue education and therefore their children's future. The report states: "For our children to understand the importance of their own education, we must demonstrate that learning is important to grown-ups, too" (1991:29). It is with these assumptions that conservatives are able to link the low educational achievement of "disadvantaged" urban youth to parental responsibility and the breakdown of the family. Conservatives argue that with respect to today's American youth, "9 percent of their first eighteen years is in school", and "the other 91 percent is spent elsewhere—at the home, playground, in front of the television" (1991:16). Immediately following this observation, *America 2000* clues us into which specific group of parents and families it has in mind when describing the situation of some children.

> For too many of our children, the family that should be their protector, advocate and moral anchor is itself in a state of deterioration.
>
> For too many of our children, such a family never existed.
>
> For too many of our children, the neighborhood is a place of menace, the street a place of violence.
>
> Too many of our children start school unready to meet the challenges of learning.
>
> Too many of our children arrive at school hungry, unwashed and frightened

And other modern plagues touch our children: drug use and alcohol abuse, random violence, adolescent pregnancy, AIDs and the rest (1991:16).

The concluding observations made by *America 2000* is that "no civil society or compassionate nation can neglect the plight of these children who are, in almost every case, innocent victims of adult misbehavior. In other words, it is the perceived "antisocial behavior" of adults and parents of color that has created the horrible conditions that inner-city children live in. Also stated is that "schools cannot replace the missing element in communities and families" (1991:17). The New Right therefore seems to put the burden of educational reform on poor and working poor inner-city black and Latino parents and families. The conservative ideology inscribed white supremcist beliefs and assumptions into the concepts "basic skills" and "functional illiteracy"; that is, their combination or articulation with the traditional family values discourse of the New Right operates to construct disadvantaged urban black and Latino communities as a social problems, as communities with antisocial behaviors that are threatening to the moral fabric of mainstream white corporate society. The significance that the New Right places on linking educational reform to traditional conservative values is seen in the following passage from *America 2000*:

Even with accountability embedded in every aspect of education, achieving the goals [of America 2000] requires a renaissance of sound American values—proven values such as strength of family, parental responsiblity, neighborly commitment, the community wide-caring of churches, civic organizations, business, labor and the media. It's time to end the no-fault era of heedlessness and neglect, and as we shape tomorrow's schools, to rediscover the timeless values that are necessary for achievement (1991:31).

What conservatives seem are claiming is that the lack of basic skills and the high rates of functional illiteracy that characterize racialized urban communities suggest disrespect for hierarchical forms of authority. In terms of education, conservatives argue that this illustrates the total disregard of racialized urban communities for "academic standards." To believe this is to claim that racialized urban communities are absent of self-discipline, and that the progressive educational reforms of the 1960s condone and encouraged this antisocial behavior by compromising academic standards in order to accommodate disadvantaged racialized urban populations. It is this compromise and accommodation that conservatives believe is responsible for the high rates of functional illiteracy in urbanized racial minority communities. Implied also in *A Nation at Risk* is that the admission of illiterate and semi-illiterate racial minorities into American universities is responsible for the serious decline in national college entrance exam scores, and the lowering of admission requirements and academic standards.

A Nation at Risk in addition believes that prior to the 1960s, before egalitarian educational reforms, that academic standards were respected; American education was at its best; and the global superiority of the U.S. economy unchallenged. The Commissions report goes on to state that "the education foundations of our society are presently being eroded by a rising tide of mediocrity that threatens our very future as a Nation and a people" (1983:5). Referring to the educational reforms of the New Right as the "conservative restoration", Ira Shor asserts that its emphasis on academic standards was a way "to pit quality against equality." He further states: "Restoration policy promotes itself as the defender of 'excellence' and 'high standards.' Such political vocabulary dominates discussion in a conservative period. It helps authority disguise the real intention of strengthening hierarchy" (1986:7). This suggest that the restoring of the traditional order's domination was done by judging the results of the "egalitarian era from the top down and [finding] it "to be dismally inferior to the quality of learning before the changes" (Shor, 1986:7).

The New Right therefore discredited the progressive and equalitarianism of the 1960s educational reform by blaming it for the high rates of illiteracy which the right-wing believed was evident given the decline in test scores. Conservatives argued that before the 1960s illiteracy was not so much of an urgent problem as it is today, and that educational reform needed to return American education back-to-the-basics. *Newsweek's* December 1979 cover story "Why Johnny Can't Write" and its misrepresentation of the National Assessment of Educational

Progress findings provided conservative educational reformers with the legitimacy to declare a Literacy Crisis (Shor, 1986:64). Shor notes that this "partisan misreading of the evidence reveal the culture war of the [conservative] restoration." He further observes: "Without a Literacy Crisis there would have been no cause for launching a traditionalist crusade for the basics. Without back-to-basics, business culture, religious fundamentalism, and authoritarianism would not have regained such a predominance in the restoration" (1986:64).

What does the predominance of this restoration suggest about the attempts of conservative educational reform to improve urban education over the last decade? To answer this question requires that we define what improvement means for the New Right regarding urban education. The focus of urban educational reform on basic skills means that improvement is about cultural homogenization and therefore the cultural assimilation of racialized urban populations into the dominant mainstream white corporate culture and way of life.. What the back-to-the-basic movement of the New Right has done in relation to urban educational reform is to establish a normative conception of culture that is white and middle class. By claiming that the progressive and egalitarian educational reform agenda was to permissive, the New Right was able to suggest that the willingness of liberal and left reformers to reconfigure the "official culture" of urban schools around the popular cultures, that is, the histories, narratives, stories, ways of learning and being, and wisdom, of racialized urban communities made them complicitous in creating the "Literacy Crisis." The back-to-basics movement of the New Right is premised on a racially exclusionary politics that interprets cultural difference as a social problem, as disruptive to traditional values and norms. Back-to-basics can therefore be taken as a "code word" for white corporate supremacist cultural domination.

The manner in which educational reform over the last decade has politicized the issues of illiteracy and basic skills is more telling about the New Right's racial politics. Both illiteracy and basic skills as defined by the New Right has functioned to construct the "new racism." Officially, the educational reform agenda of the New Right appears to be antiracist in that it does not adhere to advocating racial discrimination, and that race is not rooted in biology but in cultural differences. This view has permitted the New Right to be more flexible in their racist political practices (Winant, 1994:100-101). While the struggle of racial minority movements have taken the principle of cultural pluralism to mean the defense of difference and the rights of minorities, the New Right has reinterpreted cultural pluralism or diversity to mean the "naturalness" of racial difference. It is the different lifestyles and traditions of racialized urban communities that is incompatible with the traditional values and norms of the white majority.

For conservative educational reformers, the high rates of functional illiteracy in racial minority communities is indication of how "their" lifestyles and traditions are "culturally deprived" and therefore inappropriate for redefining the official culture of schools, and educational institutions in general. Agreeing with Stuart Hall that "hegemony is leaky" insofar that it shapes common sense understandings the New Right view of racialized urban communities influences the perceptions of undergraduate and graduate education students. In some of my classroom experiences white middle class students have shared their beliefs by asserting that the culture's of black urban students results in them lacking the communication skills and therefore insight necessary to achieve in grammar school. They draw conclusion from this that blacks are "verbally deficient" and consequently "unable to process cognitively and be self-reflective," making them unself-regulating in their behavior. These students point to the "environment" in which black youth grow up in as the cause of their perceived cultural deprivation.

Even amongst white liberal-minded scholars this perspective is supported. In their recent book *American Apartheid*, Massay and Denton argue that ghetto isolation due to the residential segregation is the cause of "black speech patterns." They point out that "black speech patterns" are the reason for low educational achievement and the lack of employment. Both authors go on to suggest that "black speech patterns" reflect the supposed values that underlie black culture, and that these values are "defined in opposition to the basic ideals and values of American society." According to Massey and Denton, "black street culture" is at variance with mainstream white cultural values such as self-relience, hard work, sobriety, and sacrifice and that his has led to the "legitimating of certain behaviors prevalent with the black community that would otherwise be held in contempt by white society" (1993:167). They conclude that "black street culture" is an autonomous culture system that devalues work, marriage, and family formation but promotes male joblessness, teenage motherhood, single parenthood, alcoholism, drug abuse, crime, violence, and school failure (1993:162:78).

Peter McLaren has referred to this particular position as "environmentalism". He points out that this "position argues that black people are not "naturally" inferior but inferior in mental skills due to their impoverished environment" (1994:26). McLaren argues that although the environmentalist position does not support biological explanations it nevertheless accept "the general premise that race and class differentials exist", thus "keeping the claim alive that cognitive differentials between blacks and whites exist" (1994:26). Enviromentalism fails then to recognize that cognitive development occurs under favorable or unfavorable conditions. According to McLaren, "development in cognition is not something that is passively acquired—people develop cognitively often during attempts to resist—to overcome disadvantageous circumstances" He makes the important observation that "cognitive processes are universal", however the problem is "not all cultures possess the same measure of equality" (1994:26).

By associating black and Latino illiteracy with their impoverished conditions the New Right has been able to use non-racist criteria to prescribe a racially exclusionary urban educational reform agenda, the back-to-basics movement. What the New Right's urban educational reform does not realize is that black and Latino illiteracy may in fact be a form of resisting the cultural colonialism of the right-wing back-to-basics movement. Henry Giroux clearly understands the racial politics being advocated by the New Right in relation to cultural difference when it uses illiteracy to construct the resistance of racially subjugated communities as an aspect of their cultural deprivation:

Within the dominant discourse, illiteracy is not merely the inability to write, it is also a cultural marker for naming forms of difference within the logic of cultural deprivation theory. What is important here is that the notion of cultural deprivation serves to designate in the negative sense forms of cultural currency that appear disturbingly unfamiliar and threatening when measured against the dominant culture's ideological standard regarding what is to be valorized as history, linguistic proficiency, lived experience, and standards of community life. The importance of developing a politics of difference i this view is seldom a positive virtue and attribute of public life; in fact, difference is often constituted as deficiency and is part of the same logic that defines the other within the discourse of cultural deprivation (1987:3).

References

Bush, George, 1991. *America 2000.* United States Government Printing Office

Frankenberg, Ruth, 1994. *The Social Construction of Whiteness: White Women, Race Matters.* Minneapolis: University of Minnesota Press

Giroux, Henry, 1987. "Literacy and the Pedagogy of Political Empowerment" in Paulo Friere and Donaldo Macedo, *Literacy: Reading the Word and the World.* Massachusetts: Bergin and Garvey Publishers, Inc.

Massey, Douglas S. and Nancy D. Denton. 1993. *American Apartheid: Segregation and the Making of the Underclass.* Cambridge, MA: Harvard University Press

McLaren, Peter, 1994. *Life in Schools: An Introduction to Critical Pedagogy in Foundations of Education.* New York: Longman

National Commission on Excellence in Education, 1983 *A Nation at Risk.* United States Government Printing Office

Omi, Michael and Howard Winant, 1994. *Racial Formation in the United States: From the 1960s to the 1990s.* New York: Routledge

Shor, Ira, 1986. *Cultural Wars: School and Society in the Conservative Restoration 1969-1984.* New York: Routledge

Stuckey, Elspeth, J. 1991.*The Violence of Literacy.* New Hampshire:Boynton/Cook Publishers

Troyna, Barry and Jenny Williams, 1986. *Racism, Education and the State. New* Hampshire:Croon Helm

Winant, Howard, 1994. *Racial Conditions:Politics, Theory and Comparisons.* Minneapolis:University of Minnesota Press

Douglas J. Simpson

Dare Schools Alter Student Values
in a Pluralistic Society?

Preliminary Remarks

The question, Dare schools alter student values in a pluralistic society?, may strike many of us as peculiar. Some of us think, for instance, that it is obvious that schools must teach students values if we are going to maintain our democratic heritage and society. Conversely, others of us believe it is clear that values are completely individual or cultural creations, and that schools should have no part in attempting to create or pass on a set of values. Still others of us may be equally convinced that the question arises from a total misunderstanding of how values should be acquired. We argue that teachers should not be allowed to impose their values upon students. Some of us, however, may question the teaching of values because we doubt that gender differences will be adequately considered and accounted for. But others of us expect schools to pass on our particular cultural, religious, gender or ethnic values and ideals. Others, nevertheless, protest that it is objectionable to indoctrinate students into a specific ethnic, gender, religious or cultural perspective. Moreover, there are those of us who claim that schools ought to be completely neutral so that no one will be offended by the values of teachers and other educators.

Even though this list of scenarios could be extended, the ones delineated illustrate the importance of our question and the difficulty of achieving consensus on the subject raised, not to mention the new questions that would arise out of our discussions if some kind of agreement were reached regarding the desirability of altering the values of students while they attend school. Even so, we seem well advised to consider anew the issue before us because various segments of society are not inclined to let the question rest. In examining our subject, we will approach it by raising a series of questions, questions that complement one another as we seek to understand and address our basic topic. Our lead question is concerned with whether it is possible to reach a consensus on the issue of whether it is appropriate for schools to change student values in a pluralistic society.

Is Consensus Possible?

In view of the differences that exist in American society and the aforementioned divergent viewpoints, some appear to think that there is no reasonable route to bringing about agreement on the teaching, changing or forming of values in a pluralistic society. If we expect *unanimity* of thought on this topic, then there probably is no reasonable road to consensus much less to action. We will be paralyzed by the somewhat and sometimes conflicting opinions that are debated by different portions of society and the education profession, for we are unlikely to convince everyone who enters the controversy to move from talking about values to seeking justifiable ways of altering values in schools. Simply stated, we are not sufficiently wise and knowledgeable—nor is everyone adequately open to alternative views—to convince everyone of practically any idea today much less a position that requires conscious attitudinal and behavioral change. But should we cease discourse in this arena merely because unanimity is missing? Do we usually insist that there be total agreement before we move forward on a public policy or educational matter? If we change our expectations in the direction of a consensus or general agreement by most people, then most of us may be able to agree that schools should assist in altering values in a pluralistic society. Any consensus regarding the desirability of changing values does not mean, of course, that the concerns of those who disagree with the majority will be ignored or exploited. Indeed, the contrary is the case: we should be more sensitive and alert to their interests as plans and programs are developed.

Initially, it seems important to state that there should be some compelling reasons for asking schools to begin or to continue with the goal of altering student values. Schools cannot do everything. Nor should they be expected to do just anything that some of us, even most of us, want done. Goals should be within the mission of the school or, at a minimum, the mission of the school should be reflectively revised to accommodate any new or revived goals we may select.

Is there a compelling rationale for asking schools to alter student values? Arguments for including values education in schools come from a wide range of perspectives and have existed throughout much of the history of formal education. Many people today, perhaps most of those who discuss the topic, think some kind of values education is needed. As noted earlier, some folk believe values must be taught if the school itself is to have an environment that nurtures intellectual, social, emotional and physical growth. Others argue that the present antisocial behavior of society and some students needs to be addressed throughout the educational careers of students so that both society and schools will be influenced in positive ways over time. Another section of society says we must teach values that will return us to a day when Judeo-Christian values permeated society. Still others argue that schools must teach values that will enable us to live intelligently and reflectively in a religiously and culturally pluralistic society. Arguments can also be found for the position that the needs of children and youth outside of school for food, love, care, housing, stimulation and nurture need to be addressed not only by social agencies, religious institutions and families but by the school to help reduce future problems in these realms. A growing body of literature, then, suggests that there is a need for and an interest in values education and the altering and formation of student values. Whether arguments found in this literature are convincing is a question that needs to be addressed at another time.

Are There Concerns That Need to be Voiced?
Let us assume—an assumption that you may wish to challenge—for the sake of discussion that there is a legitimate educational interest in values education or a compelling societal need for such. Either of these two assumptions will be sufficient to carry us forward in our discussion. Where might the teacher or school or district begin given this assumption? Or, we may say, if a general agreement is thought possible, what steps are well-advised in bringing about such agreement? No doubt, there are

many routes to the same end. So our purpose is to mention only a few possibilities. To begin with, it seems that open discussions of key questions and fears are essential. What fears do people, professional and lay, have? What reservations do people imply by their questions and comments? What are their doubts and areas of uneasiness? The concerns reflected in these questions are of critical interest, for unless they are openly approached overt and covert resistance to many kinds of values education will go unattended.

An example may stimulate us to think of a number of concerns in the area of values education. Many of us are rightly concerned that we do not impose our values, especially the moral ones, upon others. We seem to think, at least at times, that there is something morally objectionable to imposing moral values upon others. This objection to values imposition, however, opens the door to some interesting questions: On what grounds do we object to values imposition? Why is it objectionable to impose, say, aesthetic or ethical values upon students? Is it because we think each person should have a choice in selecting values? Is it also because we respect each person as an individual and do not think she or he ought to be coerced into accepting values? Do we think values imposition is inconsistent with the notions of education, educating and educated person? Or do our objections and questions arise because we fear that schools will teach our children and youth that our ethnic, cultural and religious values are wrong, inappropriate or ill-founded? Is there a fear of a covert racism, ethnocentrism or anti-religious tendencies coming out in several questions?

What Do We Mean by Values Imposition?

Whatever the concerns of people, we need to be certain that they are clearly expressed. If we are afraid of values imposition, we need to state clearly our anxieties. Likewise, it seems manifest that we need to be clear about the concept *imposition*. What does it mean for the school or teacher to impose values upon children and youth? Does it mean merely *influencing* the views of others? If values are discussed or taught are we automatically and necessarily imposing them upon students? Or does imposition mean *forcing* students to accept certain ideas, behaviors or values? Does values imposition include a *mis-educative means—* such as indoctrination, intimidation, coercion or propagandizing? If we are not afraid of values imposition, then we may well misunderstand the importance of the entire domain of values.

Are there educative ways of altering values that avoid imposing values upon others? Or is imposing values upon others sometimes appropriate or helpful? Are we imposing values upon students when we tell them they cannot steal another's lunch, fight in the corridors, bring firearms to school and sell drugs on campus? If these actions are included in the concept of imposition, should we discuss whether values imposition is *intrinsically* objectionable? Are we well-advised to look for values that we can agree *should be imposed* upon students if values imposition is not in itself unacceptable? Or are we better advised to argue that the illustrations we gave—prohibitions against stealing lunches, fighting others, bringing firearms to school and selling drugs on campus—are not examples of values imposition because we can provide *cogent reasons* for insisting that these behaviors not be allowed at school? Should we conclude that the concept of values imposition only refers to *unjustifiable* pressure to pass on values? If we have strong or convincing reasons for allowing, encouraging or prohibiting a behavior or attitude, does this mean that we can justifiably pass on values that are consistent with certain behaviors and attitudes and discourage others that are inconsistent with them? Are we well-advised to use the word *imposition* only when the passing on of values cannot be justified on publicly debatable grounds?

These brief comments and several questions may suggest that some acts of passing on values do not appear to constitute an imposition of values and, as a consequence, that we can and ought to find non-impositional or educative means of teaching values. They may also point to an inconsistency in the thinking of those who oppose every kind of values education on the grounds that all values education is impositional. That is to say, those individuals who highly prize freedom of selection of values and strongly resist all forms of teaching values may be inconsistent. Implicit in their position is the idea that schools should at least operate on the values of freedom of thought and freedom of selection. They want these values to be honored in schools. The question arises, therefore, as to whether we are not well-advised to explicitly discuss and debate these values that are unconsciously assumed in schools. Do we not need to ask what these freedoms entail, how they are to be justified and if there are any limits to them? Are we allowing values imposition to occur by not debating and clarifying these values? Are those who oppose all kinds of values education unconsciously imposing their values upon others?

Are We Afraid Religious Beliefs Will be Taught or Attacked?

We are, perhaps, concerned, if we reflect for a moment, about the possibility of both the teaching of specific religious ideas under the pretense of teaching public values and the teaching of particular values that are contrary to religious perspectives. In this realm, we may need to have discussions regarding the concept of separation of church and state as well as other legal issues that surround the teaching of religion. In these discussions, we may find that there are no legal restrictions to teaching values as long as they are taught in an educative manner and are not designed to promote a religious perspective. Even when public values and religious values coincide, overlap, or are identical, the values can still be taught or promoted if the grounds for teaching them are publicly debatable, rationally supportable and scientifically defensible, not founded upon religious teachings and a doctrinal rationale. We may also conclude that the overwhelming majority of people, regardless of whether they are religious or non-religious, highly prize many of the same values, e. g., compassion, respect of person, freedom, justice, and tolerance. The common values that are discovered often form the foundation for further discussions and plans regarding a values education program. They frequently support the conclusion that values education can be pursued without either supporting or attacking distinctively religious values. This is not to say, however, that there will not be complex issues that have to be addressed and resolved.

Discussions with all appropriate parties represented in a community and profession, including representatives of those views we personally find distasteful, often lead to a consensus of the aforementioned sort. These discussions frequently point to the thought that there are values that are shared by people of various religious positions, ethnic backgrounds, and cultural heritages.

They suggest there are *public grounds*—reasons that cut across different cultural, religious and philosophical orientations—for informed action in the areas of values education. They may also suggest that some values—respect for others, freedom, fairness, honesty and tolerance—are intrinsic features of a healthy pluralistic community, including the micro-communities we find in schools. That is to say, respect, compassion, freedom, tolerance and fairness seem to be essential values if we even expect to have a civil pluralistic society and school much less a healthy one. This observation may support the argument that schools should seek to alter the values of those who are disrespectful, uncaring, coercive, intolerant and unjust. If not, we may run the risk of cultural and religious wars indefinitely. The cultivation of respectful, compassionate, flexible, tolerant and fair people does not mean we can proceed in non-educative or unethical ways. In the realm of ideas and to a lesser degree in the realm behavior, schools and society have to tolerate to some extent both undesirable and desirable diversity. Forcing or otherwise pressuring children to accept particular viewpoints and values is neither an ethical nor educative approach to values education. In actuality, this kind of so-called values education becomes a disguised form of values imposition, for while student behavior may rightly be controlled on occasions by schools, mind control has no place in an educative school.

What Should We Do If People Claim Values Are Entirely a Personal Matter?

What should we do if there are those who argue that all values are nothing more than personal preferences and that each person should do her or his own thing and not be harassed by teachers who have been charged to pass on values? Shall we concur with them? If we concur with them, does this mean that the values of freedom of thought and selection, the values of equal respect of persons and justice, and so forth are merely personal wishes that we would like to become the wishes of others? Does this mean that our opposition to sexism and racism have no rational grounds, that our opposition to murder and child abuse is nothing more than the desire of some people in society and that contrary desires are just as creditable? Shall we decide that in a pluralistic society that it is acceptable to hate African, Asian, Arab or Anglo Americans? Do we teach that it is entirely up to each student whether she or he is prejudiced against Jews, Muslims, Christians, or Buddhists? If we draw these conclusions and decide that schools should remain neutral on value questions, are we in effect saying that this highly unusual position should be and is our values education philosophy and that our values education program should entail teaching students it is appropriate for them to do whatever they wish? If we reach these conclusions, then we seem to be yielding to an intellectual temptation that is almost uniformly resisted by those who think seriously about this subject. But should we care whether many serious thinkers about values education say this position is faulty for a number of reasons? Should we be interested in their reasons for rejecting the do-your-own-thing philosophy? If not, why?

Another consideration may throw light on these questions as well as bring to conclusion our discussion of this overall question. Many of us are familiar with the concepts of socialization, peer pressure, school ethos and hidden curriculum. Each of these concepts supports the opinion that social activities, peer influence, institutional culture, and the hidden or unofficial teachings of the school convey values to students in covert and overt ways. Values, desirable and undesirable, are changed by and in schools even when we are unaware that the process of values education is occurring. Likewise, education itself is viewed by many to be an attempt to pass on in a formal manner an entire set of values, ranging from an appreciation of the arts and a commitment to search for understanding to a high regard for evidence, reflection, courage, open-mindedness and imagination. If these interpretations of schooling are reasonably sound, then it seems to follow that schooling does alter values regardless of the nature of society, pluralistic or otherwise. From this point of view, the major question is not, Dare schools alter student values in a pluralistic society?, but How will schools alter student values in a pluralistic society? Will the alteration or formation take place in a conscious, reflective, educative and ethical manner or in an unconscious, unreflective, propagandistic, and unethical manner?

Are There Educative Roads to Action?

Are there educative roads to altering or forming student values in schools? This question arises, if we follow the previous line of thought, because (1) schools consciously and unconsciously teach many different and, sometimes, conflicting values whether we like them or not, (2) schools that attempt to be neutral on value questions obliquely suggest that the values of neutrality, freedom and tolerance are unexaminable values of the school and (3) schools that think values are a purely personal matter ultimately have their own do-your-own-thing values education programs. Thus, if we do not want to get stuck in a morass of on-going arguments and debates about every detail of a values education program, we may move beyond preliminary questions to try to determine if there are truly educative means of evaluating and passing on values to students. Perhaps it is on occasions such as this that John Dewey's thought that there are times when too much thinking and arguing is applicable; that is, if thinking and arguing paralyze us, we have conversed too long. It is important to do something other than talk. On the other hand, we should not curtail important discussions just so we can become engaged in unreflective activities.

Back to our question: Are there educative roads to altering values in education? More specifically, are there educative routes to moral education? Are there ways to avoid the imposition of values, respect the autonomy of students, respect religious diversity without teaching religious ethics and contribute to the ethical well-being of society? Can we pursue moral enlightenment and show respect for reason and diverse cultures? The answer for various individuals over the centuries has often been an affirmative one even though there have been a wide variety of disagreements over the precise means and ends. This thought brings up an important consideration: We do not have to agree upon the precise details of a moral education program or emphasis in order to proceed with it if we understand that the we keep learning about the endeavor as we move into it. We do not think that we have to agree on the details of mathematics, science, literacy and civic education before we initiate or redesign programs. Why should we have a different standard in the area of values education, especially since values are taught in all of the aforementioned fields?

Presently, there appear to be several basic approaches to teaching values in a school. Sometimes there are special sessions or efforts designed to (a) enable students to clarify their values, (b) teach them moral reasoning, (c) provide students with the skills to grapple with moral dilemmas, (d) induct students into a set of public values, or (e) initiate students into a school that is characterized by a democratic values orientation. In many cases, some attention is given to each of these five orientations. Perhaps there is a tendency on the part of many educators to integrate values education into the everyday activities of schooling since there is insufficient time to have special sessions for values education and everyday school activities are filled with value and moral issues. Regardless of the options considered and eventually selected, it seems appropriate that the criticisms of the option or options be carefully studied. In this way, weaknesses and strengths may be identified and the former may be avoided or compensated for. In addition, critics may provide invaluable insights into the approach, such as how the approach we adopt may become unreflective or impositional after the program has been instituted over a period of years. That is, they may help us understand when we are prone to drive off an educative road and onto a mis-educative one.

Concluding Remarks

The question, Dare the school alter student values in a pluralistic society? is, in one sense, a moot one. Schools change, at least to some degree, the values of students in all kinds of societies, including pluralistic ones, whether we want them to do so or not. The more appropriate questions, therefore, are as follows: If values are changing while students attend school, how can we more consciously guide and engage in the activity of change? What means of altering values are both educationally and ethically justifiable. What value ends are consequential for and can be justified in a pluralistic society? How do we show respect for different cultures and religions and remain educative in our endeavors? What steps are we well-advised to take in order to ensure that educators, parents and others understand and want the values program or emphasis that is developed? How do we ensure that the program or emphasis does not deteriorate into an indoctrination into a particular philosophy of life or an imposition of the majority opinion on value questions? How do we argue for the importance of moral education without suggesting that it is the panacea for all societal ills? Searching for answers to these and related questions explains in part why being an educator is such an important and stimulating profession.

References

Association for Supervision and Curriculum and Development. (1988). *Moral education in the life of the school*. Alexandria, VA.

Bottery, M. (1990). *The morality of the school: The theory and practice of values education*. London: Cassell Educational Limited.

Carter, R. (1988). Moral education-The debate. In W. Hare and J. Portelli (Eds.), *Philosophy of education: Introductory readings* (pp. 295-311). Calgary, AB: Detselig.

Chicago Foundation for Education. (n.d.). *A guide to successful implementation of the character education curriculum*. Chicago, IL.

Dewey, J. (1933). *How we think: A restatement of the relation of reflective thinking to the educative process*. Lexington, MA: D. C. Heath and Company.

Gouinlock, J. (1994). *The moral writings of John Dewey*. Revised edition. Amherst, NY: Prometheus Books.

Hare, W. (1993). Open-mindedness in moral education. In W. Hare (Ed.), *Attitudes in teaching and education* (pp. 57-68). Calgary, AB: Detselig.

Hare, W. (1993). *What makes a good teacher? Reflections on some characteristics central to the educational enterprise*. London, ON: Althouse.

Harmin, M. (1990). *How to plan a program for moral education*. Alexandria, VA: Association for Supervision and Curriculum Development.

Jackson, P., Boostrom, R., & Hansen, D. (1993). *The moral life of schools*. San Francisco, CA: Jossey-Bass Publishers.

Josephson, M. (1992). *Making ethical decisions*. Marina del Rey, CA: The Josephson Institute of Ethics.

Kohlberg, L. (1981). *The philosophy of moral development*. San Francisco, CA: Harper and Row.

The Network for Educational Development. (n.d.). *Personal responsibility education program*. St. Louis, MO.

Noddings, N. (1992). *The challenge to care in schools*. New York: Teachers College Press.

Peters, R. (1981). *Moral development and moral education*. Boston: George Allen & Unwin.

Piaget, J. (1965). *The moral judgment of the child*. New York: The Free Press.

Portelli, J. (1993). Dare we expose the hidden curriculum? In Portelli and S. Balin *Reason and values: New essays in philosophy of education* (pp. 171-197). Calgary, AB: Detselig.

Purpel, D. (1989). *The moral and spiritual crisis in education: A curriculum for justice and compassion*. Granby, MA: Bergin & Garvey.

Raths, L., Harmin, M., & Simon, S. (1966). *Values and teaching.* Columbus, OH: C. B. Merrill Books.

Sergiovanni, T. (1992). *Moral leadership: Getting to the heart of school improvement.* San Francisco, CA: Jossey-Bass Publishers.

Sichel, B. (1988). *Moral education.* Philadelphia: Temple University Press.

Simpson, D. (1992). The imposition of values: Reflections on a contemporary educational problem. *The journal of humanistic education and development,* 30 (3), 111-121.

Simpson, D. (1994). *The pedagodfathers: The lords of education.* Calgary, AB: Detselig.

Starratt, R. (1994). *Building an ethical school: A practical response to the moral crisis in schools.* Washington, D.C.: The Falmer Press.

Warnock, M. (1988). The neutral teacher. In W. Hare and J. Portelli, (Eds.), *Philosophy of education: Introductory readings* (pp. 177-186). Calgary, AB: Detselig Enterprises Ltd.

Chapter XII

Education as a Political Issue: What's missing in the public conversation about education?

Peter McLaren

Dennis Carlson

Peter McLaren

We live at a precarious point in time in which relations of subjection, suffering, dispossession and contempt for human dignity and the sanctity of life remain at the center of our social existence. Emotional dislocation, moral sickness and individual helplessness remain a ubiquitous feature of history. Our much heralded form of democracy has become, unbeknownst to many Americans, subverted by its contradictory relationship to the very object of its address: human freedom, social justice, and a tolerance and respect for difference. In the current historical juncture, discourses of democracy continue to masquerade as disinterested solicitations, and to reveal themselves as incommensurable with the struggle for social equality. The reality and promise of democracy in the United States has recently been invalidated by the ascendency of new postmodern institutionalization of brutality and the proliferation of new and sinister structures of domination. This has been followed by an ever fainter chorus of discontent as the voices of the powerless and the marginalized grow increasingly despondent or else are clubbed into oblivion by the crackling swiftness of police batons.

Although pain and suffering continue to pollute the atmosphere of social justice in the United States in alarming proportion to previous decades, the dream of democracy and the struggle to bring it about has taken on a new intensity, as recent events in Europe and Haiti attest. In its unannounced retreat in the United States over the past decade, democracy has managed to recreate power through the spectacularization of its after-image, that is, through image management and the creation of national myths of identity primarily through the techniques of the mass media.

The prevailing referents around which the notion of public citizenry is currently constructed have been steered into the ominous direction of the social logic of production and consumption. Buyers are beginning to culturally merge with their commodities while human agency is becoming absorbed into the social ethics of the marketplace. Social impulses for equality, liberty, and social justice have been flattened out by the mass media until they have become cataleptically rigid while postmodern images threaten to steal what was once known as the "soul."

Given the current condition of end-of-the-century ennui and paranoia, we have arrived at the zero-degree reality of the kind that once only graced the pages of surrealist manifestos or punk fanzines. Andre Breton's "simplest Surrealist act"—firing a pistol into a crowd of strangers—is no longer just a contemporary symbolic disruption of the grudgingly mundane aspects of everyday life or a symbolic dislocation circulating in avant garde broadsheets. It is precisely in this current North American historical conjuncture that people *are* really shooting blindly into crowds: at children in hamburger establishments, at employees and employers in factories, at teachers and classmates in schools, and at female engineering students in university seminar rooms. In some urban settings, children are murdering other children for their status-line foot gear—not to mention the lurid reality at L.A. 'drive-bys'. In New York City, manufacturers of bullet proof vests are starting special fashion lines for toddlers and elementary school children who might accidentally absorb stray bullets from homeboy dealers in pumps, ten dollar gold tooth caps and who carry customized AK 47 assault rifles. The guns are not fashion accessories—yet. But gas masks are. New York celebrity fashion designer, Andre Van Pier, after the Gulf War announced a spring fashion line based on the theme of Desert Storm: the "Gulf War look." Fashion accessories revealed include neon-colored camouflage pattern, canteen purses, and gas masks slung renegade-chic over the shoulder. A major New York manufacture of baseball cards revealed a new line of Gulf War cards that were supposed to be "educational." Of course, included were photos of the major American military hardware and portraits of the generals but the only item represented from Iraq in this educational collection was a "scud" missile.

Today's social ugliness that makes the bizarre appear normal is no longer just a (white, male) surrealist fantasy or proto-surrealist spin-off, or a Baudrillardean rehearsal for a futureless future. This scenario *is* the present historical moment, one that has arrived in a body bag—unravelled and stomped on by the logic of a steel-toed boot. Serial killer Ted Bundy has donated his multiple texts of identity to our structural unconscious and *we are living them*. A funky nihilism has set in; an aroma of cultural disquiet. There is a yearning for a comfortable apocalypse accompanied by forms of everyday life where salvation is unnecessary because chaos is always sublime and morality is frictionless in the age of MTV. Feelings of despair about the global condition have gone high-tech: We can not eroticize our depression and rearrange and reterritorialize our feelings by plugging our central nervous system in to the electromagnetic spectrum via tv waves and charting out our lives according to designer moods.

The erosion of the American dream has forced today's youth to occupy, if not a dystopian parody of *The Cosby Show*, then paracriminal subcultures of sardonic nihilism focussing on drugs and violence, apotheosized in movies like *Clockwork Orange* and *Colors*. Corporate rock's celebration of the subversion of adult authority gives its youthful listeners the illusion of resistance but not a language of critique or hope. It works to produce a politics of pleasure but simultaneously functions as a form of repression and forgetting—a motivated social amnesia and forced disavowal of the nation's complicitousness in racial demonization and colonialism.

The New Right has used the media effectively (and affectively) not simply to transform gangsters or actors into politicians through the services of high-tech image consultants, but even more impressively, to seduce Americans to retreat into cultural nostalgia and social amnesia as a way out of this postmodern era of retreat and despondency (many students I teach are already feeling a nostalgia for the Persian Gulf War as it was ideologically produced through CNN). At the same time the New Right has, through foreign and domestic policies shaped by the heritage of imperialism, helped the U. S. flex its global muscles in Grenada, Panama, and Iraq, setting the stage for a renewed patriotic zeal and construction of the postmodern national subject. Kellner (1990) notes that, under the control of

multinational capital, the media have effectively served as ideological mouthpieces for Reagan/Bush disinformation and have
helped to forge a conservative ideological hegemony.

Kellner (1990: 219) writes:

> It is a historical irony that the 1980s marked the defeat of democracy
> by capitalism in the United States and the triumph of democracy over
> state communism in the Soviet bloc countries. At present, the "free"
> television media in the United States are probably no more adversarial
> and no less propagandistic than *Pravda*, or the television stations in the
> Eastern European countries. Hence the very future of democracy is at
> stake—and development of a democratic communications system is
> necessary if democracy is to be realized.

Largely because of the way in which the media function to
shape and merchandise morality and to construct certain forms
of citizenship and individual and collective identities, our
understanding of the meaning and importance of democracy
has become impoverished in proportion to its dissolution and
retreat from contemporary social life. In the current historical
juncture of democratic decline in the United States, ideals and
images have become detached from their anchorage in stable
and agreed-upon meanings and associations and are now
beginning to assume a reality of their own. The world of the
media is one that splinters, obliterates, peripheralizes, parti-
tions and segments social space, time knowledge, and subjectivity in order to unify, encompass, entrap, totalize and homoge-
nize them. What is missing form the educational debate is the
way in which capitalism is able to achieve this cultural and
ideological totalization and homogenization through it ability to
insinuate itself into social practices and private perceptions
through various forms of media knowledge (see Grossberg,
1988).

Ironically, today's increasingly "disorganized" capitalism has
produced a gaudy sideshow that has managed to promote a
counterfeit democracy of flags and emblems—one that has
managed to harness the affective currency of popular culture
such that the average American's investment in being
"American" has reached an unparalleled high the likes of which
has not been seen since the years surrounding the post WWII
McCarthy hearings. The question that needs to be asked is:

How are the subjectivities (experiences) and identities of individuals and the production of media knowledges within popular culture mutually articulated?

What isn't being talked about in today's educational debate is the desperate need within our schools for creating a media literate citizenry that can disrupt, contest, and transform media apparatuses so that they no longer have the power to infantilize the population and continue to create passive, fearful, paranoid, and apolitical social subjects (McLaren and Hammer, 1991, 1995).

George Gerbner (1989/90) and others have pointed out that American television viewers are accepting a distorted picture of the real world "more readily than reality itself." Television reality is one in which men outnumber women three to one, where women are usually mothers or lovers, rarely work outside the home, and are natural victims of violence. It is a reality where less than ten per cent of the population hold blue collar jobs, where few elderly people exist, where young Blacks learn to accept their minority status as inevitable and are trained to anticipate their own victimization (they are usually portrayed as the white hero's comic sidekick or else drug addicts, gang members, or killers). It is a world in which 18 acts of violence an hour occur in children's time programs. Violence in television demonstrates the social power of adult white males who are most likely to get involved with violence but most likely to get away with it. It also serves as a mass spectacle reflecting the allocative power of the state. And this is occurring in a country that in 1990 reported the largest number of rapes against women in its history and a prison incarceration rate of Blacks that exceeds that of South Africa. A country where rich Angelenos are hiring private police, where the wealthy neighborhoods display signs warning (Armed Response!) and where security systems and militarization of urban life are refiguring social space along the lines of the postmodern film, *Bladerunner*.

What educators need to realize is that the New World Order of the New Right cannot be realistically achieved without creating a new moral order at home first (and that means in the classrooms and the living rooms of the nation)—one that refuses to challenge the received truths or accepted conventions that have provoked the current crisis of history and identity. So far conservatives have been successful in reproducing a moral order in which young people are able to resist being motivated to enter into any logic of opposition through counterpublic spheres of cultural resistance.

Missing from the debate over public education is a serious examination of the way in which contemporary forms of schooling reproduce national images of citizenship modelled on the John-Wayneing of America and captured in the renumerative cliches, Rocky Balboa's "Go for it!" and Clint Eastwood's "Go ahead. Make my day!" which adorn the discursive fountain head of United States bravado culture. These slogans have become cultural aphorism that reveal a great deal about the structural unconscious of the United States—slogans that constitute a combination of insurance company rationality, the politics of Sunday School charity drives, and the patriarchal, xenophobic and militaristic logic of terror (both Ronald Reagan and George Bush referred to "Go ahead, make my day!" during their time in office). When Clint Eastwood delivered "Go ahead, make my day!" in the movie, *Sudden Impact* (made during the Reagan presidency), he is daring a black man to murder a woman so that he (Dirty Harry) can kill him. As Michael Rogin (1990) has pointed out, Dirty Harry is willing to sacrifice women and people of color in the name of his own courage. Reagan had made women and Blacks his targets by destroying their welfare-state tax benefits—an act he was defending when he dared his detractors to "Make my day!" George Bush made the black criminal and white rapist of *Sudden Impact* into the figure of Willie Horton, as he attempted for the first time to organize American politics around the ominous image of interracial rape (Rogin, 1990). Rogin brilliantly articulates the use of movies such as *Rambo* and *Sudden Impact* as a form of political spectacle which operates as a form of social amnesia (1990, p. 107).

The kind of curriculum focus needed in today's schools is one that actively contests the historical amnesia created by contemporary cultural forms found in the mass media. Students should be invited to explore why they identify with Dirty Harry and Rambo, and begin to historicize such an identification in the context of the larger political and social issues facing the country.

It should come as little surprise that public opinion among those groups most advantaged by wealth and power is more supportive of the public school system and current reform efforts than those disempowered on the basis of race, socioeconomic status or gender. For those very populations that will be increasing in the coming decades—African Americans and Latino youth—the conditions in this country's school systems have appreciably worsened. Groups actively lobbying for minority positions on issues dealing with race, social and welfare concerns, are now being labeled within the conservative agenda by spokespersons such as Diane Ravitch, Roger Kimball, William Bennett, Rush Limbaugh, Lynne V. B. Cheney and others as "ethnocentric" or "separatist." Within this rationality, the call for diversity is sanctioned only when the converging of diverse voices collapses into a depoliticized co-existence based on capitulation to the hidden imperatives of Eurocentrism, logocentrism, and patriarchy. Those educators and students who refuse to genuflect before the Western cultural tradition and regard it glowingly as the apogee of cultural and political achievement are branded as perverse, ignorant and malicious sophists who have "defiled reason" (Kimball, 1990; see also Ravitch, 1990). What this ideological position effectively does is sound an alarm for the impending demise of white culture: "If white people have any pride in their heritage, now is the time to act because your history is under assault!" This clarion call for white authenticity embalms the past for people of color and shrouds their histories in the thinning strands of the moral and social consciousness of a nation plagued by social amnesia. It also shrouds domination in a white sheet of race, class, and gender purity by exiling questions of racism, sexism, homophobia, and class oppression.

On the other side of the educational debate we have a population that has been taught to think so extravagantly about success and power being pushed even closer to the dream of cultural and moral salvation. This dream has taken shape in Allan Bloom's colonial imagination where an "imperialist nostalgia" for the former grandeur of the empires of the center transforms itself into an inveterate fear of the unwashed masses. Bloom's highbrow petulance over *declasse* academics wanting to teach courses on popular culture translates for public schools into educational initiatives towards a national curriculum designed to maintain American "standards" in the world of international market competition (in other words, to maintain a uniform identity defined by Europe's demonization of the darker skinned populations—one that pits the Anglo "I" against the dark, forbidding "Other"). Bloom's reaction against the transdisciplinary character of much of what is occurring in recent literary theory and its capacity to reterritorialize the structure of academic discourse is really a form of pining for the loss of the authority of and consensus on the meaning of Greek and Roman Antiquity and collapse of late-Victorian highbrow academic dilettantism.

In the effete paradise of Bloom (which, of course, consists of Victorian salons and Tudor libraries populated by white bourgeois males and *belles lettristes* from Ivy League schools) the non-Western thinker becomes the debased and inverted image of the hypercivilized metropolitan intellectual. In other words, both non-Western knowledge and the uncultivated thought of the masses become, for Bloom, a primitive non-knowledge that serves as a conduit to savagery and barbarism—a descent into hell, reason's Negative Other. Bloom's collision of empires of consciousness (the radiantly civilized high culture of hellenism of which Bloom himself is a prime representative and the dark, primitive culture of the mob) occurs in a theatre of the Western mind (whose doors are being forced shut by the incursion of unholy thought into American culture) where a fantasy narrative is played out that is common to many bourgeois male academics and one in which the hegemony of the universalized and eternalized language and tropes of the colonizer makes it easier to script: Euro-American civilization is keeping the grandeur of the savage at bay in the name of Truth, and is morally policing the borders of that dark continent of the psyche where female sensuality remains unmediated by the realm of ideas and where the violence of the "blood-male" remains untempered by reason and the rule of law. For Bloom, both these savage verities of sex and violence must be cruelly trussed rather than cossetted by the Western mind.

What educators like Bloom fail to understand is that our schools are failing large numbers of minority students precisely because too much emphasis is already being placed on trading in on the status of one's cultural capital. Ironically, those students who populate urban settings in places such as New York's Howard Beach, Ozone Park, El Barrio, etc., are likely to learn more about Eastern Europe in contexts designed by *soi-dissant* metropolitan intellectuals than they are about the Harlem Renaissance, Mexico, Africa, the Carribean, or Aztec or Zulu culture. The sad irony is that test scores based on the information filtered from the Western canon and bourgeois cultural capital are used to justify school district and state funding initiatives. The reality of schooling is that U. S. society is comprised of differentially empowered publics and mainstream schooling ensures that those publics already enjoy most of the power and privilege in such a society will continue their advantage for succeeding generations. In this way, intergenerational continuity is ensured: working-class students get working-class jobs; affluent students get the kind of employment that will advantage their life chances and those of their children.

Cultural literacy spokespersons such as E. D. Hirsch have recently reduced literacy to a cultural thesaurus to be memorized by students aspiring to become active, engaged citizens. Yet when culture is despairingly viewed as a storehouse of dead facts, a time capsule of frozen memories detached from historical context, then the concept of difference, when applied to issues of race, class, gender, age, sexual preference, or disability, can be absorbed into what I call "dead pluralism." Dead pluralism is what keeps at bay the need to historicize difference, to recognize the hierarchical production of systems of difference in whose interests such hierarchies serve, and to acknowledge difference as a social construction forged within asymmetrical relations of power, conflicting interests, and a climate of dissent and opposition. The "pluralism" that supposedly already undergirds our so-called multicultural society in the vision of Ravitch and Kimball is one that is based on uncoerced consensus, interracial and intergenerational harmony and zero-degree public unity—a perspective shrouded in the lie of democratic ubiquity. When Ravitch and Kimball call for pluralism over separatism they are really buttressing the status quo against disempowered minorities seeking social justice.

The real danger facing education is not simply the refusal of the general public to recognize its embeddedness in relations of power and privilege at the level of everyday life, but rather the fact that the public prefers to act as if there exists few—or no—such political linkages. The danger is not an apathetic nation, nor a cynical one but rather the ability of the public sphere to exist relatively uncontested. Why? I believe that it has to do with the ability of the larger public sphere to mobilize desire, and secure the passion of the public, and the relative inability of progressive educators to analyze the social, cultural, moral and political implications of such an ability.

Another area of concern that relates to the ability of the schools to create a passive, risk-free citizenry is the ability of schooling to conflate citizenship values based on characteristics of nationhood and Christianity. The question not being asked in the current debate over education in this country is how nationalism and religion work together in debilitating ways to construct racist formations within the wider citizenry. For instance, self-righteous Christians who are making such an issue of curriculum censorship should be confronted by an educational system committed to curricular practices that examine the relationship among religion, nationalism and racism in our schools.

Citing the work of Alan Davies, David Seljak (1991) explores the various ways the figure of Christ has been constructed geopolitically that have had consequences for the way in which certain races have been viewed. For instance, students should be invited to examine The Germanic Christ (a combination of Lutheran pietism, romantic German nationalism and modern pseudo-scientific theories of racial purity and genetic superiority), the Latin Christ of France (a figure that embodies French nationalism, aristocratic resentment against the post-revolutionary bourgeois, classical Catholic anti-Judaism), the Anglo-Saxon Christ of the United Kingdom and Anglo North America (The United States and English Canada) which includes the incarnation of social Darwinism and the Aryan myth, the Afrikaaner Christ (Calvinist categories of double predestination and sphere sovereignty which through distortion came to justify the color dualism and racial segregation of later apartheid ideology). Students should also be invited to examine how the figure of Christ is being reconfigured in Latin America within the theology of liberation as a means of working for the empowerment of oppressed groups. Students should also be invited to examine the role Christianity has placed in the development of homophobia and violence against gays and lesbians (Sears, 1987). Religion plays an important role in the life of Americans and students should be given the opportunity to examine both the enabling and disabling effects of religious ideology in the shaping of future generations.

Needed for the coming decade is a critical pedagogy that is able to provide conditions for students to reject what they experience as a given. A pedagogy that includes a sharpened focus on the relationship among economies of capital investment, political economies, moral economies, economies of 'free' expression, sexual economies, economies of belief and identity formation and the construction of desire and formation of human will. Needed is a pedagogy of discontent and of outrage that is able to contest the hegemony of prevailing definitions of the everyday as the "way things are." A pedagogy that refuses the hidebound distinction between prosaic expression and popular culture, between art and experience, between reason and the imagination. We need a critical pedagogy in our colleges of education that can problematize schooling as a site for the construction of moral, cultural, and national identity, and emphasize the creation of the schooled citizen as a form of emplacement, as a geopolitical construction, as a process in the formation of the geography of cultural desire. Teaching in our schools must be transformed into acts of dissonance and interventions into the ritual inscription of our students into the codes of the dominant culture. It must promote structured refusals to naturalize existing relations of power. And finally, it needs to help create subaltern counterpublics.

Also needed is a curriculum that has as its focus of investigation the study of everyday, informal, and popular culture and how the historical patterns of power that inform such cultures are imbricated in the formation of individual subjectivity and identity. Pedagogy occurs not only in schools but in all cultural sites. The electronic media is perhaps the greatest site of pedagogical production that exists—you could say it is a form of perpetual pedagogy. In addition to understanding literacies applicable to print culture, students need to recognize how their identities are formed and their "mattering maps" produced through an engagement with electronic and other types of media so that they will be able to engage in alternative ways of symbolizing the self and gain a significant purchase on the construction of their own identities and the direction of their desiring. It is in such an investigation that teachers and students become transformed into cultural workers for self and social emancipation. I am calling for a pedagogy of critical media literacy that is linked to what Paul Willis (1990) has referred to a "grounded aesthetics" designed to provide students with the symbolic resources for creative self and social formation in order that they can more critically re-enter the vast, uncharted spaces of common culture.

I am suggesting that students need to make critical judgments about what society might mean, and what is possible or desirable outside existing configurations of power and privilege. Students need to be able to cross over into different zones of cultural diversity and form what Trinh T. Minh-ha (1988) calls hybrid and hyphenated identities in order to rethink the relationship of self to society, of self to other, and for deepening the moral vision of the social order. This raises an important question: How are the categories of race, class, gender, sexual preference shaped within the margins and centers of society, and how can students engage history as a way of reclaiming power and identity? The critical media literacy of which I speak is structured around the notion of a politics of location and identity as border-crossing. It is grounded in the ethical imperative of examining the contradictions in U. S. society between the meaning of freedom, the demands of social justice, and the obligations of citizenship on the one hand, and the structured silence that permeates incidents of suffering in everyday life. The politics of difference that undergirds such a critical literacy is one in which differences rearticulate and shape identity such that students can actively refuse the role of cultural servant and sentinel for the status quo in order to reclaim, reshape, and transform their own historical destiny.

References

Giroux, H. A. & McLaren, P. (1991) "Radical Pedagogy as Cultural Politics", in Donald Morton and Mas'ud Zavarzadeh (Eds.) *Theory/Pedagogy/Politics*, Urbana and Chicago: University of Illinois Press, pp. 152-186.

Gerner, G. (1989/90) "TV vs. Reality", *Adbusters*, *1*, p. 12.

Grossberg, L. (1988) *It's A Sin*, Sydney, Australia: Power Publications.

Hammer, R. & McLaren, P. (1991) "Rethinking the Dialectic", *Educational Theory*, *41*, pp. 23-46.

Hochschild, A. R. (1983) *The Managed Heart*, Berkeley: University of California Press.

Kellner, D. (1990) *Television and the Crisis of Democracy*, Boulder, San Francisco, Oxford: Westview Press.

Kimball, R. (1991) "Tenured Radicals", *The New Criterion*, *9*, pp. 4-13.

Minh-ha, Trinh T. (1988) "Not You/Like You: Post-Colonial Women and the Interlocking Questions of Identity and Difference", *Inscriptions*, *3/4*, pp. 71-77.

McLaren, P., R. Hammer, D. Sholle, and S. Reilly (1995) *Rethinking Media Literacy: A Critical Pedagogy of Representation*, New York: Lang.

Ravitch, D. (1990) "Multiculturalism", *The American Scholar*, *59*, pp. 337-354.

Rogin, M. (1990) "'Make My Day!': Spectacle as Amnesia in Imperial Politics", *Representations*, *29*, pp. 99-123.

Sears, J. T. (1987) "Peering into the Well of Loneliness: The Responsibility of Educators to Gay and Lesbian Youth", in Alex Molnar (Ed.) *Social Issues and Education*, Alexandria, Virginia, Association for Supervision and Curriculum Development.

Seljak, D. (1991) "Alan Davies on Racism", *The Ecumenist*, *29*, pp. 13-14.

Willis, P. (1990) *Common Culture*, Boulder: Westview Press.

Dennis Carlson

If, as Michel Foucault suggests, power and knowledge are inseparable, then curriculum may be studied in terms of the power relations it constitutes and by which it is constituted.[1] Furthermore, since power is always *about* something, that is, always deployed strategically to advance a particular project, the curriculum may be studied as an apparatus of power deployed within educational sites to reconstitute power in some interests rather than others, to advance one social project rather than another. Finally, since curriculum constitutes relations of power, it cannot but artificially be separated from the organization of the schools which structures curriculum use. This all implies that curriculum reform involves much more than merely changing the knowledge that students learn. It also involves changing the way teachers' work is organized and the way schools are organized and operated, and for what purposes.

In what follows I want to examine the discourse and practice of urban school reform over the past several decades—a period Ira Shor has characterized as the "conservative restoration." This examination will focus on the power relations that have shaped the schools and are embedded with the malformation of class, race, and gender oppression.[2] I argue that because reforms have not addressed the roots of crisis in urban schools or countered the inequalities that generate conflict and resistance among various groups, "basic skills" reforms are undermined by their own set of contradictions and crisis tendencies. Finally, such a perspective on the curriculum and urban school crisis directs our attention to the role the schools *might* play in reconstructing power relations consistent with democratic–progressive movements organized around agendas of "equity," "justice," "community," and "workplace democratization." In this regard I conclude with a few comments on the articulation of an alternative, democratic–progressive discourse on urban school reform.

The Conservative, Bureaucratic State Discourse on Urban School Reform

Over the past several decades, a conservative, bureaucratic state discourse has articulated urban school reform around a "basic skills" or "functional literacy" curriculum, performance and output-based program evaluation and instructional objectives, minimum competency testing, and the reorganization of urban school consistent with "effective schools" research findings. Most directly and overtly, the "basic skills" restructuring of urban schools around standardized testing and a skill-based curriculum has been a response to the changing character of work in post-industrial America, and it has participated in the construction of a new post-industrial working class. Prior to the 1960s, major urban school districts had enrolled a heavily white, ethnic, working class student population. General education and vocational programs prepared most of these students for clerical and trade union jobs in manufacturing that were available upon graduation, and a small college preparatory program was available for those who aspired to more. The jobs available to high school graduates in industry were often routine and unrewarding, but they paid relatively high wages and offered some job security. Literacy requirements often took a back seat to manual skills in these jobs, particularly for boys but also for girls. The progressive-era urban school curriculum participated in the pre-skilling and socializing of this industrial working class by teaching students how to cooperate and be "good" workers, and it emphasized manual labor, typing, and home economics skills which were more manual than mental in their orientation.

The changing character of work in post-industrial America was already becoming apparent by the 1960s when business and state leaders began to talk of a growing mismatch between the literacy skills of high school graduates and the literacy requirements of the new jobs in urban areas. Enrollments in vocational education programs and tracks were still relatively high, but graduates of these programs found fewer and fewer jobs waiting for them that required their particular skills.[3] As manufacturing moved to the Second and Third World, the "good" trade union jobs began to disappear, and they have been replaced by clerical, data processing, janitorial, and service industry jobs. The new entry-level jobs increasingly require more in the way of basic reading (word and sentence decoding), comprehension and direction-following skills.[4] Workers frequently have to refer to sets of standard operating procedures and record data on forms or punch it into a computer. They also need to be able to interact with clients and customers and categorize customer data. Thus they need generalizable literacy skills and competencies of a certain minimal level (generally defined at about the 9th grade reading level) that can be put to use and adapted to a number of diverse work settings. As D. W. Livingstone has observed, education for this new, semiskilled labor force

> ... entails instruction in general preparatory skills that are open-ended and can be built upon or refined in a range of work settings. In other words, it means the creation of labor market entrants who will be increasingly technically adaptable and capable of mobility among work settings in response to rapidly changing workplace technologies.[5]

The urban school curriculum, in response to these changes, has been reconceived in terms of the minimal language decoding, comprehension, and processing skills that students "need" to be "effective" workers in the new service industry, maintenance, data processing, and "para-professional" fields. Furthermore, the form of the curriculum, by organizing students' work in terms of direction-following and the routine production of workbook and drillsheet "piecework," orients students to the ways of working that are most typically associated with the new urban working class jobs. Many urban students are enrolled in several remedial basic skills courses to help them pass minimum competency tests, and also are placed in low ability group classes that emphasize basic skills over subject area knowledge.

While the urban school curriculum has been reconstructed by bureaucratic state reform initiatives around "basic skills," urban schools have not, after several decades of reform, been able to achieve even the very limited objective of "certifying" that their students are "functionally literate" by the time they graduate, and they have not been able to keep much more than half of all socioeconomically disadvantaged students in school long enough to graduate. In 1989, it was still possible for the New

York Times to warn of an "impending U. S. jobs 'disaster' with a "work force unqualified to work" and with "schools lagging far behind needs of employees."[6] Like the Vietnam War and the "war on poverty," the war on illiteracy and the drop-out problem in urban schools has become bogged down, and it offers no light at the end of the tunnel.

Why is it that corporate and state reform initiatives in urban education have not been more successful in ensuring that socioeconomically disadvantaged students learn the literacy skills the "need" for gainful employment in the new working class? Several factors need to be considered. First, because the basic skills curriculum is highly rationalized and regimented, it contributes to student motivation problems rather than improves them. As more and more students are enrolled in basic skills courses, where instruction is organized around routine drillsheet and workbook, "seatwork" and rounds of standardized pre- and post-testing, teachers may have to lower work demands on students even more in order to reduce conflict and keep students from dropping out. Second, not only is a "basic skills" curriculum lacking in intrinsic motivation, it fails to hold out much for urban students once they leave school. Students are exhorted to stay in school, work hard to pass minimum competency tests, graduate, and then have a chance at one of the new service industry or data processing jobs that are available to urban high school graduates. However, the new working class jobs are low paying with little room for advancement, they offer little in the way of job security or health benefits, and workers may have to work six or more hours a week at various jobs merely to maintain their families above the poverty line. Subsistence on public welfare may seem a better option that works for many who face the prospect of entry into this working world, and for welfare subsidence a high school diploma is not required. Given the growing disparities of wealth and power in America, with fewer "good" jobs available, it may become increasingly difficult to "sell" a "basic skills" education to urban students in the years ahead.

To this point, I have limited my comments to an analysis of the urban school crisis and curriculum reform that relies upon a political economic and class theory of schooling. However, urban school reform also has participated in racial power relations and dynamics in ways that are related to class but have a somewhat independent development. Racial minorities were in the 1960s reclaiming America's inner cities, and traditional white working class and middle class neighborhoods were disappearing at a rapid rate as suburbanization accelerated. To some extent racial minorities were drawn to urban areas by the new service industry and jobs which many working class white males refused (at first) to take. Minorities had been effectively excluded from the trade union movement throughout the 1950s and white working class males continued in the 1960s to enjoy a relatively privileged status, although that status was threatened as the "good" unionized, industrial jobs began to disappear very quickly in the 1970s. The new post-industrial working class thus was initially constituted along heavily racial lines, and many new low-skill and semi-skilled jobs were readily available to minorities in urban areas. Aside from economic considerations, African American and Hispanic people were drawn to America's major urban areas because they were seeking "space" within a highly oppressive society—space to assume control of their own institutions, and thus reclaim those institutions from the control of a repressive white power structure.[7] The hope was that once minority peoples became an electoral majority within a given geographical space, they could use their power to make public institutions serve new emancipatory purposes by empowering minority communities.

The state-sponsored "basic skills" reform movement, in these terms, has had the effect of overriding local control of the schools at a time when poor African American and Hispanic peoples were becoming the numerical majority in urban America. State-mandated minimum competency testing, all of the bureaucratic regulations associated with "aligning" the urban school curriculum with the new basic skills test, the growing financial dependency of urban schools on the state (resulting from chronic fiscal crisis in urban America and particularly in urban schools), and the growing threat of a direct state takeover of "failing" urban school districts have had the effect countering efforts by African American and Hispanic communities to "reclaim" urban schools. The local school board members, superintendent, and other local school leaders may be minorities, but so long as urban schools have to teach to the state test and adhere to a myriad of state funding guidelines and procedures, local or community control of urban schools is more formal than substantive or real. To challenge these curricular and educational power relations, African American and Hispanic groups will need to move beyond formal democratic control of local school boards to reclaim involvement in substantive rather than merely technical educational decisions, and this implies challenging the "basic skills" model of bureaucratic state control.

Finally, the conservative, bureaucratic state discourse on "basic skills" and urban school reform participates in gender power relations in the school. Most obviously, basic skills curricular reforms have taken for granted a bureaucratic and hierarchical chain of command in urban schools that rigidly subordinates women teachers (particularly elementary teachers) to male administrators. However, it is not merely a case of individual male administrators dominating individual female teachers. Even when women have been "promoted" from the corps of teachers to the ranks of administrators, it has generally been because they have learned how to speak a patriarchal discourse that is taken as the norm—a phenomenon that might be referred to as the "Thatcherising of women administrators.[8] It is this patriarchal discourse that is involved in the construction of the dominant models of school reform. As Michael Apple observes:

> The very program of rationalizing all important social relations in our major institutions is, in fact, pre-eminently a masculine discourse . . . Such a hierarchical conception is not neutral. It disenfranchises alternative concerns for human relations, connectedness, and care.[9]

In education, the "teacher-proofing" of the curriculum, which has been advanced through "basic skills" reforms, also has been based on the masculine presumptions that teachers are not intelligent or intellectual enough to be seriously involved in important curricular decisions, that they need to be told exactly what to do, and that they prefer leaving important decisions to administrators.[10] Basic skills reforms have also been consistent with a patriarchal structuring of power relations in education because they take for granted a rigid bifurcation of administrative and teaching roles within an asymmetrical power relationship, and because they privilege a technical rather than discursive or dialectic rationality. Consequently, teacher support for "whole language," "cooperative learning," and other progressive approaches to curriculum and instruction that hopefully return power to teachers and students to construct the curriculum through discourse, practice, and self-reflection, represent a threat to continued patriarchal hegemony in the discourse on urban school reform. In the meantime, teachers' lack of support for performance-based "teach to the test" approaches to basic skills instruction undermines the effectiveness of top-down reforms.

I have suggested some of the ways that urban school reform during the basic skills era has served to organize class, race, and gender power relations in urban schools in highly inequitable ways. The increased centralization, bureaucratization, and rationalization of curriculum and instructional decision-making has not, consequently, been a "neutral phenomenon." However, while state officials have been relatively successful in "selling" or legitimating a basic skills reform agenda by appealing to broad public support for high standards and more "accountability" in education, the conservative reform agenda has not solved or even ameliorated the basic problems that beset urban schools.

Toward a Democratic-Progressive Discourse on Urban School Reform

Over the past several decades of the "conservative restoration," progressive opposition to the bureaucratic state reform discourse has remained largely fragmented and politically marginalized. Liberal groups have exerted some influence on policy-thinking, but little on actual policy-making. Liberal discourse has advanced concerns over "equity" and "excellence," supported a curriculum organized around "higher order" literacy skills, a college preparatory curriculum for all students, emphasized the need to professionalize teachers rather than deskill them, personalize instruction rather than regiment it, and called for a decentralization and de-bureaucratization of authority through some form of "site-based management."[11] These have been important concerns, and they provide some basis for struggle in response to concrete reform proposals sponsored by the conservative, bureaucratic state. However, for a number of reasons liberalism has failed to "deliver" fully on its promises, even when liberal politicians have gained control of the state, and this has to do with a failure to take on certain "hard" questions about whose interests are served by the current system of structured inequalities and what it will take to fundamentally change the way power is arranged and distributed in schools.[12] In moving beyond these limitations in liberal discourse, without abandoning its insights, let me briefly suggest several elements of a democratic-progressive discourse in education that help us better address the crisis in urban schools and reconceptualize urban school reform in ways that move beyond the current impasse.

First, while a democratic-progressive discourse would move beyond a "human capital" or economically functional analysis of the curriculum, with its presumption that what is learned in schools must bear a rather direct functional relationship to current economic "needs," it would not completely reject economic or workplace considerations in curriculum decision-making. On the contrary, some relationship *should* exist between school work and work in other important institutional sites in society, since education serves to initiate individuals into the "productive" work of building culture and objectifying experience in useful ways. Marx argued that people make themselves and culture through work: "What they [humans] are, therefore, coincides with their production, both with *what* they produce and with *how* they produce."[13] This suggests the importance of preparing students with the discursive skills and capacities associated with non-alienating, self-enhancing, productive work within the context of the democratization of the workplace.[14]

Second, while the conservative state discourse has organized a discussion of the urban school curriculum around the notion of "functional literacy," and while the liberal discourse has emphasized "higher order" literacy skills (generally corresponding to the higher rungs of Bloom's taxonomy), a democratic-progressive discourse would reconceptualize the curriculum around notions of "critical literacy." This latter notion suggests a capacity for discursive reflection on one's own identity formation with a culture characterized by struggle and change along a number of axes, including class, gender, race, sexuality, etc.[15] In urban schools, students need to learn how to critique the discourses and practices that keep them subordinated and reflect on their own role in the social construction of inequalities. For teachers, critical literacy education implies a reconceptualization of the pedagogic roles. Henry Giroux writes that teachers need "to undertake social criticism not as outsiders but as public intellectuals who address the social and political issues of their neighborhood, their nation, and the wider global world."[16] They must engage themselves, as well, in the struggles of their students to articulate their own voices and construct identities.

Third, beyond a reconceptualization of students' work, and in order to make such a reconceptualization possible, a democratic-progressive discourse would imply a restructuring of teachers' work and the organization of the school consistent with workplace democratization. This would imply drastic changes in the way schools are organized and how educational decisions are made that shifts substantive decision-making power from bureaucratic state officials to local communities, schools, and classrooms. Workplace democratization may be consistent with some aspects of "site-based management." however, it goes beyond most such plans in that it advances a real democratization of decision-making in urban schools and communities rather than merely bureaucratic decentralization of authority within a system that continues to be overwhelmingly under the control of bureaucratic state and central office officials.

Finally, a democratic-progressive discourse would focus our attention on the need to link-up educational theory and practice with social and cultural movements. Social movements involve a collective rearticulation and reappropriation of cultural meanings and values in advancing particular agendas for changing the distribution and use of power in society. They arise out of contradictions within existing power relations and institutional structures and offer a way of moving beyond current crisis tendencies. To ward off crisis, dominant groups in education have become quite adept at crisis management and "muddling through" from one crisis to another. However, should the various groups which have been disempowered by basic skills reforms (in ways that are related to their class, gender, and race) articulate their different concerns as part of a common movement to challenge bureaucratic state discourse and practice in education, it might yet become possible to build a new democratic-progressive "voice" and movement for change that looks beyond crisis management and mismanagement towards crisis resolution.

Notes

1. Foucault, M. (1980). *Power/Knowledge: Selected Interviews and Other Writings, 1972-1977*. In Colin Gordon (ed.). New York: Pantheon Books.

2. Shor, I. (1986) *Culture Wars: School and Society in the Conservative Restoration, 1969-1984*. Boston: Routledge & Kegan Paul.

3. Gray, K. (1991, November 6) "Vocational education in high school: A modern phoenix?" *Phi Delta Kappan, 72*, pp. 437-445.

4. Levin, H. & Rumberger, R. (1986) *Educational Requirements for New Technologies*. Palo Alto: Stanford Center for Educational Research.

5. Livingstone, D. W. (1985, January) "Class, educational ideologies, and mass opinion in capitalist crisis." *Sociology of Education, 58*, p. 8.

6. Fiske, E. (1989, September 25) "Impending U. S. jobs 'disaster': work force unqualified to work." *New York Times*, p. 1+.

7. Lefebvre, H. (1979) For Henri Lefebvre, spatial conflict entails the appropriation of space by marginalized groups from its capitalist spatial organization see "Space: social product and use value." In J. W. Freiberg (ed.). *Critical Sociology: European Perspectives*, p. 293. New York: Irvington Publications.

8. Blackmore, J. (1989) "Educational leadership: A feminist critique and reconstruction." In J. Smyth (ed.). *Critical Perspectives in Educational Leadership*. New York: Falmer Press.

9. Apple, M. (1986) *Teachers and Texts: A Political Economy of Class and Gender Relations in Education*, p. 142. New York: Routledge & Kegan Paul.

10. Freedman, S. (1988) "Teaching, gender, and curriculum." In L. Beyer & M. Apple (eds.). *The Curriculum: Problems, Politics, and Possibilities*, pp. 204-218. Albany: SUNY Press.

11. As examples of the liberal discourse in education see:
    The Carnegie Foundation for the Advancement of Teaching Reports (1986) *A Nation Prepared: Teachers for the 21st Century*. New York: Carnegie Forum Task Force on Teaching as a Profession.
    The Carnegie Foundation for the Advancement of Teaching Reports (1988) *An Imperiled Generation: Saving Urban Schools*. Lawrenceville, NJ: Princeton University Press.
    Sizer, T. (1984) *Hoarce's Compromise: The Dilemma of the American High School*. Boston: Houghton-Mifflin.

12. Grubb, W. N. & Lazerson, M. (1988) *Broken Promises: How Americans Fail Their Children*. Chicago: University of Chicago Press. Gintis, H. & Bowles, S. (1988) "Contradiction and reproduction in educational theory." In M. Cole (ed.). *Bowles and Gintis Revisited: Correspondence and Contradiction in Educational Theory*, pp. 16-32. New York: Falmer.

13. Marx, K. & Engels, F. (1974) *The German Ideology, Part One*, p. 42. New York: International Publishers.

14. Davis, E. & Lansbury, R. (1986) "Democracy and control in the workplace: An introduction." In Davis & Lansbury (eds.). *Democracy and Control in the Workplace*, pp. 1-29. Melbourne, Australia: Longman Cheshire. Shuler, T. (1985) *Democracy at Work*. New York: Oxford University Press.

15. McLaren, P. & Lankshear, C. (eds.). (Upcoming) *Critical Literacy*. Albany: SUNY Press.

16. Giroux, H. (1990) "Rethinking the boundaries of educational discourse: Modernism, postmodernism, and feminism." *College Literature*, 17 (2/3), p. 42.

Chapter XIII

Educational Visions: What are schools for and what should we be doing in the name of education?

Henry A. Giroux

Maxine Greene

Henry A. Giroux

American public education is in crisis. It is not an isolated crisis affecting a specific aspect of American society; it is a crisis that is implicated in and produced by a transformation in the very nature of democracy itself. This is not without a certain irony. As a number of countries in Europe and elsewhere move haltingly toward greater forms of democracy, the United States presents itself as the prototype for such reforms and leads the American people to believe that democracy in the United States has reached its ultimate form. The emptiness of this type of analyses is best revealed by the failure of the American public to actively participate in the election of its own government officials, to address the growing illiteracy rates among the general population, and to challenge the increasing view that social criticism and social change are irrelevant to the meaning of American democracy. But the failure of formal democracy is most evident in the refusal of the American government and general population to view public schooling as fundamental to the life of a critical democracy. At stake here is the refusal to grant public schooling a significant role in the ongoing process of educating people to be active and critical citizens capable of fighting for and reconstructing democratic public life.

The struggle over public schools cannot be separated from the social problems currently facing this society. These problems are not only political in nature but are pedagogical as well. That is, whenever power and knowledge come together, politics not only function to position people differently with respect to the access of wealth and power, it also provides the conditions for the production and acquisition of learning; put another way, it offers people opportunities to take up and reflect on the conditions that shape themselves and their relationship with others. The pedagogical in this sense is about the production of meaning and the primacy of the ethical and the political as a fundamental part of this process. This means that any discussion of public schooling has to address the political, economic, and social realities that construct the contexts that shape it as an institution and the conditions that produce its diverse population of students. This perspective suggests making visible the social problems and conditions that affect those students who are at risk in our socicty while recognizing that such problems need to be addressed in both pedagogical and political terms, inside and outside of the schools.

Existing social and economic problems do not augur well for either the fate of public schooling or the credibility of the discourse of democracy itself as it is currently practiced in the United States. For example, it has been estimated that nearly 20% of all children under the age of 18 live below the poverty line. In fact, the United States ranks first among the industrialized nations in child poverty; similarly, besides South Africa, the United States is the only industrialized country that does not provide universal health care for children and pregnant women. Moreover, the division of wealth is getting worse with the poor getting poorer while the rich are getting richer. In fact, the division of wealth was wider in 1988 than at any other time since 1947. As Sally Reed and Craig Sautter (1990) have pointed out: "the poorest 20% of families received less than 5% of the national income, while the wealthiest 20% received 44% ... 1% of families own 42% of the net wealth of all U. S. families" (p. K5). At the same time, it is important to note that neoconservative attempts to dismantle public schooling in this country during the last decade have manifested themselves not only in the call for vouchers, the development of school policy based on the market logic of choice, and attacks on education for cultural diversity, but also in the ruthless cutbacks that have affected those most dependent on the public schools, i. e., the poor, people of color, minorities, the working class, and other subordinate groups. The Reagan "commitment" to education and the underprivileged manifested itself shamefully in policies noted for slashing federal funds to important programs such as Aid to Families with Dependent Children, drastically reducing federal funding for low income housing and, in general, cutting over 10 million dollars from programs designed to aid the poor, homeless, and the hungry. At the same time the Reagan government pushed the cost of military spending up to $1.9 trillion dollars. The Clinton administration has done little to reverse this trend.

Within this perspective, the discourse of democracy was reduced to conflating patriotism with the cold war ideology of military preparedness, and the notion of the public good was abstracted from the principles of justice and equality in favor of an infatuation with individual achievement. Greed became respectable in the 1980s while notions of community and democratic struggle were either ignored or seen as subversive. Absent from the neo-conservative public philosophy of the 1980s was any notion of democracy that took seriously the importance of developing a citizenry which could think critically, struggle against social injustices, and develop relations of community based on the principles of equality, freedom, and justice. In the 1990s, questions concerning democracy have been subordinated to work-related goals for training students for the workplace. This should not suggest that as educational and cultural workers we have nothing to do but wallow in despair. On the contrary, as part of the struggle to reclaim schools as agencies of critical citizenship and democratic public life, educators need to develop a new language of critique and possibility. In what follows, I want to suggest four developments such a language might take as part of a project of linking the struggle over schools to a project of radical democracy.

Reclaiming Democracy: The Missing Language of Schooling

The problems facing secondary schools in the United States need to be reformulated as a crisis in citizenship and ethics. This suggests that the solution to these problems lies ultimately in the realms of values and politics, not in the realm of management or economics. Schooling is about the production of citizens and the responsibilities of citizenship represents an ethical compact that makes primary the language of community, solidarity, and the public good. Education for democracy cannot be reduced, as some politicians have suggested, to forcing students to say the pledge of allegiance, developing good work habits, or measuring citizenship competencies through standardized cultural literacy tests. Instead, educational reformers concerned with ethics and schooling need to address more fundamental concerns of purpose and meaning such as those implied in the questions: What kind of citizens do we hope to produce through public education? What kind of society do we want to create?

If educators are to take the relationship between schooling and democracy seriously, this means organizing school life around a version of citizenship that educates students to make choices, think critically, and believe they can make a difference. It also means that educators need to affirm and critically interrogate the knowledge and experiences that students bring with them to the classroom; at the very least this means that educators need to affirm the voices, histories, and stories that provide students with a sense of place, identity, and meaning. In addition, critical educators need to offer students the opportunity to engage in a deeper understanding of the importance of democratic culture while developing classroom relations that prioritize the importance of cooperation, sharing, and social justice. The primary purpose of schooling is neither commercial nor chauvanistic; we must reject the current conservative call to make schools adjuncts of the corporation–bastions of Eurocentricism. Progressives all across the country must reclaim the importance of educating all students with the knowledge, skills, and values they will need in a democracy for the responsibilities of learning how to govern. This means organizing curricula in ways that enable students to make judgments about how society is historically and socially constructed, how existing social relations are implicated in relations of equality and justice as well as how they structure inequalities around racism, sexism, and other forms of oppression. It also means offering students the possibilities for being able to make judgments about what society might be, what is possible or desirable outside existing configurations of power.

Schooling and the Politics of Difference

Students need more than work skills and information about society, they also need to be able to critically assess dominant and subordinate traditions so as to engage their strengths and weakness. What they don't need is to treat history as a closed, singular narrative that simply has to be revered and memorized. Educating for democracy and ethical responsibility is not about creating passive citizens. It is about providing teachers and students with the capacities and opportunities to be noisy, irreverent, and vibrant. Such capacities are essential for creating the conditions necessary for dialogue, respect, and compassion to emerge as the organizing principles necessary for sustaining a democratic society. Central to this concern is the need for students to understand how cultural, ethnic, racial, and ideological differences enhance the possibility for dialogue, trust, and solidarity. Difference must be analyzed and constructed within pedagogical contexts that promote compassion and tolerance rather than envy, hatred, and bigotry. The pedagogical imperative at work here is one that demands opportunities for students to be border crossers. That is, educators need to offer students the opportunities to explore cultural difference in historical and contextual terms that open up rather than shut down partiality, possibilities, and dialogue. As border crossers, students must engage knowledge as citizens of the world. Hence, they must be provided with pedagogical opportunities to engage the multiple references that construct different cultural codes, experiences, and histories. In this context, such a pedagogy offers students the opportunity to rewrite the discourse of diversity and difference through the process of crossing over into cultural zones that provide a critical resource for rethinking how the relations between dominant and subordinate groups are organized, how they are implicated and placed in relationships often structured in dominance, and what should be changed in such relations in order to promote a democratic and just society. Difference in this case does not become a marker for deficit, inferiority, chauvinism, or inequality; on the contrary, it opens the possibilities for constructing pedagogical practices that deepen the project of a critical democracy. Rather than precluding the possibility for broader forms of solidarity among different groups, a pedagogy and politics of cultural difference can be forged in social relations rooted in compassion, trust, and generosity. As such, difference becomes the basis for developing a broader discourse of cultural citizenship. In this case, difference does not become the basis for competition, but for organizing forms of cultural democracy that serve to enlarge our moral vision.

Reclaiming the Radical Responsibility of Ethics

At the same time it is important to acknowledge that the radical responsibility of progressive educators necessitates an ongoing analyses by students of the contradictions in American society between the meaning of freedom, the demands of social justice, the obligations of citizenship and the accumulated suffering, domination, force, and violence that permeates various aspects of everyday life. In part, this suggests acknowledging that the failure of ethical discourse in our schools is rooted, in part, in viewing learning and values as merely abstract and procedural problems. The crisis in ethics is not about relativism; students are constantly subjected in mass society to the moral discourses of individualism, consumerism, and violence. What is at stake is recognizing how one is shaped within ethical forms of addresses and what the implications in terms of practice mean for violating or enhancing the quality of public life.

Educators need to insert a concern for the concrete and social back into the language of ethics. That is, moral education should be grounded in forms of learning that arise out of specific relations that connect the principles and practices of classroom life with the concrete struggles that inform community life and the dynamics of the wider society. Students should be provided with opportunities to link classroom learning with social projects that allow them to read, listen, and see the histories, stories, experiences and pains of those who are excluded from the benefits of American society by virtue of their race, class, gender, or age. By being given the opportunity through school projects to address fundamental inequalities in their communities and the wider society, students can begin to distance themselves from being implicated in power relations that are oppressive. But moral discourse as it is being formulated here is not based on simply the refusal to engage in relations structured in domination, or on the passive learning of particular rights, but on an active and discriminating participation in democratic public life. I will conclude by taking up this issue in more detail.

Recognizing democracy as a moral ideal implies an ongoing struggle to reconstruct human experience in the realization of such principles as freedom, liberty, and fraternity. Within this context, learning must be grounded in the ethical imperative to both challenge the prevailing social order while simultaneously providing the basis for students to deepen the intellectual, civic, and moral understanding of their role as agents of public formation. At one level, this means that the school curriculum must be more attentive to the issues, problems, and histories that construct the experiences of their students and the political and moral density of everyday life. At another level, this suggests that schools need to reconstruct their relations with the communities that they allegedly serve. Schools need to reach out into these communities and learn about their traditions and struggles, share power with the parents who live in them, and use their resources to empower not only dominant members of the community but also those individuals and groups that are generally excluded from school life. Progressives need to situate the meaning and purpose of schooling within a broader theory of social welfare and cultural democracy. At the very least, this means that educators can work to insert the idea of the public back into schooling and in doing so be able to defend their responsibilities as public servants by referencing and critically engaging the principles that shape their view of schooling and society *within* rather than outside of the principles and practices of a critical democracy.

Teachers as Public Intellectuals

Teachers and other cultural workers need to redefine their roles as engaged and transformative intellectuals. In opposition to dominant views of teaching defined through accountability schemes that deskill teachers while simultaneously reducing them to the status of clerks and technicians, progressives need to reclaim the role of teachers put forth by John Dewey, C. Wright Mills, Paulo Freire, Miles Horton, Maxine Greene and others. In this view teachers are seen as engaged and transformative intellectuals who combine vision, conception, and practice. This suggests providing teachers with the conditions they need to produce curricula, work productively with outside social agencies and community people, and exercise a notion of leadership that combines a discourse of hope with forms of self and social criticism. Teachers and other cultural workers dedicated to reforming all spheres of educating as part of a wider revitalization of public life need to raise important questions regarding the relationship among knowledge and power, learning and possibility, social criticism and human dignity, and how these might be understood in relation to rather than in isolation from those practices of domination, privilege, and resistance at work in the larger society. This is essentially a question of not only what people know but also how they come to know in a particular way within the contexts and constraints of specific social and cultural practices. Teachers need to become bearers of public intellectuals and engaged critics capable of resurrecting traditions and memories that provide new ways of reading history and reclaiming power and identity in the new interests of creating a democratic society that affirms difference, justice, equality, and freedom. Not only does this suggest that educators develop a vision that enables rather than dismantles the possibility for critical citizenship, it also suggests that educators make connections with other cultural workers in order to form alliances, create critical public cultures, and collectively struggle for work conditions which enable them to function and engage as principled educators.

The struggle for democracy is never over, and the complacency and indifference to the language of democracy as it is often expressed in the United States signals an important reason for educators to once again reclaim the language of schooling as an ethical and political imperative. If democracy is not to fall victim to a growing ethnocentricism, individualism, and consumerism, at the very least educators and others can work together to develop a political and ethical discourse that provides a rationale for students and others to comprehend democracy as a way of life that consistently has to be fought for, struggled over, and rewritten as part of the practice of critical citizenship.

References

Reed, S. & Sautter, C. (1990, June). "Children of Poverty: The Status of 12 Million Young Americans," *Phi Delta Kappan*, pp. K1-K11.

Maxine Greene

Education, as both concept and undertaking, is in continuing tension with the institutions called schools. Education, after all, has to do with engaging live human beings in activities of meaning-making, dialogue, and reflective understanding of a variety of texts, including the texts of their social realities. Growing, becoming different, becoming informed and articulate: all these are involved in the project called education, a project that must be chosen by persons intentionally and cooperatively involved in learning to learn. Schools, speaking largely a transitive language, were established to work upon the young from without, to shape the raw material of human nature (as Horace Mann saw it) into the forms required by a society caught in material pursuits, divided by class and gender and color boundaries, fragmented in commitments to values and to faith. Control was demanded, along with what was called "voluntary compliance" with the laws of righteousness and with (illegible though it often was) the dominant ideology. That meant agreement with meritocratic arrangements; it meant stratifications even in classrooms. For a long time, there was a general acquiescence with hierarchy and distinction because of the promises continually offered: promises of equity, upward mobility, a chance at pecuniary success. Immigrant parents, poor parents, dislocated parents could not but accept the goal of accommodating to market demand.

There were, of course, signs of alienation from the beginning, stirrings of discontent. Not all were specifically oriented to schooling; but many, like the critiques of the socialist Robert Owen and Frances Wright, or of the Catholic reformer Orestes Brownson, struck directly at those dimensions of the system the common school was invented to serve. We might say the same of some of the great Black leaders like Frederick Douglass, Sojourner Truth, and Dr. W. E. B. Dubois. We might summon up the voices as well as of women protesting subordination and exclusion within and outside society's dominant institutions. Out of these and other articulations of discontent, like many of those that followed after in the 20th century, we might work

forward to an educational vision appropriate to a nation so
poorly served by the metanarratives of progress, so entangled
in its own myths at a moment of erosion and decline.

Avoiding both functionalism and determinism, we see
schools defining themselves variously in different regions of the
country and, indeed, in different localities. Schools in homoge-
neous communities (in the Cumberland mountains, in the
midwestern prairies, on lake shores and northern peninsulas)
are likely to transmit the codes and value patterns that have sus-
tained particular groups sometimes over generations. What
Pierre Bourdieu calls "cultural reproduction" has taken place in
such schools, sometimes on the basis of a shared investment in
"cultural capital," on the model of the early common schools.
Factory closings, failures on the farms, the impacts of technology, the effects of media and popular culture have often created
great gulfs between what the schools believed they were "for"
and what changing communities required if they were to survive. Mark Twain's steamboat plowing down the river in *The
Adventures of Huckleberry Finn* still provides a fitting metaphor
for what happened and what is happening today. Huck and Jim,
having been swept south by the current, are waiting for the fog
to lift when they hear the steamboat pounding along. "She
aimed right for us," says Huck. "Often they do that and try to
see how close they can come without touching; sometimes the
wheel bites off a sweep, and then the pilot sticks his head out
and laughs, and thinks he's might smart." In all that indifference and impersonality, with her furnaces blazing and her
steam whistling, "and as Jim went overboard on one side and I
on the other, she came smashing right through the raft." It is
not only the violence and carelessness of technology that has
overwhelmed the face-to-face community represented by Jim
and Huck. It is the lack of anything like an empowering education that renders them so powerless once they reach the river
banks, so vulnerable to hypocrisy and mystification and greed.
Huck has been taught the skills and pieties of a slave society in
school. He has felt "cramp'd up" by it all, perhaps especially by
the norms of a society that sold children away from their mothers, decorated houses with genteel sentimental sketches,
allowed gun-toting landowners to listen to sermons on broth-

erly love on Sundays across the land. But he has not been helped to interpret in such a fashion that would bring him in contact with a community of restless ones, those trying to transform. At the end, he refuses to be "sivilized"; and he can only "light out for the territory ahead," territory long closed. Still, there is a vision in the making, as we shall see, a kind of vision that might lead to the enfranchisement of boys and girls like Huck, a trust in the meanings to which they give voice, the shaping of a critical community.

Huck has, to a degree, been schooled and been miseducated by what he could bear to learn. There are other examples in the 19th century literature: Herman Melville's Bartleby who could not cope with a walled-in, commercial society where free choices were inefficient and unacceptable. He could only survive (at least for a while) by repeating "I prefer not to," by becoming a living negation of what schools were intended for—and with no recourse but death. His employer, whose story it is, experiences a moment of fraternity; but, in the midst of the bustling city, in the law offices of Wall Street, he can find only lifelessness and barriers. There is Edith Wharton's Lily Bart, schooled perhaps, but ending with the feeling of being a mere cog in a machine or "of being swept like a stray uprooted growth down the heedless current of the years." Here, too, there is the intimation of a vision. Lily, "rootless and ephemeral, mere spindrift of the whirling surface of existence, without anything to which the poor little tentacles of self could cling. . . And as she looked back she saw that there had never been a time when she had had any real relation to life." She has lived from house party to house party, bridge game to bridge game, loan to loan in a burgeoning New York; and nothing binds her to "the mighty sum of human striving." So is it with Edna Pontellier in Kate Chopin's *The Awakening*, another woman schooled to passivity and thoughtlessness, caught (she is convinced) between the "soul's slavery" of domesticity and a future of promiscuity. In some terrible way fixated, she swims out to sea with images of her far-off childhood in mind, all future possibilities closed.

The stories in and out of imaginative literature are multiple: stories of schooling standing in the way of educating, of critical consciousness, of legitimate awakenings. Of course, for those sometimes called the "fortunate fifth," for suburban children and wealthy children, the schools have built upon the cultural capital brought in by the students. They have used the invest- ment to produce the inventors and discoverers and bankers and superintendents and military men even Horace Mann had seen emerging from the schools. The irony has been that resources made available to suburban and exurban schools have allowed them to institute enriched curricula, interdisciplinary studies, arts and humanities experiences. Here, too, school people have felt themselves able to "afford" an encouragement of critical thinking, problem-solving, field work of various kinds. Here, where a tracking system reaches a kind of grim apotheo- sis, schooling and educating now and then mesh.

In the declining cities, where calls for equality contest with calls for more child-centering in the schools, where structural disintegration threatens the very survival of the young, efforts to restructure by involving more of those affected in the schools themselves now and then become educative in the deepest sense. Parental involvement, "family groups" within the schools, outreaches into community, journal keeping and field research, bilingual experiences, experiential learning: all become indica- tions of what can be done and should be done if we are serious about educating the young. They open towards possibility, in fact, because they ground learning in situated life. They release the young to tell their stories, to "name" the world they hope to transform. This occurs, as is well known, in the Foxfire schools, in Central Park East in New York City, in various schools repre- sented by the "network" for democratic education. Whether or note they depend upon tests to determine their "success," they nonetheless offer evidence that committed people working in small communities can make schools habitable, stimulating, sus- taining—and sometimes resistant to a society that too obviously does not care.

The signs point to a lack of care where poor and minority children are concerned, as does the erosion of financial support since the beginnings of the Reagan administration. The Rea- ganite stress on deregulation, privatization, uniform standards, and technical norms had, it turned out, an almost immediate and malign effect on schools. The so-called "reform" reports, beginning to emerge in 1983 and following after a period of shallow preoccupation with behavioral objectives, competencies, and the rest, focused on measurable achievement. More often than not, the inability to achieve, or to show evidence of "higher cognitive skills," was blamed upon the child, usually the poor child or the child's family. She/he was not read to; not enough time was spent on homework; American youth lacked "background knowledge," there was insufficient "cultural literacy."

The decade saw a convergence of end-of-the-world warnings of a decline in technological dominance and economic competitiveness with laments about what 17-years old did not know, what teachers could not do on their own, what relativism and immorality and banality were doing to national greatness and national pride. The young were repeatedly spoken of as human "resources," with obvious implications that they were to be grist for the market, for the nation's technocratic mills. It was made clear enough in a number of the reports that those who could not master the skills required, those who could not adjust to the new technologies could not expect to be supported by public funds. Little mention was made of the fact that the actual future for thousands of the young was to be found in the service industries, in places where the deskilling process was at work, as in hamburger shops and supermarkets. Not expected to use their capacities or to develop new potentialities in a society where energies were to run down narrower and narrower channels, they were scarcely thought of as *persons* to be educated. When the Department of Education issued a monograph called "What Works" early on in the decade, presumably showing what research was contributing to education of the young, they left a general impression of the most sterile pragmatism. Incurious about the newcomers in society, disinterested in the suppressed talents and energies distributed through the country, obsessed by the raw-edged individualism associated with *laissez-faire*, federal bureaucrats and certain academics came together to fashion a myth about a rejected golden age. Below the surface of what they were doing and saying was a call for a conformist, untroubled, unquestioning, stratified society. People would be lulled by the media into becoming passive audiences while they were being attacked for what they did not know. Their own stories, their own meaning structures would be scorned and set aside, as education was reread to mean a return to some absolute, to a realm accessible mainly to the well-to-do.

The great popularity of books like Hirsch's *Cultural Literacy* and Bloom's *The Closing of the American Mind* is not to be attributed to any conspiracy. Hirsch's book speaks out of a conservative dread of fragmentation in what was never the kind of "language community" Hirsch speaks of preserving. Moreover, the discrete pieces of information that compose the "knowledge" ostensibly necessary for any kind of "excellence" in this country are arbitrarily selected from what seems to be an objectively existent body of concepts and facts. Calling for an emphasis on content (officially selected), oversimplifying and actually distorting the work of Rousseau and Dewey in order to condemn and emphasis on "process," Hirsch offers a kind of reassurance to those troubled by the profound changes in our culture. Not only does there exist a dependable body of knowledge, he says; we can overcome the great rifts and uncertainties in our society by identifying a specific content and thereby make sure that the young are equipped for the economic demands of the "modern" world.

Bloom, in contrast, is mainly concerned with elite young people. They become the exemplars for him of what is happening in a society he believes is being corrupted by feminism, rock music, the persisting spirit of the Sixties, and German philosophy. Challenging all that along with banality and lack of commitment, he asks even the humblest among us to look upwards, to fasten our small wagons to a Platonist star, to a universal notion of the Good (not to speak of the True and Beautiful). Diversity, perspective, situatedness, plurality: all are cancelled out by this elementary kind of classicism that appeals so much to those who are fearful of youth, of the new music, of racial harmony, of questioning and unrest.

These books and many other books and articles following in their wake are today focusing on the evils of "multiculturalism," on changes being made in the traditionally male and Eurocentric canon. Moreover, they have invented a new scare term called "P.C." which is being used to silence increasing numbers of people and keep others in their places. The initials stand for "politically correct," now attached to what is called a posture of indoctrination and intolerance on the part of a radical few. Unfortunately (and significantly) those working to make "P.C." a cure for relativism and radicalism and multiplicity are beginning to focus on far more than inclusion in the curricula, the introduction of Women's Studies and Black Studies, the rewriting and reconsideration of texts. On some level in tune with those who intend to make the schools more than ever before training grounds for the "Deltas" who will presumably make up the majority in the post-industrial society, these conservatives try to cloak themselves in the mantle of esoteric, almost priestly scholars. They present themselves as guards of the House of Intellect against the barbarians in the garden. Never have the engines of economic power installed themselves so shamelessly and obviously in the inner halls of that House. The irony, of course, is that the House is ancient and probably sinking into the ground. Here and there, the sunlight hits a window-pane, or a branch strikes against a sagging door. It may be ready to be brought to a new life if the need and restlessness of this country can be recognized again, if enough people have the courage to ask themselves what they should be doing in the name of education.

Pursuing a vision, deeply aware of the war just ended, the war that scars everyone of us, I can only think of what education should be in terms of a refusal of what that war entailed. First, there was the assumption of the value of the "technological fix." If our technology is powerful enough, it can solve all problems; and value questions must be held irrelevant when the "fix" is in sight. Technology, of course, in the case of the Gulf War, signified the most powerful destructive machines yet seen in history. It made possible a distancing, a terrible depersonalization that infected most of those who paid heed with what Albert Camus called "plague." Indifference, distancing, lack of responsibility, a making living beings into things—or "targets," or diagrams. Dr. Robert Lifton would describe what happened as an almost fatal psychic numbing.

Coupled with that was a use of language to distort, disguise, deny. We all recall "collateral damage," "sortie," "take out"; and many of us still shudder at the sound of "victory," given the circumstances of the war. None of this, of course, is intended to defend or justify the brutal actions of the leader of Iraq. All of it argues, however, for an ability to hold opposing and sometimes contradictory ideas in mind at the same time. All of it argues powerfully for the use of imagination, at least in the posting of alternative possibilities. Surely, there are alternatives to mass killing, to fires, to withholding of the basic goods human beings need to live.

Considering all that, I can only shape an education vision that demands moral judgment when it comes to the uses of technology, and the learning of self-reflectiveness when it comes to the kind of thinking described as technical rationality. To speak of moral judgment today, however, is to remind ourselves of the ways in which significant moral values are grounded in lived life and realized when persons choose them in their coming together, in the making of face-to-face communities. The shaping of narratives, the telling of stories help persons to identify their moral purposes, to orient themselves to some vision of what they believe to be decent and good and right. So does the gathering together in classrooms and corridors to play together, to sing together, to make decisions together that affect all involved. There must be moments for recognition, moments for face-to-face encounters among the diverse newcomers in our schools. It is when spaces open among them, when their diverse perspectives are granted integrity that something they can hold in common may begin to emerge. It requires imagination; it requires involvement with the arts and the personal presentness the arts invite. It demands, as well, the identification of deficiencies in the world around (the addictions, the illness, the abandonments, the devastations) and a shared effort in some manner to repair. It is when this occurs that values are created, that persons with diverse backgrounds can come together. Camus talks in his novel about how important it is, in time of pestilence, to take the side of the victims. I can imagine no vision more important than a vision of transformation for the sake of fighting plague.

Giving what we see—the neglect, the cold carelessness, the rampant greed—it will take outrage if we are to succeed in education. It will take a new kind of hope, a new shaping of possibility, a new venture into the unpredictable. But, then, utopias are never predictable. We can only choose ourselves for something caring and humane and daring. We can only begin.

List of Contributors

Clinton B. Allison is Professor of Education in History of Education, University of Tennessee, Knoxville. He is an expert in the history of southern education, having published numerous articles on the topic. His latest publications include a chapter in *Curriculum as Social Psychoanalysis* (SUNY: 1991) and *The Past and the Present: Issues in American Educational History* (Lang: 1995).

Kathleen Berry is Associate Professor at the University of New Brunswick, where she teaches literacy and drama. She taught both elementary and secondary school for fifteen years. She is the author of *Creative Curriculum: The Mythological Roots* (World Council of Curriculum and Instruction: 1990) and her forthcoming book, *Thinking and Acting Critical in Non-critical Schools: Misbehaving in a Behavioral World* (with Shirley R. Steinberg, Lang).

Deborah P. Britzman is an Associate Professor in the Faculty of Education at York University, in Toronto, Ontario with cross appointments in Social and Political Thought and Women's Studies. She writes on questions of identity, social difference, and education and is author of *Practice Makes Practice: A Critical Study of Learning to Teach* (SUNY: 1994) and recent articles in *The Harvard Educational Review* and *Curriculum Inquiry*.

Dennis Carlson is Assistant Professor of Education at Miami University (Ohio). Carlson has published numerous articles on the critical analysis of power relations within educational contexts. His "Teachers as Political Actors" published in the *Harvard Educational Review* is a highly-regarded example of the application of critical social theory to the analysis of the institutional and social roles of teachers. He is the author of *Teachers and Crisis: Urban School Reform and Teachers' Work Culture* (Routledge: 1992).

Dalton B. Curtis, Jr. is Director of the University Studies Interdisciplinary Program at Southeast Missouri State University where he also teachcs history of education, philosophy of education and European history. He is a co-author of *Lives in Education*, a book of biographical essays on the history of educational thought and practice. He also has published articles on Jacques Maritain and the Social Reconstructionists.

Henry A. Giroux is a former secondary school teacher and currently holds the Waterbury Chair Professorship in Secondary Education at Penn State University. He is the editor of several book series which cover the fields of pedagogy, cultural studies, and educational reform. He is the author, co-author, and editor of numerous books and articles. His most recent books include: *Border Crossings*, *Living Dangerously* (Lang: 1993) and *Disturbing Pleasures*. He is on the editorial board of many journals.

Andrew Gitlin is Associate Professor of Educational Studies, University of Utah. He has taught and published in the areas of curriculum, critical theory, and teacher education. His major areas of interest include the effects of school structure on teachers' work, evaluation, and school reform. He is the author of *Teacher Evaluation: Educative Alternatives*, (co-authored with John Smyth) and of *Becoming a Student of Teaching* (with Robert Bullough, Garland: 1995).

Maxine Greene is the William F. Russell Professor of Philosophy and Education at Teachers College, Columbia University where she teaches social philosophy, aesthetics, and the Arts and American Education. In addition to many articles, she is the author of *The Teacher as Stranger*, *Landscapes of Learning* and *The Dialectic of Freedom* (Teachers College Press).

Madeleine R. Grumet is Dean of the School of Education of Brooklyn College, City University of New York. She is a curriculum theorist who brings phenomenological, psychoanalytic, literary, and feminist studies to research in education. Her book *Bitter Milk: Women and Teaching* (Teachers College Press:

1989) is a study of the relation of our reproductive projects to epistemology, curriculum, and pedagogy.

Walter P. Gutierrez is an Academic Counselor/Advisor in the Office of Multicultural Student Affairs at the University of Wisconsin-Parkside; he is also Coordinator of Social/Cultural Programs on campus and writes grants for cultural programming. A former high school Spanish teacher, he serves as Adjunct Instructor in Spanish at the University of Wisconsin-Parkside and at the College of Lake County in Illinois.

Stephen Nathan Haymes teaches in the social foundations program in the School of Education at DePaul University. His research interests are in the areas of critical education theory, cultural studies and urban studies. He is the author of *Race, Culture and the City: A Pedagogy for Black Urban Struggle* (SUNY), and of the forthcoming book, *Black Critical Pedagogy/Black Social Movement* (Lang).

Eleanor Blair Hilty is an Assistant Professor of Education at the University of Western Carolina. She has written several articles on moonlighting teachers and has a chapter on public television and children in *Kinderculture: Exploring Cults of Childhood* (Westview, 1995). Her forthcoming book is entitled *Political Dimensions of Educational Psychology: Learning in Critical Perspective* (Lang).

Harvey J. Kaye is the Ben and Joyce Rosenberg Professor of Social Change and Development and Director of the Center for History and Social Change at the University of Wisconsin-Green Bay. Kaye is author of *The British Marxist Historians* (1984) and *The Powers of the Past* (1991); and, with K. McClelland, the co-editor of *E.P. Thompson: Critical Perspectives*. He is currently working on the question of intellectuals and the development of a popular democratic historical memory, consciousness and imagination.

Joe L. Kincheloe teaches Cultural Studies and Education at Penn State University. He is the author of *Getting Beyond the*

Facts: Teaching Social Studies in the Late Twentieth Century (Lang: 1989), *Curriculum as Social Psychoanalysis: Essays on the Significance of Place* (with William F. Pinar, SUNY: 1991), *Teachers as Researchers: Qualitative Paths to Empowerment* (Falmer, 1991), *The Stigma of Genius: Einstein and Education* (with Shirley R. Steinberg and Deborah J. Tippins, Hollowbrook: 1992), *Toward a Critical Politics of Teacher Thinking: Mapping the Postmodern* (Bergin and Garvey: 1993), and *Toil and Trouble: Good Work, Smart Workers and the Integration of Academic and Vocational Education* (Lang: 1995).

Joyce Elaine King is Associate Vice Chancellor for Academic Affairs and Diversity Programs at the University of New Orleans. Her research and publications address ideology and consciousness in education, curriculum transformation, the sociocultural foundations of teaching and learning, as well as the theory and practice of community-mediated and African-centered research. She is the author of *Black Mothers to Sons: Juxtaposing African American Literature with Social Practice* (with C.A. Mitchell, Lang: 1990 and 2nd edition in press: 1995), *Teaching Diverse Populations* (with E.R. Hollins and W.C. Hayman, SUNY: 1994) and many articles and chapters in scholarly journals and books.

Magda Lewis is Queen's National Scholar and Assistant Professor of Sociology in the Faculty of Education at Queen's University, Kingston, Ontario where she teaches Feminist Theory, issues in social class, gender and race in education and qualitative research methods. Her publications, most recently in the *Harvard Educational Review*, reflect her long and active interest in feminist politics and pedagogy. She is the author of *Without a Word: Teaching Beyond Women's Silence* (Routledge: 1993) and of a forthcoming volume in *Counterpoints*.

Donaldo Macedo is professor of English and graduate program director of bilingual and ESL (English as a Second Language) Studies at the University of Massachusetts-Boston. He is a leading authority in language education and has published widely in the area of critical literacy. His new book, *Literacies of Power:*

What Americans are not Allowed to Know (Westview: 1994) has been an instant success. He is co-author with Paulo Freire of *Literacy: Reading the Word and the World* and is working on a new book entitled *Cultural Illiteracy Dictionary: What Americans Are Not Allowed to Know.*

Peter McLaren is an Associate Professor in the College of Graduate Studies in Education at UCLA. He is author of *Cries from the Corridor: The New Suburban Ghettos* and *Schooling as a Ritual Performance, Paulo Freire: A Critical Encounter* (with Colin Lankshear) His book, *Life in Schools* (now in 2nd edition: Longman) was named by the American Educational Studies Association as one of the most significant books on education for the year 1989. His most recent book is the fourth volume in the *Counterpoints Series, Rethinking Media Literacy: A Critical Pedagogy of Representation* (with Rhonda Hammer, David Sholle and Susan Reilly, Lang: 1995).

Janet L. Miller is Professor in National College Of Education's Department of Interdisciplinary Studies, National-Louis University. She serves as Managing Editor of *JCT: An Interdisciplinary Journal of Curriculum Studies.* Her teaching, writing, and research interests include curriculum theory, feminist studies qualitative inquiry, and critical and collaborative forms of teacher education research. In addition to many articles in these areas, she is the author of *Creating Spaces and Finding Voices: Teachers Collaborating for Empowerment.*

Clara Ann New is Assistant Professor of Teacher Education at the University of Wisconsin-Parkside. She teaches various courses in the early childhood, elementary and secondary certification programs, and her primary research interest is identifying and changing prospective teachers' perceptions of culturally different student classroom behavior.

Joseph W. Newman is Professor of Educational Foundations at the University of South Alabama, where he was voted Outstanding Professor in 1986 and Outstanding Scholar in 1991. He teaches social foundations and multicultural education and the history of American education. He is author of the textbook, *America's Teachers: An Introduction to Education* (1990, Longman). He is author of a chapter in *Curriculum as Social Psychoanalysis* (SUNY: 1991).

Jo Anne Pagano is Professor in the Department of Education at Colgate University. She has written extensively in the fields of curriculum theory, teacher education and feminism. Drawing upon feminist psychoanalytical theory and literary criticism, Pagano has provided a unique perspective on the educational enterprise. Her works include *Exiles and Communities: Teaching in the Patriarchal Wilderness* (SUNY: 1991), *Adolescent Culture, Knowledge, and Gender in Contemporary Film and Music* (Garland, forthcoming), and a volume in *Counterpoints* (Lang).

William F. Pinar is Professor of Education at Louisiana State University in Baton Rouge. He is the editor of *Contemporary Curriculum Discourses* (Gorsuch Scarisbrick: 1988) and of *Curriculum as Social Psychoanalysis* (with J. Kincheloe, SUNY: 1991). Pinar is the author of *Autobiography, Politics, and Sexuality: Essays in Curriculum Theory 1972-1992,* Lang: 1994) an *Understanding Curriculum* (with W. Reynolds, P. Slattery and P. Taubman, Lang: 1995). He is the co-editor (with William M. Reynolds) of *Understanding Curriculum as Phenomenological and Deconstructed Text.* The founding editor of *JCT: An Interdisciplinary Journal of Curriculum Studies,* Pinar founded the yearly Conference on Curriculum Theory and Classroom practice formerly held at the Bergamo Conference Center; "Bergamo" is now held at the Dubose Center, in Chattanooga, Tennessee.

Eugene F. Provenzo, Jr. is a Professor in the Social and Cultural Foundations of Education at the University of Miami and the author of the wide-selling, *Video Kids: Making Sense of Nintendo* (Harvard University Press: 1991), and two chapters in *Kinderculture* (Westview: 1995). An eclectic scholar and frequent guest on national television, he has written many books and articles dealing with different aspects of educational and cultural theory.

Douglas J. Simpson is Dean of the School of Education, Texas Christian University. Simpson has brought an educational philosopher's perspective to the study and reform of teacher education. He is the author, co-author and editor of a number of books including *The Educated Person, The Teacher as Philosopher* (with Michael J.B. Jackson) and *The Pedagodfathers: The Lords of Education* (Detselig: 1994).

Christine E. Sleeter is Professor of Teacher Education at the University of Wisconsin-Parkside. Formerly a teacher in Seattle, Washington, she teaches courses in multicultural education, and consults nationally in this area. She has published numerous articles about multicultural education in various journals, including *Harvard Educational Review, Journal of Education, Phi Delta Kappan, Journal of Teacher Education,* and *Teachers College Record.* Her most recent books include *Empowerment through Multicultural Education* (SUNY, 1991), *Keepers of the American Dream* (Falmer, 1992), *Turning on Learning* (with Carl Grant, Merrill, 1993). She also edits a series of books for SUNY Press entitled "The Social Context of Education."

William Stanley is Chair of the Department of Curriculum and Instruction at the University of Delaware. Having published numerous important articles in social studies education, Stanley has brought the insight of critical social theory to the analysis of the purposes of social studies education. His recent work in social studies education has focused on the implications of postmodernist social theory for the field.

Shirley R. Steinberg developed the "In-Process Collective" which employs dialogue and social drama in a constantly evolving format. She is the co-editor (with Joe L. Kincheloe) of the new Peter Lang Series, *Counterpoints* and is author of *The Stigma of Genius: Einstein and Education* (with Joe L. Kincheloe and Deborah Tippins, Hollowbrook: 1992). She is the general managing editor of *Taboo: The Journal for Cultural Studies and Education* (Lang: Volume 1, No. 1, 1995). An educational consultant and lecturer, Steinberg is the author (with Joe Kincheloe) of *Kinderculture: Exploring Cults of Childhood* (Westview: 1995).

Susan R. Takata is Associate Professor of Sociology at the University of Wisconsin-Parkside. She has directed a series of undergraduate student-run research projects focusing on gangs and delinquency in small cities. One of her most recent publications is *Using Sociology to Understand Your Life: Theories, Methods and Strategies for Career Planning* (co-authored with Jeanne Curran, 1993). She is the author of several works in the fields of criminology, delinquency, sociology and education.

 Joe L. Kincheloe and Shirley R. Steinberg, General Editors

Studies in the Postmodern Theory of Education

AVAILABLE TITLES:

Living Dangerously: Multiculturalism and the Politics of Difference, *Henry A. Giroux;*
Vol. 1, ISBN 0-8204-1832-3, 1993, paper, 187pp./$19.95.

Autobiography, Politics, and Sexuality: Essays in Curriculum Theory, *William Pinar;*
Vol. 2, ISBN 0-8204-1849, 1993, paper, 288 pp./$24.95.

A Radical Democratic Critic of Capitalist Education, *Richard Brosio;*
Vol. 3, ISBN 0-8204-2189-8, 1994, paper, 635 pp./$39.95.

Dogs Playing Cards: Powerbrokers of Prejudice in Art, Education, and Culture, *Dennis Fehr;*
Vol. 5, ISBN 0-8204-2325-4, 1993, paper, 232 pp./$29.95.

Present and Past: Essays for Teachers in the History of Education, *Clinton Allison;*
Vol. 6, ISBN 0-8204-1780-7, 1995, paper, 232 pp./$29.95.

Toil and Trouble: Good Work, Smart Workers, and the Integration of Vocational and Academic Education, *Joe L. Kincheloe;*
Vol. 7, ISBN 0-8204-1787-4, 1995, paper, 376 pp./$29.95.

Understanding Curriculum, *William Pinar, William Reynolds, Patrick Slattery, and Peter Taubman;*
Vol. 16, ISBN 0-8204-2601-6, 1995, paper, 1144 pp./$49.95.

Black Mothers to Sons: Juxtaposing African American Literature with Social Practice, *Joyce King and Carolyn Mitchell;*
Vol. 20, Rev. Ed., 0-8204-2815-9, 1995, paper/$24.95.

Rethinking Media Literacy: A Critical Pedagogy of Representation, *Peter McLaren, Rhonda Hammer, David Sholle, and Susan Reilly;*
Vol. 4, ISBN 0-8204-1802-1, 1995, paper/ $29.95.

FORTHCOMING TITLES:

Critical Black Pedagogy and the Urban Cultural Worker, *Stephen Haymes;* Vol. 8

Ain't We Misbehavin'? Thinking and Acting Critically in a Behavioral World, *Shirley Steinberg and Kathleen Berry;* Vol.9

"It's Alright Ma (I'm Only Bleeding)": Education as the Practice of Social Violence against the Child, *Alan Block;* Vol. 10

In Addition to the Mathematics: The Politics of Knowledge, Breaking Down Dichotomies, and Challenging the Taken-For-Granted. *Marilyn Frankenstein and Arthur Powell;* Vol. 11

Consciousness Construction and the Postmodern Zeitgeist: The Struggle with Place, *Julia Ellis;* Vol. 12

Gender and Schooling: Uncovering the Varied Structures of Education, *Jo Anne Pagano;* Vol. 13

The Political Dimensions of Educational Psychology: Learning in Critical Perspective, *Eleanor Blair Hilty;* Vol. 14

Pedagogy as an International Narrative Practice. *David Smith;* Vol. 15

The Changing Curriculum, *Ivor Goodson;* Vol. 18

To the Lighthouse and Back: Ruminations on Teaching and Living, *Mary Aswell Doll;* Vol. 19

Daredevil Research: Breaking the Boundaries in Educational, *Nicholas Paley and Janice Jipson;* Vol. 21

James B. Macdonald, A Retrospective, *James Macdonald;* Vol. 22